CIVIL
WAR
BARONS

CIVIL

WAR

BARONS

THE
**TYCOONS, ENTREPRENEURS,
INVENTORS, AND VISIONARIES
WHO FORGED VICTORY
AND SHAPED A NATION**

JEFFRY D. WERT

Da Capo Press

Da Capo Press
Hachette Book Group
1290 Avenue of the Americas, New York, NY 10104
dacapopress.com
@DaCapoPress, @DaCapoPR

Printed in the United States of America

First Edition: November 2018

Published by Da Capo Press, an imprint of Perseus Books, LLC, a subsidiary of Hachette Book Group, Inc. The Da Capo Press name and logo is a trademark of the Hachette Book Group.

The Hachette Speakers Bureau provides a wide range of authors for speaking events. To find out more, go to www.hachettespeakersbureau.com or call (866) 376-6591.

The publisher is not responsible for websites (or their content) that are not owned by the publisher.

Print book interior design by Amy Quinn

Library of Congress Cataloging-in-Publication Data has been applied for.

ISBNs: 978-0-306-82512-5 (hardcover), 978-0-306-82513-2 (ebook)

LSC-C

10 9 8 7 6 5 4 3 2 1

To Gloria, who makes all in life worthwhile
and whose love sustains me

CONTENTS

PREFACE

As the secession crisis deepened in the winter of 1860–1861, William T. Sherman penned a letter warning Southerners of the consequences of a possible civil conflict brought on by their acts. In it, the former army officer stated: "You are rushing into a war with one of the most powerful, ingeniously mechanical and determined people on earth—right at your doors. . . . If your people would but stop and think, they must see that in the end you will surely fail."

Sherman's words and similar predictions went unheeded in the descent into the bloodbath of the Civil War. After the attack on Fort Sumter on April 12, 1861, both sections embraced the whirlwind. Northerners suddenly confronted a formidable challenge of conquering fellow Americans in the Confederate States of America, a vast region of 750,000 square miles. The preservation of the Union required a mobilization of manpower and resources on an unprecedented scale.

The Union military's demands unleashed the agricultural and industrial might of the North, from New England west to Minnesota and beyond. The region had been undergoing a transportation and industrial transformation during the antebellum decades. Fort Sumter awakened an economic giant.

The federal government and private enterprises in the North created an organization that linked the resources of the home front to the conduct of military operations and campaigns. In the end, after four years of fighting, this combination achieved victory. Military power and a capitalistic economy waged the struggle against the redoubtable Confederates, which ended at Appomattox.

The administration in Washington, DC, depended on private business in mustering the region's natural and man-made resources. Firms, large and small, produced the war materiel that made Union forces the best armed and best equipped, arguably, in the world at that time. American businessmen and workers met the challenges of an unparalleled undertaking.

This book chronicles the accomplishments of nineteen of these businessmen. Undoubtedly, this is an eclectic group, inclusion in which rests solely with me. They were administrators, inventors, dreamers, tinkers, organizers, entrepreneurs, investors, patriots, builders, improvisers, and a visionary. Their contributions to the Union war effort varied in size and importance. Some of them contributed directly, whereas others supplied materiel. All of them were remarkable individuals in their era and, most likely, would be in ours.

Some of these men are not familiar to most Americans today—Henry Burden, Jay Cooke, James B. Eads, Abram Hewitt, Collis P. Huntington, Gordon McKay, Robert P. Parrott, Thomas A. Scott, Christopher M. Spencer, and J. Edgar Thomson. Others, however, are well known to millions of contemporary Americans because of their creations or their wealth—Philip D. Armour, Gail Borden Jr., Andrew Carnegie, John Deere, Cyrus McCormick, Edward Squibb, the Studebaker brothers, Cornelius Vanderbilt, and Frederick Weyerhaeuser.

The common factor that links them was the Civil War. Unquestionably, each man was affected uniquely by the conflict, but each man has a fascinating story to be told. Some of them have been the subject of singular biographies, and others have received far less historical attention. My book is the first to combine their stories, set amid America's greatest saga, into one account. Their individual achievements during the four-year struggle left a legacy that has endured even until today.

As always, my book has benefited from the gracious assistance of others. All errors of omission and commission are entirely mine.

The following individuals merit my particular gratitude and recognition:

Rachel Ornstein, Director of Administration, and her staff and volunteers, Putnam History Museum, Cold Spring, New York, for their assistance and graciousness in researching West Point Foundry.

Michelle Tom, Librarian/Archivist, Windsor Historical Society, Windsor, Connecticut, for her kindness and cooperation in providing me material on Christopher Spencer.

Gregory Gill of the New Jersey State Archives, Trenton, for assisting me in securing pertinent copies of the Ringwood Manor Papers.

Dr. Thomas Carroll of Troy, New York, for giving leads on sources related to Henry Burden.

Dr. Joseph Whitehorne, a fellow historian, for providing me with important contacts related to Henry Burden.

Dr. Clarence Geier, Emeritus Professor of Anthropology at James Madison University, Harrisonburg, Virginia, for the encouragement and for educating me about horseshoes.

Childs Burden of Middleburg, Virginia, great-grandson of Henry Burden and staunch Civil War preservationist, for his advice and contacts on his ancestor's company.

Nicholas Picerno Sr. of New Market, Virginia, a dear family friend and devoted Civil War preservationist and collector, for his advice and assistance with research material.

Amber Morris, project editor, and Christina Palaia, copyeditor, for their excellent efforts on my behalf.

Don Fehr, my agent, for endorsing the idea of my book and for his counsel.

Bob Pigeon, my editor, for believing in my work.

Our family—our son, Jason Wert; our daughter-in-law, Kathy Wert; our grandchildren, Rachel and Gabriel Wert; our daughter, Natalie

Wert Corman; our son-in-law, Grant Corman—for all that truly matters in life and for their love and support.

My wife, Gloria, who has been with me through all these years of research and writing and who has typed every page, found my mistakes, offered advice, and has been my best friend and cherished love. For all these reasons and for so much more, this book is dedicated.

Jeffry D. Wert
February 2018

Prologue

UNCERTAIN GIANT

————⚭————

AUGUSTE LAUGEL ARRIVED IN NEW YORK IN SEPTEMBER 1864. A French professor and author, he had crossed the Atlantic Ocean to visit both the military front and the Northern home front. A perceptive observer, Laugel kept a diary during his eight months in the divided, war-torn country.[1]

At the time of Laugel's arrival, the Civil War was nearing the end of its fourth summer of fighting. When the conflict had begun in April 1861, many, if not most, Americans, both in the North and in the South, felt as a volunteer soldier from Maine wrote to his mother: "It is generally believed that the contest will be a short and decisive one. It is thought that it will be a comparatively bloodless one." At roughly the same time, a private from Wisconsin concluded otherwise, telling a friend, "in my opinion this war will not be brought to a close as a great many immagine [sic] I think we will have some hard and bloody fighting, and a great many Companies will lose some of their number from the muster Roll before they return."[2]

The Wisconsin recruit had it right, but even he could not have foreseen how deep a descent into darkness the war would bring. Three years later hundreds of thousands had fallen across terrible landscapes, with the darkest and bloodiest of days—like an unrelenting nightmare—occurring during the spring and summer of 1864. By early September, however, the Federals' capture of Atlanta, Georgia, appeared to ensure the reelection of Abraham Lincoln and ultimate Union victory.

The Frenchman had arrived, then, at a propitious time for a foreign visitor, as a witness to a presidential election and the conflict's end. He traveled across the Northern states, from Maine to Missouri, visiting cities and towns, hearing the clang of machines in factories, and watching farmers at work in fields. All the while he filled the pages of his diary with his observations.[3]

"The American seems at first a tissue of contradictions," he wrote. He possesses an "insatiable curiosity," but his and fellow Americans' "minds are not cast in uniform molds." Laugel thought that the American "has looked at the realistic sharp side of things" since his childhood. "The American is not systematic; he always subordinates the means to the end; he can profit by circumstances, by men, even by chance."[4]

This American pragmatism was coupled with confidence, nonconformity, and egalitarian principles. Even within the tragedy of the appalling struggle between the Union and the Confederacy, the region beyond Pennsylvania from Ohio to Wisconsin "is joyous, impatient, and intoxicated with chronic enthusiasm."[5]

Perhaps it was the sense, if not the certainty, that federal armies would triumph, that the union of states would endure, and that the decisive issue of slavery would be settled which caused the optimism Laugel saw. Perhaps, too, it was the knowledge of folks living along the Ohio and Mississippi rivers and those residing in New England and the Mid-Atlantic of their home-front contributions to the defeat of the Confederacy. They had gathered the harvests on farms, forged the cannon, stitched together the shoes, and sewed the uniforms.

During his stay in the North, Laugel visited Pittsburgh, Pennsylvania. "A heavy smoke hangs constantly over the innumerable workshops," the Frenchman recorded in his diary. The sides of nearby hills "crop out the black layers of coal." What Laugel saw in this vibrant, working city epitomized the foundation of the Union's military prowess.[6]

THE SIGNS HAD BEEN THERE FOR YEARS HAD ADVOCATES OF SECESSION chosen to see them in their quest to leave the Union and to risk a civil conflict. Since the establishment of the republic, the hallmark of the American economy had been growth. To be sure, from the early years of the century until the winter of 1861, cotton had dominated the economy and Southern politics. Following the War of 1812, the country underwent a revolution in transportation with the building of the Erie Canal and the construction of rail lines. With this revolution, the economy underwent a transformation.[7]

In two decades, from 1839 to 1859, the country's gross national product more than doubled, spurred certainly by the expansion of the railroad industry. The rail companies required tens of thousands of machinists, toolmakers, engine builders, and repairmen. North of the Mason-Dixon Line and Ohio River, railroads dominated business growth. In the ten years before the war, railroad mileage tripled. By 1861, 31,500 miles of track crisscrossed the nation, with 22,000 miles in the North and 9,500 miles in the South.[8]

While rail lines lengthened, fundamental factors also shaped the nature and size of the economy—natural resources, a sixfold increase in population from natural births and a flood of immigrants, interchangeable parts, an array of new inventions, and public schools. "By 1860," according to historian James McPherson, "the nascent outline of the modern American economy of mass consumption, mass production and capital-intensive agriculture was visible."[9]

In a way, since its beginning, America's story has rested on farms. Blessed with deep, rich soils and a moderate climate, agriculture formed the bedrock of the nation's economy for more than two centuries. Whereas "King Cotton" reigned for most of the 1800s, by 1860 grain farmers in the Mid-Atlantic and in the states of the old Northwest Territory were challenging cotton's dominance. At that time, the Free States boasted more than 1.3 million farms. Railroads had opened up new markets for crops, and John Deere's steel plow and Cyrus McCormick's reaper, among other inventions, expanded harvests. Chicago was shipping, for instance, nearly ten million bushels of wheat and oats each year, and Cincinnati had earned the nickname "the metropolis of Pig" for its meatpacking industry.[10]

Deere and McCormick epitomized a certain breed of fellow countrymen. Necessity had bred pragmatism; pragmatism had bred inventiveness. Between 1830 and 1860, the number of patents submitted to the Patent Office increased fivefold. The vast majority of the new ideas came from the North. Writing about the ironmaking industry, a newspaper bragged: "There is no lack of genius or skill among us. The world has admitted that Americans can undoubtedly rival their neighbors in this art as well as the rest."[11]

American ingenuity, combined with vast forests, deposits of iron ore and coal, and skilled workers, created a rapidly expanding industrial base. In this the Free States dominated. By 1860, more than 128,000 manufacturing firms existed in the United States and, of these, only about 18,000 were located in the eleven states that would form the Confederacy. For example, private gunmakers in just one Connecticut county produced more firearms than gunsmiths in the entire slaveholding South.[12]

The North's industrial ascendancy was staggering in comparison to the South's development of manufacturers whose products were vital to a country at war. Iron rolling mills and foundries, cotton and wool mills, ready-made clothing firms, boot and shoemakers, and meat packers numbered in the thousands from New England to Wisconsin. Other small firms built wagons, tanned leather, cast cannon, stamped out horseshoes, canned foodstuff, and crafted guns. Large businesses increased in number, but the typical American company was owned by a man or a family.[13]

As historian Jay Winik notes, the antebellum years witnessed "the stunning emergence of industrial capitalism." The center of this "emergence" lay in Massachusetts west through Connecticut, New York, New Jersey, and Pennsylvania to Ohio. The North's investment in manufacturing rose during the 1850s from slightly more than $500 million to $1 billion, or by nearly 90 percent. The new technologies helped to energize the economy, and the United States military's need for interchangeable parts increased further and faster the rise of mechanized mass production.[14]

Persistent difficulties plagued the economy during the antebellum years, however. Periodic "panics" or recessions caused disruptions that led to bank failures, factory closures, and personal and business bankruptcies. Corruption affected every level of government, with politicians accepting bribes and granting favors, notably to railroad companies and larger firms. The lack of a standard national currency exacerbated the fluctuations in the amount of available specie, which roiled financial markets. Speculation in land and commercial enterprises seemed to be a mania.[15]

Although railroads and telegraph lines widened markets and linked towns and cities as never before, the nation's economy remained largely decentralized. It might have been so, in part, because of the independent-minded character of Americans. In his travels, Laugel noticed this trait, writing, "In the United States there is a horror of all trammels, systems, and uniformity."[16]

The Founding Fathers had their doubts about whether a republic of America's size could endure. Their reading of the past had convinced them of its fragility. In his first inaugural, President George Washington had cautioned his fellow citizens that the new nation was an "experiment." That it had survived the tumults for six decades likely would have surprised them.[17]

During those six decades, the "experiment" had been increasingly tested as the issue of slavery tore open a broader, if not unbridgeable, divide between North and South. A civil war was not inevitable, however, because the Americans in the two sections were not that much different from each other socially and culturally. Arguably, the fundamental basis for the division between them rested in the emerging and contrasting free-labor industrial North and the slave-labor agricultural South.[18]

Although the capitalistic North grew more vibrant with each successive decade, the slaveholding states dominated the American economy from 1800 to 1860. The American South supplied three-fourths of the world's supply of cotton, grown primarily in a swath of states from South Carolina through Georgia and Alabama to Mississippi. Cotton fed the textile mills of New England and filled the hulls of ships on their passage to Europe. "King Cotton" had earned its preeminence in the country's economic life. In 1853 a planter boasted: "Our Cotton is the most wonderful talisman in the world. By its power we are transmitting whatever we choose into whatever we want."[19]

The planter's observation might have been true then, but for the previous decade or more his region had been confronting a rising section to the north, both industrially and demographically. Immigrants from Europe arrived by shiploads, with seven out of eight of them settling north of the Mason-Dixon Line and the Ohio River. Birth rates in the North exceeded those in the South. By 1860, more than twice as many men, women, and children lived in the Free States and territories than in the fifteen slave states and District of Columbia, including the indentured population.[20]

The impact of the disparity in population had resulted already in the Free States' majority in the House of Representatives. The implications of further admission of Free States into the Union were not lost on Southern political leaders. The Constitution protected slavery legally without naming it specifically, but it did not guarantee its continued existence. If opposition to the "peculiar institution" garnered a majority of votes in both houses of Congress, bondsmen could be given their freedom by law.[21]

A myriad of political issues and crises, all inexorably linked to slavery, had plagued the country for forty years. Each decade came worse, it seemed, than the one before, eroding the viability of Washington's "experiment." Each one seemed to be accompanied by a louder sound of a tocsin in the night—Missouri Compromise of 1820, nullification crisis of 1832, rise of the abolitionist movement, Compromise of 1850, Kansas-Nebraska Act, "Bleeding Kansas," Dred Scott Supreme Court decision, John Brown's raid on Harpers Ferry.[22]

Unhealed, the divisive wounds festered until it was too late, climaxing in the 1860 presidential election. During the campaign, Southern voices warned of the consequences if Republican candidate Abraham Lincoln won the office. Although Lincoln assured Southerners that he had no intention of trying to abolish slavery, the region's political leaders did not heed his words. Just days before the election in Louisiana, broadsides appeared on streets predicting: "The slavery agitation will soon make the North and South *two separate nations,* unless it can cease, of which we have little hope. We can never submit to Lincoln's inauguration."[23]

Finally, after decades of vitriolic speeches, political and constitutional crises, and bloodshed, the division between Free States and slave states could not be resolved. As the Louisiana posters forewarned, the election of President Lincoln resulted in the secession of seven states and the formation of the Confederate States of America. When Confederate gun crews fired on Fort Sumter in the harbor of Charleston, South Carolina, the internecine struggle began. A day after the garrison formally surrendered, on April 15, Lincoln called for seventy-five thousand state militia to suppress the rebellion. The attack and the president's act galvanized both sections, as tens of thousands of men rushed to enlist and four more states seceded.

Though illusions of a brief conflict persisted for weeks, there was no turning back. Each section confronted formidable obstacles in conducting a war, but the greatest burden rested, arguably, with the Northern states. Time soon brought the realization that to save the Union, federal armies and navies, backed by the economic might of the citizenry, would have to conquer the vast Confederacy.

Referring to the North, historian Allan Nevins describes the section as "the shambling, uncertain American giant of 1861." Ahead of it and its government was an unprecedented struggle, whose breadth and depth could hardly be perceived. If the Union was to be restored, the giant, in all its might, had to stir.[24]

Weeks before the attack on Fort Sumter, a former army officer, William T. Sherman, warned Southerners of what lay across the Mason-Dixon Line. "The North can make a steam engine, locomotive, or railway car," he declared, "hardly a yard of cloth or shoes can you make. You are rushing into a war with one of the most powerful, ingeniously mechanical and determined people on earth—right at your doors. . . . If your people would but stop and think, they must see that in the end you will surely fail."[25]

But, as the French visitor Auguste Laugel witnessed during the war's final year, Southerners had not stopped. Instead, they had summoned forth a slumbering American giant in the North.

Chapter One

STIRRINGS

——————~\\\~——————

ESTIMATES PLACED THE CROWD AT 250,000 FOLKS IN NEW YORK City on April 20, 1861. They covered city blocks from Fourteenth Street to Seventeenth Street and from Broadway to Fourth Avenue. Several stands for orators rose above the throngs. When Major Robert Anderson, the "hero" of Fort Sumter, appeared, the people cheered even louder. A prominent city attorney, George Templeton Strong, called the entire scene "an event," adding, "Few assemblages had equaled it in numbers and unanimity." A week later he reported, "Here the flag is on every public building, every store, every house almost." Historian George Bancroft exclaimed, "I witnessed the sublimest spectacle I ever saw."[1]

New Yorkers were not alone in their reaction to the outbreak of civil war and the threat to the Union. Across the entire North, in villages and cities, similar rallies occurred. Husbands, fathers, and sons hurried to enlist in volunteer units. In New York, more than 13,000 men joined the ranks of seventeen regiments, and nearly 21,000 Pennsylvanians signed up in twenty-five regiments. Without legal authority, on May 3, President Abraham Lincoln requested 42,034 volunteers to serve for three years. An angry wind had been embraced.[2]

In Massachusetts, Ralph Waldo Emerson remarked on the "whirlwind of patriotism, not believed to exist, but now magnetizing all discordant masses under its terrific unity." Brigadier General Jacob D. Cox recalled, "The wonderful outburst of national feeling in the North in the spring of 1861 has always been a thrilling and almost supernatural thing to those who participated in it." It was that "national feeling" that brought Cox and his fellow Northerners into the ranks, or, as a private put it, Southerners had "insulted our flag and we must insult theirs" and "stand by the Union and constitution of the states."[3]

Defense of the Union seemed to be the common motivation behind enlistments. One volunteer told his brother, "If I fall, I die in defence of the Flag I was born under and which I will die under." A Wisconsin recruit asserted to his parents, "With thousands of others I was so much excited at the thought of treason breaking out in our Old Union that I thought nothing but to be if possible the first to enroll my name amongst those of her defenders."[4]

A member of the 38th New York Infantry invoked Revolutionary War patriots in explaining to his parents why he had volunteered: "Don't feel sorry that one of your sons enlisted in this struggle for our rights and the rights of our forefathers who died for their country and made it free and now we are duty bound to protect it and keep it free, for without Union there cannot be Peace so down with Secession."[5]

One of Lincoln's secretaries, twenty-two-year-old John Hay, visited the camp of the 1st Rhode Island Infantry and declared afterward, "When men like these leave their houses, their women, their wine, harden their hands, eat crackers for dinner, wear a shirt for a week and never black their shoes—all for a principle, it is hard to set any bounds to the possibilities of such an army."[6]

The volunteers gathered at training camps, generally located in state capitals. The War Department in Washington, DC, ordered regiments to the capital in concern for the security of the city. By early June, thousands of troops had arrived in the national capital, and any immediate threat had disappeared. A New Jersey soldier asserted at the time, "Things look very mutch like war here but there is so mutch military that it cant look other ways."[7]

President Lincoln soon became a familiar figure to many of the arriving troops. Whenever the opportunity beckoned, Lincoln escaped from his second-story office above the East Room in the Executive Mansion and visited with the officers and men in their camps. An acquaintance of the president described him as "eminently human," and the soldiers came to see this in him. When he went among their tents—he had a "forward-bending form" when he walked—Lincoln greeted all that he could with some words.[8]

An officer recounted an incident during one of Lincoln's visits when "a boy came by with a pail of water for us, and the President took a great swig from it as it passed." Another officer said of the commander in chief: "It is easy to see why he is so popular with all who come in contact with him. He gives you the impression of being a gentleman." It was this common touch of his that impressed the rank and file.[9]

The president's reported homeliness drew inevitable remarks. A lieutenant decided that "he is ten times a homlier man than I expected he was." A fellow officer contended otherwise, "It is really too bad to call him one of the ugliest men in the country for I have seldom seen a pleasanter or more kind-hearted looking one and he has certainly a very striking face." With each visit, with the speaking of words or shaking of hands, Lincoln established a bond that he would need in the fearful days ahead.[10]

Before the floodtide of soldiers, slightly more than sixty-one thousand folks resided in Washington City, as it was termed at the time. Nearly fourteen thousand persons lived in Georgetown or in the district's rural areas. Free blacks and slaves comprised one-fifth of the population. The Capitol, Executive Mansion, General Post Office, Patent Office, Treasury, and Smithsonian Institution were the city's impressive structures. A pair of small brick buildings housed the State and War departments.[11]

A politician or visitor described the capital as a "city of magnificent distances." When he came to Washington before the war, British novelist Anthony Trollope believed the streets were a baffling maze. Pennsylvania Avenue, "*the* avenue" to locals, had earned a distinction as "'the worst' street in the country." A journalist thought that it had been called that "with justice," for "in dry weather [it was] a highway of choking dust, in the rainy season a quagmire of yellow mud and many pitfalls." Older residents remembered that a large billy goat had charged Senator Henry Clay on "*the* avenue."[12]

Albert Gallatin Riddle, a congressman from Ohio, described the nation's capital in the spring of 1861 "as [an] unattractive, straggling, sodden town." He noted also, "The Washington Monument, the Capitol, and the Treasury building were melancholy specimens of arrested development." Both the monument and the Capitol dome remained unfinished at the time.[13]

A visitor shared Riddle's sentiments, writing: "Everything worth looking at seemed unfinished. Everything finished looked as if it should have been destroyed generations before." Inside the Capitol, however, both houses of Congress had flowered carpets, ornate mirrors, and chairs of morocco leather. Along Fourteenth Street stood the Willard Hotel, an impressive private building.[14]

Washington City struck Dr. George William Bagby, a physician-turned-reporter from Virginia, as "a paradise of paradoxes—a great, little, splendid, mean, extravagant, poverty-stricken barrack. . . . The one and only absolutely certain thing is the absence of everything that is at all permanent." Bagby went on, claiming it "has the reputation of Sodom . . . a monument that will never be finished; a capitol that is to have a dome, a Scientific Institute [the Smithsonian] which does nothing but report the rise and fall of the thermometer."[15]

Most of the soldiers, if not nearly all of them, had never been to the capital. When the opportunity arose, they roamed the streets as sightseers, visiting the public buildings. "Washington is the prettiest place in the World," thought one of them. A chaplain contended, "The Capitol is beyond the possibility of description."[16]

Some of the officers and enlisted men expressed different impressions to folks back home. A volunteer used a common expression at the time, calling the city "just no place at all." A lieutenant believed that it resembled "a half grown tree withered by the premature extraction of *sap*." Another soldier grumbled to his parents, "Hogs run around the street just like dogs."[17]

Whether the city impressed them or not, their presence, in numbers unprecedented, spoke to a grim reality ahead of them and the Northern home front. The government that they had come to defend was woefully unprepared and undermanned for the approaching struggle. Americans had seemingly always possessed a deep ambivalence to war and, ironically, Congressman Abraham Lincoln had described military glory in the Mexican War as a "rainbow that rises in showers of blood." When the conflict began, the Regular Army consisted of approximately sixteen thousand officers and men strewn in forts and outposts across the frontier and along the coasts. Barely more than thirty-six thousand civilian employees worked for the government and, of this force, 85 percent worked for the post office.[18]

John Hay recalled the days before the president-elect's inauguration: "The picture was as confused and bewildering as a dissolving view. The old time was passing away, and all things had not become new." Then came Fort Sumter and, with it, war and a shattered past. New was afoot everywhere. Writing after the conflict's beginning, Hay understood the stakes: "The North will not have mercy, for mercy would be cruelty now. The Government must die or crush its assailants."[19]

THE FOUR-STORY BRICK WAR DEPARTMENT SQUATTED ON SEVENTEENTH Street due west of the Executive Mansion, or the White House. District residents called it "the lunatic asylum." The building housed the offices of Secretary of War Simon Cameron and Secretary of the Navy Gideon Welles. Across the street stood a more imposing structure, Winder's Building, where Commanding General Winfield Scott and the quartermaster and ordnance bureaus were located. As the war progressed and the demands increased, War Department employees eventually occupied eleven buildings.[20]

Scott served as the president's military adviser. The brevet lieutenant general had been a soldier for nearly four decades and was a hero of the Mexican War. He was now, however, seventy-four years old, his physical stature—he stood six feet five inches tall—wracked by time and obesity. He could neither work long hours nor mount a horse without assistance. Proud and vain, Scott still possessed a brilliant intellect.[21]

The commanding general had no illusions about the daunting task that awaited Union forces. A native Virginian, Scott regarded the Confederacy as a formidable opponent. Geographically, the Rebel states covered an area of more than 750,000 square miles. The Appalachian Mountains ran nearly the length of the Confederacy in the east and would be a towering barrier to military operations. Numerous rivers scarred the Southern landscape, offering natural defensive lines. The conflict's outcome would depend on the Union army's and navy's ability to conquer the Confederacy.[22]

Scott informed Lincoln that it would require three years and incalculable men and resources to defeat the Rebels. The army commander proposed a three-prong plan—a naval blockade, capture and control of the Mississippi River, and offensive invasions into the Confederate heartland. When Scott's plan was made public, Northern newspapers derisively dubbed it the "Anaconda Plan." The press demanded an immediate advance against the enemy, clamoring for "On to Richmond," the Confederate capital.[23]

The Federals went forth from Washington in mid-July, marching toward a Confederate force near Manassas, Virginia. The clash came on Sunday, July 21, and, before the Battle of First Manassas, or Bull Run, had ended, the Yankees were fleeing back toward the capital in a demoralizing rout. Concern for the security of Washington mounted. Officials earlier had sandbagged and stocked with food and ammunition the Treasury as a final stronghold for the president and cabinet members if the enemy entered the city.[24]

MUCH MORE THAN MEN DIED ON THE PLAINS OF MANASSAS ON THAT July Sabbath. Gone were the illusions of a brief and bloodless conflict and of a weak opponent. In turn came the realization of a prolonged struggle, as Scott had predicted, and, with it, the further realization that a war effort required a mobilization of the entire Northern society. As never before in America, on an unprecedented scale, the fortunes of the Union military were linked to the production of the home front.[25]

That linkage between the civilian producers and the Union's army and navy required a mobilization never before undertaken in the country. It became necessary to convert industrial capacity into military might. The North's advantages in a conflict—manpower, natural resources, factories and farms, railroads, and taxable wealth—had to undergird the war effort. Union military strategy had to be predicated on the ability of the government and the home front to muster, arm, supply, and transport ultimately more than two million men. Invading Union armies and the navy had to rely on an economy whose industrial foundation had materialized only within the past two decades.[26]

Responsibility for this mobilization of an entire society rested with a federal government woefully unprepared for it in the spring of 1861. Henry Adams wrote: "The government had an air of social instability and incompleteness that went far to support the right of secession in theory as in fact, but right or wrong, secession was likely to be easy where there was so little to secede from. The Union was a sentiment, but not much more."[27]

Secretary of War Simon Cameron put in stark terms what the administration faced after the attack on Fort Sumter: "I found the nation without an army; and I found scarcely a man throughout the War Department in whom I could put my trust." The adjutant general and quartermaster had joined the Confederacy, and "more than half the clerks were disloyal." Even President Lincoln confessed, "I hardly knew who to trust any more."[28]

Congressman Riddle asserted that the civil service was "in a bad condition." To the Ohio Republican, work in all of the government's departments appeared to be "sadly in arrears." He continued, "The public offices were apparently used chiefly as lounging-places, where men gathered to read Democratic papers, smoke, chew tobacco, and damn Lincoln and his myrmidons."[29]

No matter how inadequate the government was to the onslaught of volunteers, it and state governments endeavored to fill the supply needs of the soldiery during the war's initial weeks. Responsibility for the efforts remained uncertain, causing much confusion. Legislatures in the state capitals issued bonds or borrowed from banks or wealthy individuals to raise money for supplies. The national government owned armories and some factories, and several states operated clothing factories. None of the facilities could fill the escalating demands.[30]

When Lincoln called for the volunteers on May 3, supply needs doubled seemingly overnight. Behind the regiments arriving in the capital came hordes of civilian suppliers in search of contracts. The granting of contracts fell initially to agents of the War Department appointed by Secretary Cameron.[31]

A powerful Pennsylvania politician, Cameron had sought the Republican nomination for the presidency in 1860. But the odor of corruption clung to him because he combined elective office with personal financial gain. Along with William H. Seward, Salmon P. Chase, and Edward Bates, Cameron owed his cabinet seat to machinations at the 1860 Republican convention.[32]

Cameron's appointment surprised Congressman Riddle, who said later of the secretary, "I did not then know so well that intellectual ability was a small factor in selecting a Cabinet Minister." Riddle thought that Cameron "was not at home" at the department.[33]

Lincoln's secretaries, John Nicolay and John Hay, offered contrasting opinions of the Pennsylvania politician. In a memorandum, Nicolay declared, "Cameron [is] utterly ignorant and regardless of the course of things, and the probable result." He described the secretary as "selfish and openly discourteous to the President" and "obnoxious to the Country," adding that he was "incapable either of organizing details or conceiving and advising general plans."[34]

Hay contended otherwise, arguing that much of the opposition to

Cameron rested outside of the administration. The secretary "never is vindictive," wrote Hay. "There has never been the slightest unkindness or distrust between him and the President." It appears that Hay had it right because Lincoln and Cameron got along personally, and the president granted his cabinet members rather wide latitude in the conduct of their departments.[35]

Unfortunately for Lincoln and his administration, Cameron appointed political friends and supporters as purchasing agents. It took some time before it was revealed that contracts had been given to spurious businesses that sold poorly fabricated uniforms and shoes, in particular, to the War Department and the states. "Shoddy" became a household word throughout the North. It referred to fabric made of cuttings and waste gathered from the floors of clothing factories and then glued together to resemble a sturdy fabric. In foul weather and heavy use, shoddy uniforms fell apart.[36]

Lincoln endeavored, however, to bring organization to the purchase and transport of supplies as early as June 1861 with the appointment of Montgomery C. Meigs as quartermaster general. Meigs had led a secret expedition to reinforce Fort Pickens in the harbor of Pensacola, Florida, during the crisis before the firing on Fort Sumter. When the president was considering Meigs for the post, he wrote about the officer to Winfield Scott, "I do not know one who combines the qualities of masculine intellect, learning and experience of the right sort, and physical of labor and endurance so well as he." This proved to be one of Lincoln's finest personnel choices.[37]

Meigs was forty-five years old, an 1836 graduate of West Point, and a career engineer officer. His mother said of him as a six-year-old that he was "high-tempered, unyielding, tyrannical toward his brothers, and very persevering in pursuit of anything he wishes." He could be arrogant and demanding with others, but his talent was unquestioned. Gideon Welles described him as "prudent, cautious."[38]

Meigs's major antebellum feats remained unfinished at the war's outset. He had designed and overseen the construction of the capital's main aqueduct a dozen miles up the Potomac River at Great Falls. He worked on the building of the Post Office and served as a designer and primary engineer of the Capitol dome. The aqueduct and the dome remain as legacies of Meigs's brilliance as an engineer.[39]

The new quartermaster general found his department and the supply system in disarray. States continued to purchase arms and equipment. Three days after the Union defeat at Bull Run, Meigs claimed: "The nation is in extremity. Troops, thousands, wait for clothes to take the field. Regiments have been ordered here [to Washington] without clothes. Men go on guard in drawers."[40]

With his experience and administrative abilities, Meigs brought order to the mobilization undertaking. In the fall, he directed state governments to cease the purchases of supplies, leaving his bureau primarily responsible for the massive procurement of uniforms, boots and shoes, blankets, and other equipment. He established large clothing depots in New York City, Philadelphia, Cincinnati, and Saint Louis under the direction of army officers. Small depots branched out from the principal installations.[41]

Congress had passed a law that required open bidding for government contracts, and Meigs demanded compliance. Although he wisely dispersed orders throughout the states to satisfy senators, representatives, and governors, his department retained relative independence from the politicians and their supporters in the patronage business. Meigs established new guidelines for manufacturers, including standard measurements, or sizes, for uniforms.[42]

By the beginning of 1862, a military bureaucracy managed the North's supply system. In addition to Meigs's department, the Subsistence Department oversaw the acquisition of food supplies, and the Ordnance Department purchased or manufactured cannon, firearms, and ammunition. In time, however, the Quartermaster Department consumed nearly one-half of the Northern industrial output and spent more money than any agency or bureau of the federal government. Within another year, Meigs employed a hundred thousand civilian workers.[43]

"Meigs's role in managing the expansion of the Quartermaster Department and supervising officers in the field cannot be overestimated," in the judgment of historian Earl J. Hess, "He and his officers were responsible for Union logistical success in the Civil War." He submitted budgets for his department to Congress, scrupulously oversaw disbursement of funds, ensured that paperwork was handled properly, and kept the War Department current on the conflict's mounting demands.[44]

A chief quartermaster of the Third Corps of the Army of the Potomac grumbled after the war that Meigs's department was "the most abused and the least understood of any in the army, though the most important by far of all the staff departments." This ultimately vast bureaucracy linked the North's private enterprises to its military forces. The department and its officers, enlisted men, and clerks procured and then distributed mountains of war materiel to Union armies and the navy.[45]

The result, unprecedented in the nation's past, was "a mixed military economy," according to historian Mark R. Wilson. A "decentralized national network of depots and officers" stood between the needs of the War Department and the thousands of private suppliers in the North. A biographer of Meigs, Robert O'Harrow Jr., has argued that the Quartermaster Department "provided momentum to the nation's economy for years to come."[46]

No one could have foreseen during the war's initial months that vital and enlarging role of Meigs and his department. New York attorney George Templeton Strong met the quartermaster general in August 1861 and recorded in his diary: "He is an exceptional and refreshing specimen of sense and promptitude, unlike most of our high military officials. There's not a fibre of red tape in his constitution."[47]

Four years later at the war's end, the accomplishments of Meigs "should be given a place near that of Seward and Stanton, Chase and Gideon Welles," historian Allan Nevins argues. Historian James McPherson believes the ranking quartermaster to be "the unsung hero of northern victory," and fellow historians Herman Hattaway and

Archer Jones claim, "Meigs performed tasks monumental in the annals of military history."[48]

~

IN 1861, JOHN HAY PENNED—ANONYMOUSLY—AN ARTICLE FOR A pro-administration Saint Louis, Missouri, newspaper near year's end. "The whole inventive genius of the American people is now centered upon a single object," the president's secretary contended, "and if they do not work out some miracles in the use of iron, lead and 'villainous salt petre,' they will belie their past history and all the idiosyncrasies of the universal Yankee nation."[49]

Hay decried the fact that American "genius" was devoted almost entirely to "the great work of human slaughter." New cannon were being forged; new firearms were being designed and tested. But the "Yankee nation" was at work in quantities of products far greater than "death-dealing instruments."[50]

The transition from America's economic past to a yet-to-be-determined future was ongoing. The improvisation of the conflict's early days slowly gave way to expansion and organization, from the antebellum local, state, and regional economies to a national organization of resources and production. The federal government and business enterprises, large and small, became partners in the struggle to save the Union.[51]

Most critical to the undertaking, private enterprise in the North "believed in its obligation to preserve the nation." The administration and the home front had to engineer victory by combining the output of farms and factories with the advance of Union forces into the Confederacy. "As the first two years of the struggle might be called the improvised war," Nevins states, "the last two could be termed the organized war. The transition from one to the other was a transition from the old America to the new, and not in material terms alone, but in psychological terms also."[52]

At the foundation of the monumental undertaking lay the "Yankee nation"—the farms and factories from Maine to Minnesota—and "the whole inventive genius of the American people." The entrepreneurial talent of businessmen and the ingenuity and skill of Northern workers—men and women—resulted in, according to McPherson, "war production on a scale that would make the Union army the best fed, most lavishly supplied army that had ever existed."[53]

WHILE TRAVELING EAST, SOLDIERS FROM WISCONSIN DETRAINED BRIEFLY in Pittsburgh, Pennsylvania. "You can smell smoke," one of them asserted in a letter, "feel smoke & I will go so far as to say you can taste it." The volunteer from the West believed that newsboys looked "as if they had [been] suspended over the funnel of some blacksmith's shop."[54]

It was the autumn of 1861, and the smoke from the city's factories heralded an awakening, a stirring of the giant. Three and a half years later, at war's end in April 1865, the federal government had spent more than $3 billion on the victory. Two-thirds of that amount had gone for the purchase of materiel. On some items, the numbers were staggering: 1 billion rounds of small arms ammunition, 1 million horses and mules, 1.5 million barrels of pork, 100 million pounds of coffee, 6 million woolen blankets, and 10 million pairs of shoes. The War and Navy departments also bought or manufactured hundreds of heavy ordnance, more than a million firearms, hundreds of naval vessels, and millions of accoutrements.[55]

This level of mobilization could not have been possible without an American business culture, natural and man-made resources, a skilled and trainable workforce, and leaders in private industry. The North's economy had been moving increasingly toward industrialization during the two prior decades. These changes needed and created individuals who developed skills of finance, organization, and innovation. The administration in Washington relied on them to marshal the region's economic capacity.[56]

The Civil War brought forth their talents as they also strived to preserve the Union. They were tinkers, inventors, improvisers, builders, organizers, entrepreneurs, and even dreamers. They created their own companies or expanded other enterprises. They were instrumental as private individuals in forging victory and recasting the past and heralding the future. They were among those who stood astride the transformation of a nation.[57]

Chapter Two

THE ADMINISTRATORS

—⟋⟍—

THOSE WHO SAW IT AND EVEN THOSE WHO READ ABOUT IT RE-
garded it as the engineering marvel of its day. A nearly two-mile-
long semicircle, the Horseshoe Curve, as it became known, lay outside
of Altoona, Pennsylvania, carrying the tracks of the Pennsylvania Railroad. It had been created by constructing a huge fill, a man-made em-
bankment, over one ravine and slicing off the face of a mountain to fill
in another.[1]

When completed in February 1854, Horseshoe Curve reduced travel
time by rail between Philadelphia and Pittsburgh to fifteen hours. It
solved the decades-old problem of getting a direct line across the Allegheny Mountains. Horseshoe Curve owed its construction to the labor
of several hundred mostly Irish immigrants and to the engineering brilliance of one man, John Edgar Thomson.[2]

J. Edgar Thomson was born on February 10, 1808, to John and
Sarah Lewis Thomson on the family farm ten miles south of Philadelphia in Delaware County, Pennsylvania. The Thomsons were Quakers,
and John Thomson was a noted surveyor and civil engineer in the region. He surveyed the route for the "historic" Thomas Leiper Railroad,
the first line in the state and the second in the country where horse-
drawn cars ran on the tracks. This line eventually became a spur of the
Baltimore & Ohio Railroad. Perhaps as early as 1809, he built a three-
quarter-mile-long line from a quarry.[3]

The elder Thomson was a "strict, exacting father," but he and his son were "unusually close." By the time he was a youth, J. Edgar accompanied his father on surveying and engineering projects, learning the rudiments of both trades. What formal schooling the son received is uncertain, but he became well educated. He expressed to his parents at one point a desire to attend the military academy at West Point, but the family's pacifist beliefs likely precluded an effort to receive an appointment.[4]

The younger Thomson worked briefly on a canal before serving as engineer on the Philadelphia & Columbia Railroad at age nineteen. He hired on later as engineer with the Camden & Amboy Railroad in New Jersey. In 1830, he left the job and visited Europe to examine public works. Four years later, he was hired as chief engineer for the Georgia Railroad, which was under construction from Augusta to Marthasville. The Georgia legislature, meanwhile, had approved another railroad, the Western Atlantic, from Marthasville to Chattanooga, Tennessee. When the board of directors of the Western Atlantic sought to rename Marthasville, Thomson suggested Atlanta as an alteration of Atlantic.[5]

Thomson spent nearly thirteen years in Georgia before returning to his native state and accepting the position of chief engineer at the recently incorporated Pennsylvania Railroad. The charter for the new rail company had been pushed through the legislature and signed by the governor to prevent the Baltimore & Ohio Railroad from building a line from Cumberland, Maryland, to Pittsburgh. The Pennsylvania Railroad was organized by lawyers, bankers, speculators, and politicians.[6]

Earlier governors and legislatures in the Keystone State had endeavored to duplicate the economic success of the Erie Canal. In the 1820s, the politicians authorized the Main Line of Public Works, which consisted of canals and railroads from Philadelphia to Pittsburgh. The first leg of the Main Line was the eighty-two-mile-long Philadelphia & Columbia Railroad, which Thomson had worked on as the company's principal assistant engineer. In the line's early years, passengers rode in horse-drawn cars and it took nine hours to complete a one-way trip. From Columbia on the east bank of the Susquehanna River, canal boats carried passengers and goods to the foot of the Allegheny Mountains, where the thirty-six-mile Allegheny Portage Railroad used an incline plane system to cross the barrier. More canal boats on the western slopes completed the tedious journey.[7]

When the Main Line of Public Works opened in 1834, it extended more than 390 miles between Pennsylvania's two major cities, requiring three trans-shipments of cargo and passengers along the route. Winter weather closed the canals three or four months each year. In the end, the Public (or State) Works proved to be a failure and incurred financial losses. On April 13, 1846, the state legislature granted a charter to the Pennsylvania Railroad. The body also authorized three possible routes around the Allegheny Mountains portage to decrease the time required to cross the state.[8]

After conducting surveys of the proposed routes, the railroad's chief engineer, Thomson, chose the middle one at a site known as Kittanning Point outside of Altoona. The construction of Horseshoe Curve consumed six years. Thomson designed it so that the track would rise gradually from the valley below at a grade of 1.8 feet in 100 feet. His ingenious plan reduced the danger of a train wreck on a steep mountainside. A newspaper stated years later that Horseshoe Curve helped to establish Thomson's "reputation of being a veritable railroad genius."[9]

While at work on the massive undertaking near Altoona, Thomson clashed with the company's president, Samuel Merrick. They disagreed, apparently, on nearly all aspects of the project, with Thomson threatening to resign. He wrote, "The old president and me cannot get along cordially." Merrick was not an engineer and likely opposed the cost of the enterprise near Altoona. Eventually, the difficulties between the two men resulted in a vote of the stockholders, who elected Thomson president on February 3, 1852, two years before Horseshoe Curve opened for traffic. Ironically, the chief engineer had told Merrick years earlier, "I am naturally indisposed to seek authority."[10]

According to a biographer of Thomson's, "He rose to power on the Pennsylvania by reason of his professional skills and wide experience, which combined to serve his company well." His brilliance as an engineer and his talent as an administrator contributed undoubtedly to the stockholders' confidence in him. His personality made him, however, an unlikely choice for such an important position.[11]

"I found Thomson so taciturn that I could get nothing out of him," Herman Haupt, a business associate, told a colleague. "He was noncommittal in everything." The fellow worker, assistant engineer Samuel Mifflin, replied: "I know Thomson intimately. He is a queer fish." In time, a joke circulated among office employees that the company president spoke only twice a day.[12]

He possessed an intense shyness, which combined with professional caution. Mifflin might have believed that he knew Thomson intimately, but, even so, few others in the company or railroad business did. In public, particularly, Thomson could be icily aloof and brusque. His conservatism resulted in his thorough examination of ideas. He had that pragmatic businessman's attitude and was a stickler for facts. Once he had settled on a course of action, nothing seemed to stop him in its implementation.[13]

Thomson's outward reticence belied internal passions. Although he was an unimposing man physically at five feet nine inches tall, he burned with a devotion to the company. He married, and he and his wife adopted a daughter, but his existence revolved around the railroad's headquarters in Philadelphia. In a biographer's estimation, the firm became "the center of Thomson's life."[14]

Thomson worked tirelessly on behalf of the company during the 1850s, with a goal of expanding the firm into a rail system. They double-tracked 136 miles of the line at a cost of more than $18 million. In 1857, he purchased the assets of the Main Line of Public Works at auction for $7.5 million. He consolidated three rail lines into the Pittsburgh, Fort Wayne and Chicago Railway, completing the passage from Pittsburgh to Chicago. He also bought stock in other companies and in May

1861 secured a 999-year lease on the unfinished Philadelphia & Erie Railroad.[15]

The railroad company's investments and purchases required the sale of new shares of stock to raise funds. The state legislature, however, had to approve such stock issuances. Newspaper publisher Horace Greeley contended that Pennsylvania's legislature was "then one of the rottenest and the surrounding lobby the most rapacious and shameless on earth." Unquestionably, Thomson pressured members and did favors for them. Samuel Mifflin confided that Thomson "is in a tight place with that location," meaning the state capital.[16]

Thomson did not trust the politicians and the lobbyists and described them as "the land sharks at Harrisburg." In most business matters with the legislature, he seemed to be guided by a particular strategy, as he stated to a United States congressman: "It has been my policy to say as little as possible." It was the legislators who, in turn, pressured him to bid on and buy the Public Works.[17]

The company's major battle with the politicians during the 1850s involved the tonnage tax. The legislature had levied a tax on the number of tons hauled and the miles traveled by railroad firms. Thomson hated the tax, but it was a complex issue. Voters opposed a repeal of the tax, and newspapers conveyed that viewpoint across the state. The company's vice president, Thomas A. Scott, managed to get a repeal through the legislature in 1860.[18]

Scott typified the talented associates that Thomson either hired or promoted, including Herman Haupt, Samuel Mifflin, and Andrew Carnegie. The president valued loyalty and rewarded accomplishments. If a man could be of help to Thomson, said Mifflin, "he will not be ungrateful." He and his closest colleagues invested in real estate and coal and timber companies along the railroad's line. Haupt's investments were worth $473,160, for instance, by 1856.[19]

During the 1850s, Thomson colluded with the presidents of the New York Central, New York & Erie, and Baltimore & Ohio railroads to fix rates and ensure profits for each company. In 1859, the four men met privately in Washington, DC, endeavoring to agree further on "a uniformity of action" among them. The effort failed, yet two years later the demands on their lines and others rapidly accelerated.[20]

OHIO CONGRESSMAN ALBERT GALLATIN RIDDLE MET THE VICE PRESI-dent of the Pennsylvania Railroad, Thomas A. Scott, in Washington, DC, after the Civil War had begun. "Slight but symmetrical," Riddle remembered the Pennsylvanian, "with a face as sharply and beautifully cut as a cameo, he was the embodiment of energy, intellect, and wise unerring judgment. Whenever he was to be found in the office [at the War Department], what a relief to deal with him, with his electric brain and cool, quiet manner."[21]

Scott had been summoned to the capital by a fellow Pennsylvanian, Secretary of War Simon Cameron, "to take charge" of railways and tele-graph between Washington and Annapolis, Maryland. Pro-secessionists in Maryland had disrupted the passage of troops, arms, and supplies through Baltimore, and the situation demanded resolution. A close friend of Cameron's, the thirty-seven-year-old Scott had a well-deserved reputation for fixing problems and removing obstacles.[22]

Scott was born on December 28, 1828, in Loudon, Franklin County, a village consisting of "a few straggling houses" at the time. His father owned an inn along a well-traveled road. Scott attended a local com-mon school until his father died in 1835. For the next two years he lived with an older sister and then an older brother. Scott clerked in various country stores for nearly a decade until he secured a job with a commis-sion house as a collector of tolls on the Main Line. It was in this posi-tion that he came to the notice of Herman Haupt, who recommended him to J. Edgar Thomson, president of the Pennsylvania Railroad.[23]

Scott's ascendancy in the company paralleled the railroad's growth and increasing economic and political power in the state during the 1850s. He served as agent of the firm's Eastern Division and then its Western Division. While in the latter post, he oversaw the consolidation of the Pittsburgh, Fort Wayne and Chicago Railway. When the company's general superintendent died, Scott filled the office, and, in 1859, upon the death of its vice president and on Thomson's urging, the board of stockholders picked him for the vacancy. His reputation in the company was nothing short of "phenomenal."[24]

It was Scott, not Thomson, who directed the campaign for the repeal of the tonnage tax. He possessed the requisite personal attributes that the taciturn president did not. Scott was "a clever political creature," according to a biographer of Thomson's. The repeal of the tax faced fierce political and public opposition. The levy on tonnage had been imposed on the company's original charter to protect Public Works.[25]

Scott waged an unrelenting campaign, utilizing tactics common to the era. He manipulated the press with stories favorable to the railroad and directed the bribery of members of the legislature. "Scott was not so much tainted by corruption as impregnated with it," historian Richard White asserts. In the end, the legislature rescinded the tax and replaced it with a flat annual payment of $460,000 until July 31, 1890.[26]

Scott's victory in the legislature indicated, if not confirmed, the company's political influence. By the winter of 1861, the Pennsylvania Railroad stood as the dominant business enterprise in the state. In fifteen years, the company had double-tracked 423 miles of rail and controlled the stock of three railroads in Ohio, Indiana, and Illinois, which added another 465 miles to its lines. Thomson and Scott were arguably the preeminent railroad executives in the North on the eve of the Civil War, having "attained a more extensive dominion than most people realized," according to historian Allan Nevins.[27]

J. Edgar Thomson considered the outbreak of civil conflict in the United States as absurd. He believed that the Lincoln administration had done nothing to justify secession and the attack on Fort Sumter. He also thought, as he wrote to Simon Cameron on April 27, 1861,

"This war can be brought to a close in ninety days, if pushed with the vigor that the people now seem disposed to sustain it."[28]

A crisis in rail travel to the capital had begun on April 19, when a mob assailed the 6th Massachusetts Infantry as it passed between railroad stations in Baltimore. Officials in Washington wanted a secure route opened to the city for the passage of troops and supplies. Cameron appointed Thomson as his personal agent, responsible for all transportation to Washington, DC. According to a newspaper report, Thomson informed government officials that his railroad could transport sixty thousand troops and baggage from Pittsburgh to Harrisburg in nine hours if given twelve hours' notice.[29]

The secretary of war had initially tried to shift rail traffic to the North Central Railroad, which ran from Sunbury, Pennsylvania, dozens of miles up the Susquehanna River from Harrisburg, through York to Baltimore. Cameron, his brother, and Thomson held a major financial interest in the line, but, with a terminus in Baltimore, it was closed to traffic. Instead, Thomson and Samuel Felton, president of the Philadelphia, Wilmington and Baltimore Railroad, proposed bypassing Baltimore and to ship men and materiel by rail to Perryville, Maryland, at the mouth of the Susquehanna River. From there, loads could be hauled by steamboat down the Chesapeake Bay to Annapolis, and on by railroad to the capital.[30]

The plan worked. Regiment after regiment followed the detour around Baltimore, which Union troops occupied in early May. Felton reminded Cameron that he and Thomson had "assumed great responsibility" financially in the successful implementation of the plan. For his part, Thomson stockpiled supplies in Philadelphia, expedited the transport of troops to Perryville, and rushed arms from the Allegheny Arsenal in Pittsburgh to the national capital.[31]

THE MAN RESPONSIBLE FOR KEEPING OPEN THE ROUTE BETWEEN ANnapolis and Washington was Thomas A. Scott. When the war began,

Pennsylvania governor Andrew Gregg Curtin appointed Scott to his staff, directing the railroad executive to equip and to forward troops to the national capital. On April 27, however, Secretary of War Simon Cameron requested him to oversee the rail and telegraph lines between Annapolis and Washington. On May 3, Scott was appointed colonel of the District of Columbia militia unit.[32]

Herman Haupt, who had recommended hiring Scott on the Pennsylvania Railroad, wrote to Scott, seeking his endorsement for a position in the War Department. When Haupt read in the newspapers of Scott's assignment, he wrote to Congressman John Covode: "This accounts for the milk of the coconut. I did not understand why it was that Scott did not seem to favor the idea of my appointment." Haupt added, however, that "no better appointment could have been made than [Scott]."[33]

The occupation of Baltimore by Union troops ended Scott's duty with the Annapolis–Washington route. On May 23, Cameron assigned him to further work and broader authority. The order read: "Col. Thomas A. Scott has been appointed to take charge of all Government railways and telegraphs or those appropriated for Government use. All instructions in relation to extending roads or operating the same on Government account must emanate from his department."[34]

Initially, Scott convinced Cameron to leave railroads under civilian management. In turn, he informed rail companies that they were to conduct their business as "direct adjuncts" of the War Department. On July 12, he issued a directive establishing rates for troops and quartermaster supplies. A railroad could charge two cents per mile for troops or passengers, while rates for supplies were to be determined by weight and distance. In time, profits for railroads soared.[35]

Congress authorized the office of the assistant secretary of war, and Cameron appointed Scott to it on August 3. Before he accepted the position, Scott consulted Thomson, who evidently approved. Scott followed with a letter to the president and board of directors of the railroad, explaining "my protracted absence from Philadelphia [company headquarters]." In his and Thomson's discussions, he had agreed to leave the War Department by October 1 if either he or the board desired it. "I have endeavored," professed Scott, "by my labors at Washington and to our struggling company and at all times when possible have been careful to protect the interests of our Company." The board accepted his "temporary" appointment.[36]

Scott continued as assistant secretary of war for another ten months. By the time he left the War Department, his benefactor, Cameron, had been forced out as secretary. Charges of corruption had swirled around the Pennsylvania politician since the spring of 1861. Cameron had rewarded friends and supporters with contracts and had routed as much traffic as he could on to the North Central Railroad, which benefited him, his brother, Thomson, and Scott. He also had proved to be a poor administrator or, as Lincoln intimated to John Nicolay, Cameron was "incapable either of organizing details or conceiving and advising general plans."[37]

Cameron had committed a major political blunder in December, when he advocated the arming of slaves in his annual report to Congress. He distributed copies of the report to several newspapers before submitting it to the president for approval. Lincoln had the paragraph deleted and ordered all copies seized. Finally, a month later, after more intrigue, Cameron accepted the post of minister to Russia. Then, after discussion with cabinet members, Lincoln appointed Edwin Stanton as Cameron's successor.[38]

Newspaper correspondent Noah Brooks described the new cabinet secretary as "a shortish, full-fed man with spectacles, black, and full, grizzled beard." Brooks added that Stanton was "opinionated, implacable, intent, and not easily turned from any purpose." Herman Haupt, who came to know Stanton well, recalled: "He was a man of marked ability and of strong characteristics. He was, I believe, honest, patriotic and fearless, but at times impulsive and headstrong."[39]

Stanton was in almost all respects the antithesis of his predecessor. Tireless, capable, and zealous in devotion to the Union cause, Stanton transformed the workings of the War Department. Both Brooks and

Haupt had him right, for he ruled, rather than directed, the department and was a terror to its employees, civilian and military. What characterized Stanton more than anything was, in the estimation of Secretary of the Navy Gideon Welles, fondness of "power and of its exercise."[40]

One of Stanton's initial actions was to appoint Colonel Daniel C. McCallum and Herman Haupt to the newly authorized United States Military Rail Road. The USMRR was created to build or rebuild and to operate railroads in Union-occupied Confederate territory. McCallum served as its administrator, and the former Pennsylvania engineer, Haupt, oversaw the construction of and transportation on the rail lines. Both men proved to be brilliant choices by the new secretary of war.[41]

The creation of the USMRR relieved Scott of his duty with railroads and telegraphs. Although Scott must have had the odor of Cameron about him, Stanton utilized the Pennsylvanian's talents on other missions. In March 1862, Scott traveled to Fort Monroe at the tip of the Virginia Peninsula to arrange the transfer of the hundred-thousand-man Army of the Potomac and all its artillery, wagons, and supplies from Washington to the peninsula. It was a massive undertaking, "the stride of a giant" to a British observer, that took nearly three weeks to complete.[42]

Scott also conducted several inspection tours for the War Department in Pennsylvania, Ohio, Illinois, and Tennessee during the spring. But on June 1, Scott resigned as assistant secretary of war. In Pennsylvania, the legislature had been investigating his efforts in the repeal of the tonnage tax and, in Washington, a congressional committee sent notices to newspapers that he and Cameron had defrauded the government of public funds. The latter charge against him had no basis in facts.[43]

Before Scott departed for Philadelphia, he stopped at the White House to see Lincoln. Finding the president, in Scott's words, "besieged by the million," he scribbled a brief note to Lincoln. He had called, Scott wrote, "to say 'good bye' and to thank you for your past Courtesy and Kindness." Scott concluded that if he would be needed in the future to "render you some special service without seriously interfering with my Railway duties," he would do so at Lincoln's request.[44]

Scott's contact with the War Department continued after his resignation. During the Antietam campaign in September 1862, he kept Major General George B. McClellan, commander of the Army of the Potomac, informed of intelligence as General Robert E. Lee's Confederate Army of Northern Virginia entered Maryland and approached Pennsylvania. To allay fears of a Rebel advance into the Keystone State, Scott asked Stanton to send fellow Pennsylvanian, Brigadier General John F. Reynolds, to command Pennsylvania emergency units. Despite McClellan's objections, Reynolds reported to Governor Andrew Gregg Curtin.[45]

Months later during an actual Confederate incursion, the Gettysburg campaign, Scott traveled to Harrisburg to help Curtin organize emergency units and to intercede with the War Department for arms and equipment. Scott and Thomson asked Lincoln to appoint McClellan to command the state's defenses. The president had relieved McClellan of command the army in November 1862 and refused to reinstate him in any capacity. "Tom Scott and Edgar Thomson," as a War Department official put it, "will find it harder than ever to manufacture public sentiment to bear upon the President for the restoration of McClellan."[46]

In September 1863, Lincoln and Stanton requested Scott's assistance. A Union army in the West suffered a major defeat at the Battle of Chickamauga on September 19–20, and it had retreated into Chattanooga, Tennessee. With the war stalemated in Virginia, General Lee had acceded to the transfer of two infantry divisions and an artillery battalion to the Confederate Army of Tennessee. The arrival of these troops was instrumental in the Rebel victory. In reaction, the Lincoln administration ordered the transfer of the Eleventh and Twelfth corps from the Army of the Potomac to the West.[47]

The War Department dispatched Scott to Louisville, Kentucky, where he had the authority "to do what he deems necessary for the service, subject, however, to approval by this Department." He shuttled units of the two corps through Louisville and south, handling one hundred or more railroad cars a day. Scott followed the corps to Nashville, Tennessee, where he forwarded them on to Chattanooga. His expertise expedited the transfer with few glitches and, by the end of October, Scott had returned to his duties with the Pennsylvania Railroad.[48]

THE CIVIL WAR OFFERED AN OPPORTUNITY THAT WAS PERHAPS EVEN beyond the expectations of J. Edgar Thomson. He had labored tirelessly to make the Pennsylvania Railroad into a rail system. The restoration of the Union intertwined with the interests of Thomson's company. Patriotic work meant burgeoning profits and the possibility of a dream fulfilled.[49]

Thomson maintained separate accounts for hauling troops and government supplies. He managed to secure the bulk of the government's livestock trade. Newspapers and some elected officials accused him of fixing rates and defrauding the public, but those allegations could not be substantiated at the time. Unquestionably, he billed the government all that he could, believing correctly that the conflict had to end sometime.[50]

Gross revenues of Pennsylvania Railroad soared from $5.9 million in 1860 to $17.4 million in 1865. Net earnings increased from $2.3 million in 1860 to $4.2 million in 1865, and the company issued its first stock dividends in 1863. The Pennsylvania Railroad donated $270,000 to hospitals, soup houses, and the work of the Christian and Sanitary commissions. The rail firm also gave the commonwealth $50,000 toward Soldiers' Orphan Schools.[51]

Much of the profit went toward the purchase or consolidation of other rail lines. Soon after the war began, Thomson and Simon Cameron had the Pennsylvania legislature pass a special act that allowed Thomson's company to secure the Northern Central Railroad. Thomson obtained possession of the Philadelphia & Erie Railroad in the winter of

1862. By the war's end, he had reorganized the Steubenville and Indiana Railroad, finished the double-tracking of his own line, reorganized the Pittsburgh, Fort Wayne and Chicago Railway Company, and acquired branch railroads in Pennsylvania. The rails Thomson controlled extended from Philadelphia as far west as Chicago and Saint Louis.[52]

Problems plagued the carrier, however, throughout the four years of warfare. Inflation gnawed away at profits, and the costs of repairing the track beds and purchasing steel rails further eroded gains. The company's primary challenge was finding and keeping skilled workers. The increased traffic made for long workdays and overburdened facilities. The burdens of the presidency forced Thomson to take a respite for his health, and he spent several months in Europe in 1862. During the Confederate advance into Pennsylvania in the summer of 1863, Thomson shifted all the company's rolling stock to Philadelphia and suspended traffic throughout the state.[53]

When the war ended in April 1865, the Pennsylvania Railroad ranked as the preeminent rail system in the reunited country. The company's success could only be attributed to Thomson and Thomas Scott. Although they were, as a newspaper noted, as unlike personally "as it would seem to be possible," both men possessed farsightedness, strong wills, tireless energy, intense ambition, and administrative talent matched by few others.[54]

A few years after the war, the Philadelphia *Ledger* gave a description of the railroad executive, whose home was on the corner of Eighteenth and Spruce streets in "fashionable" Rittenhouse Square. "He looks like an Episcopal bishop," the paper stated about Thomson, "wears a white necktie, and is robust and rather handsome specimen." Continuing, "Silence and thinking are his specialities . . . indeed [he is] a thinking man, and . . . also [a] man of great energy action." He has the "entire confidence" of his company, and "neither his word nor purpose is ever questioned."[55]

A fellow railroader asserted: "We are specialists, that is pygmies. Thomson was great in everything—operating traffic, motive power, finance, but most of all in organization." An economic historian claims, "Thomson was indeed one of the most brilliant organizational innovators in American history." A biographer, James A. Ward, contends, "Thomson's noteworthiness was that he was in the vanguard that reshaped these impulses [for progress] into the institutional embodiments they ultimately assumed, which are so familiar to us today."[56]

Like Thomson, Scott had a similar aptitude for administration. Superintendent Daniel McCallum of the USMRR professed in an 1866 report, "The fact should be understood that the management of railroads is just as much a distinct profession as is that of the art of war." McCallum's words could have unquestionably applied to Scott. He was, according to historian Richard White, "the quintessential railroad man of his generation." The two railroad executives were among "the first group of modern business administrators in the United States." Amid the fires of civil war, they reforged a company and framed its future.[57]

Chapter Three

THE VISIONARY

—∿—

USTOMERS CAME TO E. W. CLARK AND COMPANY, A BANKING firm on Third Street in Philadelphia, often inquiring, "Where is the counterfeit clerk?" In the 1840s, counterfeit scrip, or "wild cat money," as it was called, circulated throughout the country. The paper bills were usually old and dirty, and most banks would not exchange them for specie. The banking house on Third Street, below Market Street, accepted the "wild cat money" because it employed the "counterfeit clerk."[1]

The clerk was, remembered a young onlooker, "tall, slender, light-haired, blue eyed, fair complexioned, and a radiant countenance." He possessed an uncanny, some said flawless, ability to detect counterfeits amid stacks of bills while conversing with clients, asking or answering questions. "The like I had never seen," asserted the eyewitness, "and it astonished me." Simply put, Jay Cooke "was a revelation."[2]

He had joined the banking firm and brokerage founded by Enoch W. Clark and Edward Dodge at the age of nineteen. By then, the young man had been a clerk in various stores for a decade. His first job had been in a dry goods store owned by an uncle, who allowed him to sell tin toys and picture books on his account. Cooke remarked later that he could "earn all my spending money through their sale. In fact, I was quite a capitalist . . . this when I was not over nine or ten years old."[3]

Born August 10, 1821, at "Ogontz Place," later Sandusky, Ohio, Cooke was the third of six children to Eleutheros and Martha Caswell Cooke. His parents named him after John Jay, the first chief justice of the Supreme Court. The family traced its lineage to Puritan Massachusetts, but his parents had emigrated from New York into the Northwest Territory, settling in Ohio by 1819. Eleutheros Cooke practiced law and served in the state legislature and one term in Congress.[4]

Young Jay attended a private school and then an academy until age fourteen, when he was hired as a clerk in a new dry goods store in Sandusky. An owner of the store, a Mr. Hubbard, taught his employee double-entry bookkeeping and chess. Cooke helped his family assist runaway slaves en route to Canada. In 1836, he accepted a clerkship with a store in Saint Louis, but the Panic of 1837 closed the doors of the establishment.[5]

Cooke claimed later that when he returned home from Saint Louis at the age of sixteen, "I came back with more cash in my pockets than any Sandusky boy ever possessed before." Within a year, he joined his brother-in-law, William G. Moorhead, in the latter's newly formed packet boat business in Philadelphia. Cooke stated in his memoir that he created advertisements and "editorial notices" for the firm. Unfortunately, the business soon failed, and Cooke returned once again to Sandusky. He had not particularly cared for Philadelphia.[6]

Ironically, Philadelphia became his home for the rest of his life when he accepted a clerkship with E. W. Clark and Company in 1839. Enoch Clark and Edward Dodge met Cooke when he worked for his brother-in-law. As he wrote later, the banking business "proved to be my life work." The firm had branches in Saint Louis, New Orleans, and New York. Clark and Dodge made Cooke a partner in 1843. "The business I am engaged in is the most respectable kind and the house is the first in the city," he boasted to a brother in a letter.[7]

During the Mexican War, the federal government sought $10 million in loans, and E. W. Clark and Company and a Washington, DC, banking house were awarded the bids. In a complicated but legal arrangement, the Philadelphia firm deposited money in government subtreasuries and made "a large profit" on exchange premiums above its earnings on the loans. It was a business practice Cooke learned well.[8]

Enoch Clark died in 1856, and Cooke served as executor of the estate. When the Panic of 1857 ravaged the country economically, the banking house closed all its branches except its Philadelphia office. Cooke assisted Clark's sons with the business's reorganization before leaving the firm in 1858.[9]

He had spent nearly two decades with the banking and brokerage house. In 1844, he had married Dorothea Elizabeth Allen, and when he left the firm, he had acquired "a fair fortune." He had learned, as he put it: "Through all the grades [social ranks] I see the same all-pervading, all-engrossing anxiety to grow rich. This is the only thing for which men live here."[10]

The former banking partner lived "Free Foot" the next two years, hunting, fishing, and restoring his health. "I have often reflected," Cooke recalled about these years, "that this preparation of rest and of disentanglement from all business providentially fitted me to carry cheerfully, energetically, as well as faithfully and trustingly, the most enormous financial burdens I verily believe that were ever placed on the shoulders of any one man."[11]

JAY COOKE & COMPANY OPENED FOR BUSINESS IN A BROWNSTONE AT 114 South Third Street in Philadelphia, on January 1, 1861. Cooke claimed that he reentered the banking business at the suggestion of his brother-in-law and then partner, William Moorhead. The company began with capital of perhaps $10,000, with Cooke having two-thirds interest and Moorehead one-third.[12]

Cooke conducted the firm's business affairs. "It was not expected," wrote Cooke, that his partner would be in the office. Moorhead was president of the Philadelphia & Erie Railroad and oversaw its interests. Although Cooke claimed later that he had disentangled himself from "all business" during his two-year respite, he had reorganized sections of the state's canal system and invested in at least one railroad company. It seems likely that he had some financial investment in his brother-in-law's rail line.[13]

Jay Cooke & Company had its doors open less than four full months when the war began. In Pennsylvania, volunteers flooded to a training camp in Harrisburg, but the state had a debt of $40 million and a low credit rating. On May 15, 1861, the legislature passed an act for a reserve force and authorized the sale of $3 million in bonds at 6 percent interest. Bankers informed Governor Andrew Gregg Curtin that the bonds had to be sold at less than par. Cooke, meanwhile, told Curtin that he could sell the bonds at par "on *patriotic* principles."[14]

On May 28, Curtin officially designated Cooke's company and A. J. Drexel's Drexel & Co. as commissioners to secure bids for the loan. Cooke sent agents into the state's counties and used "liberal advertising" in newspapers. In less than three weeks, the two firms obtained subscriptions for $3.3 million, saving the state more than a half million dollars. "I have always regarded [it] as one of the greatest in my financial experiences," Cooke declared years later.[15]

Cooke's sales campaign was an unquestioned success. He considered it to be "an achievement as great or greater than Napoleon's crossing the Alps." Its methods were inventive. He used patriotism, not self-interest, as a primary motivator for the purchase of the bonds. He discovered that the widespread publication of advertisements in the press "proved vastly the cheapest method" of informing the public. Hiring agents to canvass the mostly rural counties enabled Cooke to reach a broad swath of the state. Such a campaign, he believed, could succeed across the North if necessary.[16]

Ambition burned within Salmon P. Chase with an intense flame. He had sought the Republican Party's presidential nomination in 1860 but settled for a position as Treasury secretary. He could be stubborn, pompous, and rather humorless, with a self-importance, even a self-righteousness, that seemed to be as much a part of him as his well-tailored suits. Fellow cabinet member Gideon Welles believed Chase had "capacity," noting that he committed few mistakes "but persevered in them when made, often to his serious detriment."[17]

Fellow Republican Carl Schurz remarked that Chase "looked as you would wish a statesman to look." The secretary was tall, broadshouldered, with a head that seemed to belong to a bigger man. A newspaper reporter who knew him well wrote, "Mr. Chase is easy and gentlemanly in his manners, though he has a painful way of holding his head straight, which leads one to fancy that his shirt collar cuts his ears."[18]

Chase inherited a national treasury nearly depleted of funds. As recently as December 1860, the government had not possessed enough money to pay members of Congress. On February 8, 1861, Congress authorized the sale of bonds, but banks did not accept them at par. In turn, the Treasury received only gold and silver as payments, which removed much specie from circulation. An estimated 7,000 different bank notes from approximately 1,600 banks comprised much of the money in circulation.[19]

"Mr. Chase has a good deal of ability," Gideon Welles confided to his diary, "but has never made finance his study." Like his predecessor, the Treasury secretary used the February legislation to offer another $8 million in bonds, requiring payment in specie. The offering secured barely more than $3 million. Chase then hired a New York City brokerage to sell $15 million in Treasury notes.[20]

Jay Cooke watched these bond and notes sales with keen interest. His family and Chase's had been linked socially, politically, and financially in Ohio for a number of years. Eleutheros Cooke, Jay's father, had supported his fellow Republican and abolitionist when Chase won the governorship and through his candidacy for president at the party convention. Henry Cooke, who was four years younger than his brother Jay, was editor and publisher of the *Ohio State Journal*, which Chase had a financial investment in. The relationship between the Cookes and the cabinet official soon proved to be timely and mutually beneficial.[21]

Jay Cooke had never met Chase but, using his family's connections, offered advice to the Treasury secretary. He wrote a letter on April 8, 1861, to Chase, which his brother Henry delivered to the secretary. Cooke recommended "not to try too much to save the pennies but to keep on the right side of the capitalists who are disposed to dabble in the loans etc., of the government, and if they do make sometimes a handsome margin it is no more than they are entitled to in such times as these."[22]

Henry Cooke served as liaison between Jay Cooke and Chase during the initial weeks of the conflict. "My brother knew little of financial matters," Jay stated in a memoir but, most importantly for the Cookes, Henry and Chase were "warm personal friends." In fact, when Chase died in 1873, Henry acted as executor of his estate.[23]

It was through Henry, then, that Jay offered his services to the government, confiding to his younger brother, "Pay or no pay, I will do all I can to aid him [Chase]." The Treasury secretary offered Jay the assistant treasurer's position in Philadelphia, but Cooke declined, informing Chase that he would act as "a secret agent of the Treasury Department." According to Cooke, he began selling government bonds without taking a fee or commission. He also sent a telegram through Henry to Chase outlining a plan to reduce the federal debt, closing with, "If he [Chase] would give me a chance I could show him a way to raise money."[24]

Congress convened in a special session on July 4, 1861. Chase submitted an estimate of expenditures for a year, placing the figure at $320 million. He proposed to raise $80 million through indirect taxation and $240 million through loans. The legislature approved the proposal, granting the secretary broad authority in the kinds of loans. Chase sought initially $50 million from banks.[25]

Cooke, meanwhile, informed Chase by letter that he and Drexel & Co. were planning to open an office in Washington, DC. Then, Cooke boldly proposed to the secretary "that you will give us the management of the loans to be issued by the government during the war, allowing us a fair commission on them." Chase wisely rejected Cooke's proffer because it would have given the two firms a monopoly on commissions.[26]

The Union army's defeat at Bull Run on July 21, ended the myopic belief in a short, bloodless conflict and accelerated the federal government's need for funds. Cooke acted immediately and without authority, canvassing banking firms in Philadelphia for subscriptions to a government loan. He raised nearly $2 million within a few hours. Much more was required, however.[27]

Chase turned to financial firms in New York and Boston, traveling to the cities and seeking personally their subscriptions to government loans. The Treasury secretary invited Cooke to accompany him and to negotiate with the bankers. These investors were reluctant to purchase bonds unless they were discounted below par. Cooke distrusted them, believing that they put profits ahead of patriotism with the nation in crisis.[28]

Cooke must have made convincing arguments because he and Chase secured subscriptions for $45 million from the bankers in both cities and in Philadelphia. On their return to the capital, Chase appointed Cooke a subscription agent to sell the bonds, restricting his area to Philadelphia and the surrounding environs in Pennsylvania and New Jersey. Cooke's firm was one of hundreds appointed throughout the North.[29]

Cooke opened his agency at his Philadelphia office on September 5. As he had done with the Pennsylvania bond sales, he geared his campaign toward ordinary folks, placing advertisements in newspapers and blanketing the region with agents. On September 7, he boasted to Chase: "This has been a hard day. I have been at it from 8 A.M. till after 5—a continual stream, clergy, draymen, merchants, girls, boys and all kinds of men and women. Some of our citizens who came in—I mean those of mark—went out almost with tears in their eyes, so overjoyed at the patriotic scene. . . . I am glad to say that they all went away happy and delighted and we bagged over 70,000 as the day's work."[30]

Common folks kept coming through the office door over which Cooke had hung a flag inscribed with the words "U. S. Subscription Agency for the National Loan." One thousand employees of the Philadelphia and Reading Railroad purchased bonds and notes by having the company deduct an amount from their monthly wages to pay for them. By year's end, Cooke's agency had sold more than 20 percent of the entire $45 million.[31]

In January 1862, meanwhile, in Washington, DC, the Treasury wrestled with a crisis. Chase was unbending in requiring the government be paid in gold and silver. Reserves in banks were depleted, and members of Congress argued that the Treasury would have no money in a month. Despite Chase's opposition, Congress passed the Legal Tender Act on February 25, 1862, authorizing the printing of a national paper currency, or "greenbacks," as they soon became known. In the end, the hard-money man Chase endorsed the act out of necessity.[32]

Congress also authorized additional borrowing. The Treasury offered notes, bonds, and certificates at varying rates and maturity dates. The primary issue were three-year notes at 7.30 percent interest, so-called "seven-thirties." While seven-thirties remained, bonds redeemable in not less than five years or more than twenty years at 6 percent—"five-twenties"—became the major issue.[33]

The sales of five-twenties lagged, however, throughout the spring, summer, and into the fall. With banks discounting the bonds below par, it was estimated that the Treasury had lost $10 million to $15 million. For his part, Cooke continued to sell mainly seven-thirties. He had predicted earlier in the year that bankers would only subscribe to bonds at a discount. By October, Chase realized that changes had to be made in the marketing of the bonds and designated Jay Cooke & Company as the sole agent for the sale of five-twenties.[34]

Chase's decision to grant a monopoly on the bond sales to Cooke's firm raised questions and rightfully opened their personal and professional relationship to criticism. To be sure, the Cooke brothers had ingratiated themselves to the Treasury secretary. Henry Cooke often met privately with Chase and, when visiting Washington, Jay Cooke frequently stayed at the Chase residence. Since at least February 1862, Jay had given the secretary investment advice and had loaned him money. In one exchange after Cooke lent Chase $2,000, the banker wrote, "Command me at all times in any matter for your own, or the public good."[35]

"Please in your correspondence," Chase cautioned his fellow Ohioan, "to keep public & private matters entirely distinct. I wish to file every letter relating to your agency for the government." But it appears that that distinction blurred at times. Cooke evidently loaned him more money, invested it, and then paid him dividends and profits on the funds. In one case, Cooke earned a $1,000 profit for the secretary in sixty days on an investment of $13,000. In turn, Chase kept the money with Cooke's banking house, earning interest on it until he needed some or all of it.[36]

In time, Cooke's monopoly and his and Chase's close association elicited criticism. The Detroit *Free Press* offered a not untypical judgment: "Jay Cooke & Co., Washington bankers (notorious for their connection with Secretary Chase)." New York bankers were particularly hostile to Cooke's sole agency, and they were not alone when politicians across the region voiced their concerns.[37]

Less than a month after his appointment, Cooke confided to Chase, "I of course expect to meet with obstacles arising from the jealousies of others, but I shall take good care that the public interests do not suffer & as far as possible give satisfaction to all."[38]

THE CAMPAIGN TO MARKET FIVE-TWENTY BONDS BY JAY COOKE & COMpany had exceeded the most sanguine of expectations within several months. On many days, subscriptions to the loan amounted to more than a million dollars; on the busiest of days, more than $2 million. By May 10, 1863, sales totaled nearly $69 million. The relationship between the national government and its citizenry was undergoing a redefinition.[39]

Cooke expanded his sales methods across the entire North on a scale never before witnessed. In fact, he arguably pioneered the mass marketing of government bonds and notes. From his Philadelphia office, where thirty-three clerks handled the volume of customers, to the firm's second office at No. 452 Fifteenth Street, opposite the Treasury building, in Washington, DC, the banking house's tentacles spread across the loyal states.[40]

This larger campaign's success resulted from Cooke's genius in offering the bonds once again to ordinary Americans, couching their appeal in patriotism and personal financial gain. He sold subscriptions in denominations as low as $50 and $100. The purchase of bonds by common folk promoted the idea of support for the administration and the Union cause.[41]

He blanketed the North with advertisements in newspapers and with flyers that educated citizens in a question-and-answer format about the purchase of a bond. Cooke placed his promotions in the press and journals favorable to the Lincoln administration, or as he explained to Secretary Chase, "My advertising shall not discriminate, but give to all parties who will speak a good word for the government and finances—the same patronage." He asked newspapers to print daily sales figures and endeavored to create competition between towns, counties, and even states. His efforts were, according to historian Melinda Lawson, "unprecedented."[42]

Cooke employed twenty-five hundred subagents, who took the solicitation door to door into hotels, courthouses, post offices, factories, farms, reading rooms, and railroad stations. They worked on commissions of 0.125 percent of subscriptions. A newspaper claimed: "The old saying was that 'wherever the Union army went, the printing press accompanied it.' The new saying will be, 'Wherever Rebel territory is conquered, JAY COOKE'S agents will appear.'" Subscriptions flowed in so rapidly that government printers could not meet demand for the actual bonds.[43]

The vast sums of money and the Philadelphia bank's alleged profits elicited harsh criticisms. The Cooke brothers' close association with

Chase sharpened the public censure. Anti-Lincoln newspapers led the attacks. The New York *World* described Cooke's company as "this favored house" and speculated that the relationship between the firm and the Treasury secretary "will be a useful matter of inquiry." After seeing reports in the New York press that Cooke was earning $10,000 each day, the Detroit *Free Press* offered a blistering denunciation: "Such a palpable fraud upon the Treasury will shock the people of this country."[44]

According to historian Lawson, Cooke "was, in effect, the government's banker." Unquestionably, he worked tirelessly in the promotion of bonds, adding to the amount subscribed and increasing his profits. He kept his offices open frequently from 5:00 A.M. until midnight. He also kept the money from sales in his and other banks for days, even weeks, earning interest on the funds and further enhancing his personal gains. Chase did, however, prod him to deposit the money more expeditiously into the Treasury. But the cabinet member continued to seek advice from the Cookes and offered his counsel on investments.[45]

In January 1864, the mounting criticism and opposition from other banking firms convinced Chase to terminate the agreement with Cooke on five-twenty bond sales. Ironically, a month earlier in his annual report, the secretary declared, "The history of the world may be searched in vain for a parallel case of popular financial support to a national government." In April 1864, Chase replied to a request from the House of Representatives on "what have been the services of Jay Cooke & Co. to the Government." In it, Chase stated that subscriptions for five-twenty bonds amounted to $361,952,950.00, with payment of $1,350,013.15 to Cooke and his subagents. After expenses, Jay Cooke & Company realized a net profit of $220,054.49.[46]

Bond sales lagged during the spring and summer of 1864. Chase offered subscriptions at less than the allowed rate, worsening the situation. On the military front, the fighting in Virginia exacted fearful casualties, and the Union forces in Georgia seemed to have bogged down in a fruitless campaign. Speculation raced across the North that Lincoln would not be reelected. The gold bullion market collapsed, and the dollar fell to a wartime low.[47]

Cooke watched the fluctuations in the price of gold and the value of greenbacks for months. He argued publicly in newspaper editorials and in printed circulars against speculation in gold, believing that it "was decidedly injurious to the cause of the North." At one time when the price of gold rose rapidly, he convinced Chase to sell a few million dollars of gold from the New York subtreasury. Gold prices stabilized. "I have always regarded this as one of my most successful efforts for the preservation of the national credit." He could not, however, control outcomes on battlefields, which often caused speculative market actions.[48]

In June, Congress authorized an additional $400 million loan in seven-thirties, with interest redeemable every six months. On June 14, Cooke wrote to his father, "I hope soon to see the Rebellion suppressed we are today working hard to give it a financial KNOCK—we shall bid for several millions of the new Loan tomorrow."[49]

Chase's overweening ambition and self-importance finally ended his tenure as Treasury secretary. For nearly a year, the former Ohio governor had plotted to wrest the Republican presidential nomination from Lincoln. The president knew of his machinations and tolerated them. It was, however, a clash over the appointment of an assistant treasurer in June 1864 that led Chase to submit his fourth letter of resignation in which he asked for an apology from the president. Lincoln could not tolerate such presumptuousness and accepted the resignation, to Chase's surprise. Six months later, after his reelection, Lincoln nominated Chase for chief justice of the Supreme Court.[50]

Chase's departure elicited protests from members of Congress and from many newspapers. The Senate Finance Committee convened an emergency meeting and came to the White House to raise its concerns with Lincoln. The Chicago *Tribune* called Chase "the great magician of the treasury, his name will be handed down to history as the greatest financier of his century." Horace Greeley's New York *Tribune* asserted, "Mr. Chase is one of the very few great men left in public life since the almost simultaneous decease of Messrs. Clay, Webster and Calhoun," a triumvirate of senators who had dominated that body for three decades, from the 1820s into the 1850s.[51]

Lincoln selected Maine senator William Pitt Fessenden, chairman of the Finance Committee, as Chase's successor. Cooke preferred his political ally and fellow Ohioan, Senator John Sherman. The Cooke family had supported Sherman in his 1861 campaign for the Senate and conferred often with him on legislation during the past three years. Sherman replaced Fessenden as chairman of the Finance Committee.[52]

With the sales of seven-thirty bonds faltering, Fessenden approached Cooke and Morris Ketchum of Ketchum, Son & Company, a New York City banking firm. Ketchum and other bankers had been trying to depress the securities market on the remaining five-twenty bonds. The new Treasury secretary proposed a united effort by Cooke and Ketchum to stabilize and to maintain the five-twenties at par. Ketchum rejected the idea.[53]

Months passed, with the federal government compiling a daily debt of $2.5 million. Cooke, meanwhile, kept busy, claiming that he was a "shuttlecock" between Philadelphia, Washington, and New York City trying to revitalize the bond issue. By January 1, 1865, the Treasury had received only $115 million in subscriptions for the seven-thirties. On January 28, however, like his predecessor, Fessenden appointed Cooke as sole agent for the sale of the seven-thirty loan. Cooke announced his agency for the issue on February 1.[54]

Months before, Eleutheros Cooke described his son's sales campaign methods: "You have built the *Rail Road*—prepared the process—the depots, water stations—Engines Cars & Agents & familiarized the people with the character of these securities." Now, with the government's dire need of money, Cooke rebuilt his "*Rail Road*." He hired Samuel Wilkinson of the New York *Tribune*, paying the newspaperman $6,000 annual salary to lead the new advertising campaign. Eleutheros Cooke, having died in December 1864, did not live to see this undertaking.[55]

From its Philadelphia office and from its office in a new Italianate-style building on Fifteenth Street—"Not only has Washington nothing else approaching it" or likely other cities, editorialized a city newspaper—the Cooke company oversaw the campaign. Cooke doubled the number of sales agents to five thousand. By the end of February, sales reached $9.5 million per day, the demand once again swamping the Treasury's capacity to print the certificates. The two major Confederate armies surrendered in April, but the bond drive continued into the summer. By July 26, Cooke had sold $830 million of seventy-thirty bonds and another $23 million of five-twenty bonds. It was a staggering accomplishment.[56]

Union victory was achieved across a landscape of destruction and carnage. At war's end, deaths from disease and combat of Americans killing and maiming fellow Americans exceeded six hundred thousand. The loyal states incurred an unprecedented financial cost of approximately $3.2 billion. Perhaps upward of $1.75 billion had been secured by the federal government with the sale of bonds and Treasury notes. Authorities in Washington issued an estimated $450 million in greenbacks.[57]

The contribution of Jay Cooke & Company to the financial underwriting of the Union war effort can hardly be overstated. Though figures vary, it seems that the firm obtained subscriptions for five-twenties and seven-thirties that totaled roughly $1.275 billion. Cooke sold the bonds at par and guaranteed them at "enormous financial risk" to his banking house. He supported publicly the Legal Tender Act of 1862 and the National Banking Act and National Currency Act of 1863. "Popular loans had never been tried," contended a newspaper, "and their nature was not generally understood" until Cooke launched his campaigns.[58]

Within weeks of the conflict's end, newspapers in the North praised the Philadelphia banker. "Without Jay Cooke or some other equally clever and equally enterprising dealer in Government loans," argued one newspaper, "financial ruin would have been brought on the country. Jay Cooke has made a fortune. We are glad of it." The Milwaukee Daily News noted that there was criticism of the arrangement between Cooke's firm and the Treasury but also that "the successful seller adopted an extensive and a judicious system of advertising—the unsuccessful did not." Cooke possessed, the daily added, "a princely competence to himself."[59]

The Boston *Transcript* stated: "The greatest banking firm in the world is Jay Cooke and the American people. . . . Jay Cooke and Company have run the Treasury machine and run it with more safety, and with immensely more speed, than the official engineers." Years later, the Louisville *Courier-Journal* observed that when the war began, Cooke "was little known outside of Philadelphia. A few years later his name had become a household word." In the financial world, he was "colossal in the midst of colossal events."[60]

Ulysses S. Grant reportedly remarked to Cooke's son, "Tell your father that it is to his labors, more than those of any other man that the people of this country owe the continued life of the nation." Likewise, an unidentified former Confederate leader allegedly claimed, "He [Cooke] won the war for the North, just as surely as the men in the field, and it was in the Treasury Department that the South was really defeated."[61]

Like a stream at flood tide, the Civil War carved new channels, sweeping away debris from the past. In financing the Union war effort, Cooke fashioned a revolution. He linked patriotism, in part, not only to civic duty or self-sacrifice but also to citizens' self-interest. On the home front, ordinary folks who could afford them purchased bonds, binding themselves in their own way to the cause of the Union. When the time came, and it surely did, Americans financed future conflicts as Cooke had demonstrated with singular accomplishment and remarkable vision.[62]

In his memoir, written in 1894, Cooke affirmed, "Like Moses and Washington and Lincoln and Grant, I have been—I firmly believe—God's chosen instrument, especially in the financial work of saving the Union during the greatest war that has ever been fought in the history of man." He went on, "I absolutely by my own faith and energy and means saved the nation financially and did not realize any profit

therefrom. . . . The public should know even at this late period the un-
selfishness and sacrifices made by myself and [my] firm."[63]

It was an astonishing statement because he was a wealthy man at
war's end. He groused in the memoir that his company received less
than $8 million to cover expenses and commissions to subagents. Ex-
actly how much of a profit the firm netted remains unclear. During the
conflict, he and his brother Henry invested in railroads and other enterprises. As a young man, Cooke had proclaimed, "I look upon riches
but as naught more than the means whereby one can display his social
and generous spirit, and, if I should ere be one I may be, I'll be a friend, a
man." In time, he would have the opportunity to be true to his words.[64]

Chapter Four

THE INVENTORS

—〰〰—

As the *Carrolton*, an Ohio and Mississippi River steamboat, approached the landing at Saint Louis, suddenly a chimney flue collapsed onboard, igniting a fire. Passengers and crew deserted the sinking vessel, but eight persons were either consumed by the flames or drowned in the waters. Among the survivors was the Eads family, whose members escaped with only the clothes they wore.[1]

It was September 1833, and Thomas C. Eads had brought his wife, daughters, and son with him in search of another new beginning. The family began their wanderings in Indiana, proceeded through Cincinnati, Ohio, and on to Louisville, Kentucky, before arriving in Saint Louis. Failed business ventures clung to Eads like an old, worn suit.[2]

The family evidently scraped by financially in their new city. What the father did remains unclear, but his thirteen-year-old son peddled apples on the streets before being hired as a clerk in the Williams and During dry goods store. In 1836, Thomas Eads, his wife, and daughters moved to Davenport, Iowa. But James B. Eads stayed behind and, perhaps unknowingly at the time, had found a home.[3]

James Buchanan Eads was born on May 23, 1820, in Lawrenceburg, Indiana. His parents had journeyed west from Maryland, and he was named for his mother's cousin, future president James Buchanan. As a youth, he constructed models of steam engines, sawmills, and steamboats. His schooling was limited, but one of the owners of the mercantile firm in Saint Louis, Mr. Williams, allowed his clerk use of his personal library. Eads stayed with the business for five years before signing on as a purser on a Mississippi River steamboat.[4]

At some point, Eads visited Washington, DC. Since his early years building models, he had an abiding interest in engineering and mechanical things. "Patent Office with the models of machines which have been patented most absorbing," he wrote in a letter while in the capital. "I could spend five days at the Patent Office," he exclaimed, "and find something new and interesting every day."[5]

While working on a steamboat, Eads witnessed firsthand the dangers on the Mississippi River. Snags or branches of fallen trees posed particular hazards because a collision with one could gouge a hole in the hull of a steamboat. Accidents occurred rather frequently on the river. Eads served as purser on two vessels sunk by crashing into snags; the second one happened in 1842 while he was on board the *Knickerbocker*.[6]

After that latter mishap, Eads designed a diving bell that could be used by divers to salvage cargoes from wrecks on the river bottom. He took his plan to Calvin Case and William Nelson, boatbuilders. Case and Nelson constructed the diving bell by knocking out the bottom of a forty-gallon whiskey hogshead, fastening lead weights to it, and rigging it to a derrick on a boat with air pumps. The bell enabled Eads to walk on the river bottom and salvage the cargoes. He called it a submarine.[7]

Eads, Case, and Nelson formed a partnership and tested the diving bell on a sunken vessel near Keokuk, Iowa. Eads admitted later that "shifting sands and rapid current" made any salvage operation difficult and dangerous for him in the diving bell. He was a rather slender-built man but, an acquaintance claimed, "he was one of the strongest men physically I ever saw."[8]

Eads bought out his partners within the next year or two. But in 1845, suffering from unspecified health problems, he quit the business. Eads borrowed money and built the first glass factory west of the Mississippi River at 2300 North Broadway in Saint Louis. The venture failed in 1848, leaving him $25,000 in debt. His creditors, however, extended him another loan of $1,500 to resume his former salvage work.[9]

The new enterprise was a far more extensive operation than the previous business. Eads built larger, twin-hulled boats with two engines, a derrick, and air pumps that could pump out mud and sand and lift entire sunken vessels to the river's surface. He called his firm the Western River Improvement and Wrecking Company. He and his crews salvaged boats in the river from Galena, Illinois, to south of New Orleans, Louisiana, and up the tributaries of the Mississippi.[10]

Eads wrote an account of one of his efforts at "wrecking," as it was known then:

> Five miles below Cairo [Illinois] I searched for the wreck of the *Neptune* for more than sixty days, in a distance of three miles. . . . My boat was held by a long anchor line, and was swung from side to side of the channel, over a distance of five hundred feet, by side anchor lines, while I walked on the river bottom, under the bell, across the channel. The boat was then dropped twenty feet further downstream and I walked back again as she was hauled towards the other shore. In this way I walked on the bottom four hours, at least, every day (Sunday excepted) during that time.[11]

He located the *Neptune* on the Ohio River bottom fifty-five feet below the surface. Eads retrieved a cargo of lead, various articles, and, as he noted, a jar of butter "in a good state of preservation." It was not much of a haul for a typically difficult salvage operation.[12]

In 1856, Eads traveled to Washington, DC, with a proposal to remove snags and other obstructions from the Mississippi River. He had prepared a bill in which he agreed to keep the river clear of the dangerous debris for five years. He lobbied members of both houses, but, in the end, only the House of Representatives approved the measure.[13]

Nevertheless, the salvage business prospered, and profits increased dramatically. But, once again, health maladies plagued Eads and, in

1857, he retired from the firm, with a personal fortune of $500,000. As a successful and wealthy businessman, he had become involved in the state's Democratic Party, and for the next four years, he involved himself in the issues that were roiling the sections.[14]

Eads believed that slavery was a matter of state authority. At a Democratic convention in Saint Louis in 1858, the delegates nominated him for the Missouri legislature. He declined but stood and spoke: "I feel earnestly impressed with the importance of relieving our State of an evil [slavery] which I believe to be cramping the energies of our people and retarding the growth of the commonwealth, by checking the tide of capital and immigration which our wonderful resources would otherwise secure."[15]

Folks who knew Eads during these years described him as dignified and faultlessly attired but a noted jester and storyteller. He gave a lecture to the students at a night school, the Polytechnic Institute of Saint Louis. "Labor, when coupled with knowledge," he told the group, "becomes a mighty engine of power." He went on, stating, "True greatness is found in other places than on the battle field or in the Senate Chamber."[16]

RESIDENTS OF TROY, NEW YORK, MARVELED AT THE STRUCTURE. No one in the county, state, or nation had seen a waterwheel of such size and power. It had a diameter of sixty-two feet and a width of twenty-two feet, and it held thirty-six large buckets. The circular edifice weighed 250 tons and had an output of up to perhaps a hundred horsepower. Folks had dubbed it the "Niagara of water wheels."[17]

It was 1851, and the "inventive genius" who had designed and built the water wheel had come to America from his native Scotland more than three decades earlier. Henry Burden was born on April 22, 1791, on his family's farm near Dunblane, Stirlingshire, Scotland. He constructed a threshing machine for his father before attending the University of Edinburgh, where he studied mathematics, drawing, and engineering.[18]

Although the circumstances remain unknown, in 1819 Burden met Richard Rush, American minister to the court of Saint James in London. Burden must have impressed the American diplomat, who suggested that the twenty-eight-year-old Scotsman look to the United States for a career. Rush gave Burden letters of introduction to three prominent American politicians at the time—John C. Calhoun, Thomas H. Benton, and Stephen Van Rensselaer.[19]

Burden arrived in New York, where he sought out Van Rensselaer. A former lieutenant governor of the state, Van Rensselaer owned a twelve-hundred-square-mile manor in the Hudson River Valley. He directed Burden to Townsend and Erastus Corning, owners of the Albany Iron Works, which manufactured cast iron plows and other agricultural implements.[20]

Burden worked for the Corning brothers for three years. During that time, he invented what he claimed later to be the first cultivator. He also designed improvements to plows, threshing machines, and grist mills and received a patent for a hemp and flax machine. In 1822, he left the firm and joined the Troy Iron and Nail Factory as its agent. Before long, he became its superintendent.[21]

The Troy Iron and Nail Factory, roughly two miles south of the village on the creek Wynants Kill, had been established in 1809. The original mill had a pair of rollers powered by two small water wheels to forge nails. The firm was a stock company with capital of $96,000. It was not long, however, until Burden's inventiveness transformed the manufacturing of iron products.[22]

The Scottish immigrant received a series of patents: for a furnace to heat iron bars and for machines to make wrought iron railroad spikes and horseshoes. His "rotary concentric squeezer" rolled puddled or purified iron into bars, revolutionizing the industry in America and Europe. The commissioner of patents acclaimed the machine to be the first original American invention in ironmaking.[23]

In 1833, Burden built a boat three hundred feet in length, with a pair of paddle wheels thirty feet in diameter. Because of its length and shape, the vessel was dubbed a "cigar boat." He put considerable money

into the project, believing it would earn a profit hauling cargo on the
Hudson River. On its initial trip, however, the pilot miscalculated and
the boat either ran aground or hit an object in the river. The cigar boat
sank and, with it, Burden's entire investment.[24]

Undaunted, Burden advocated for a line of steamships for crossing
the Atlantic Ocean. He wanted large ships for the times, the 1830s,
capable of hauling fifteen thousand tons of passengers and cargo. No
American or European shipbuilders expressed interest. Years later, in
1845, Burden and a group of Scottish investors sought shareholders in
"Burden's Atlantic Steam Ferry Company." It, too, failed to secure financial support.[25]

During the winter of 1836, Burden traveled to England. By this
time, he owned nearly half the shares of the Troy Iron and Nail Factory
and was earning 30 percent of the profits from his patented machines.
During his stay in England, he observed that railroad companies had
replaced flat rails with H or I types. These new rails needed a bent or
hook-headed spike to be nailed to the ties.[26]

Upon his return to Troy, Burden designed a machine to make offset
spikes. The hook-headed spikes negated the necessity of drilling holes in
ties and soon were in demand by railroad firms. The Long Island Railroad Company made the initial purchase of ten tons of spikes. The production and sales of spikes paralleled the expansion of railroad mileage
across the country. In fact, the spikes became the Troy Iron and Nail
Factory's second most profitable product, trailing only its manufacture
of horseshoes.[27]

Burden did not secure a patent for his machine until 1840. By then,
other iron manufacturers were making the spikes, including Erastus
Corning's Albany Iron Works. In 1844, Burden filed a suit against Corning and other ironmakers to prevent them from using his machinery.
The litigants settled on October 14, 1845, with the defendants agreeing
not to manufacture horseshoes in return for permission to make the
spikes. It was, however, the beginning of bitter legal disputes between
Burden and Corning.[28]

By 1848, Burden had acquired sole ownership of the Troy company and renamed it Burden Iron Company. Three years later, he constructed a series of reservoirs on Wynants Kill for a steady supply of water for his mammoth water wheel. (Tradition holds that a student at a local institute, George W. G. Ferris, was inspired by Burden's creation with its large buckets, to create his amusement ride.)[29]

The "Niagara of water wheels" was a marvel in its day. Folks from Troy and the surrounding towns and counties came to watch the giant wheel turn and its six-foot-deep buckets dump water. The wheel made two revolutions a minute, generating between 500 and 600 horsepower. Burden's invention operated the entire mill and adjacent shops until replaced by steam engines.[30]

During the 1850s, Burden expanded his company's operations and erected more structures at what became known as the Upper or Water Works. He purchased an abandoned factory along the Hudson River and, by the decade's end, the complex of buildings covered both sides of Wynants Kill. A Troy newspaper boasted, "Few men in the country are so well qualified for the [iron] business as Mr. Burden." His creative and engineering brilliance and business acumen prepared the company for the forthcoming and unparalleled demands on it.[31]

THE APRIL 17, 1861, LETTER FROM UNITED STATES ATTORNEY GENeral Edward Bates to James B. Eads was marked "Confidential." "Be not surprised if you are called here suddenly, by telegram," Bates, a fellow Missourian, wrote to his friend and political supporter. "In a certain contingency, it will be necessary to have here, the aid of the most thorough knowledge of our river the use of steam upon it. And, in that event, I have advised that you be consulted." If summoned, Bates advised, Eads should "come instantly."[32]

No summons came from Washington, DC, but the retired Mississippi River salvage operator developed his own strategic plans for the war on the western waters. Within weeks of Bates's letter, on

April 29, Eads submitted his ideas in a report to the Navy Department. Like Winfield Scott, Eads believed that Union forces had to control the Mississippi River. He proposed establishing a base of operations at Cairo, Illinois, and erecting artillery batteries on both banks of the river.[33]

"The effect of this blockade would be most disastrous to the South," Eads asserted in the report, "as it would effectually close the main artery through which flows her food. It would establish a tollgate through which alone her dutiable goods could enter, or through which her products could find their way to market." Once the blockade had been completed and the Tennessee and Cumberland rivers and the railroad from Louisville, Kentucky, to Chattanooga, Tennessee, had been seized, "starvation is inevitable in less than six months."[34]

Control of the Mississippi River had obvious strategic importance, but starving the Confederacy into submission appeared rather farfetched. Nevertheless, his report drew a response from Secretary of the Navy Gideon Welles. The cabinet official replied that he had "referred it [the report] to the War Department, to which the subject more properly pertains." Welles did not mention that he had ordered Commander John Rodgers to develop a naval force on the Mississippi River.[35]

Eads, meanwhile, sought Bates's help in securing the post of commissary of subsistence in Saint Louis, for which Brigadier General Nathaniel Lyon and several colonels had recommended him. Bates wrote to President Lincoln on his friend's behalf, stating, "I really think he ought to receive the appointment, being, as I am confident, highly qualified." Bates noted, however, that Eads's civilian status had raised objections. Could the president commission Eads a captain or major in the army, the attorney general inquired.[36]

The president endorsed Bates's letter before forwarding it to the War Department. "I wish to oblige Mr. Attorney General Bates in the matter mentioned within," but he also wanted General-in-Chief Winfield Scott's opinion about whether the president had "the lawful power, and that there will be no military impropriety in it." Whether Scott replied is unknown, but Eads did not receive the post. Lyon was killed in the Battle of Wilson's Creek on August 10.[37]

At roughly the same time, Eads sold his Submarine No. 7 to the government. It was to be outfitted as a gunboat. The condition of the large salvage vessel and its monetary worth resulted in a dispute between the owner and the navy. Eventually, upon the intervention of Major General John C. Fremont, Lyon's successor as department commander, a three-man civilian panel of experienced river pilots awarded Eads $26,850. It took months, however, before Eads received payment.[38]

Implementation of a strategy for the Mississippi River and its tributaries required a fleet of gunboats, which the Navy Department did not possess. Earlier, Eads had traveled to Washington to propose an armored river fleet. It appears that Bates presented the idea to the cabinet, which approved it. Whether Eads's advocacy factored into the department's decision to construct a fleet is uncertain. Secretary Welles requested bids from companies for the construction of seven vessels, built on the design and specifications of the department. Eight firms submitted bids.[39]

Quartermaster General Montgomery Meigs awarded the contract to Eads on August 7, 1861. Although Eads had influential supporters in Bates and Welles, he had submitted the lowest bid. The terms specified that the seven gunboats were to be completed by October 10, in sixty-four days. The builder would be paid $89,600 for each vessel but would forfeit $250 "per day for each and every boat that is delayed beyond that time." Eads was required to post four sureties of $30,000 each against loss or default.[40]

The gunboats were to be constructed on the primary design of Samuel M. Pook, a naval architect under contract to the Navy Department. Each boat was to measure 175 feet in length and 51 feet in breadth at the beam. They were to be flat-bottomed, paddle-wheeled, with a sloping casemate made of 24-inch-thick oak covered with 2.5-inch iron armor plates. A pair of steam engines would provide power, and thirteen cannon of three different calibers would comprise the armament. When finished, they would appear like no other gunboats in existence.[41]

Reportedly, Eads pledged to Lincoln that he would meet the deadline, but the president expressed doubts. In a memoir, the former salvage operator stated, "None but a bold and self-reliant man would have ventured to make such a contract." A pro-Republican newspaper in Saint Louis, the *Democrat*, opined, "The contract has fallen into good hands." When he secured the contract, he owned no factories or other facilities needed in the construction of such boats.[42]

By the third week in August, Eads had leased foundries, machine shops, boatyards, and sawmills and hired subcontractors and four thousand carpenters, ironworkers, and engineers. He established the construction sites—at Carondelet, Missouri, eight miles south of Saint Louis, and at Mound City, Illinois, up the Ohio River from Cairo. Firms in Pittsburgh, Pennsylvania; Cincinnati and Portsmouth, Ohio; Newport, Kentucky; and Saint Louis built the steam engines and boilers and rolled armor plate. The Thomas G. Gaylord Company in Saint Louis rolled the first iron plating in the war.[43]

The construction continued twenty-four hours a day, seven days a week. If the crews met deadlines, Eads paid them bonuses. The casement on each gunboat sloped at a 35 degree angle, and Eads instructed the workmen to have the white oak's "grain running up from the water instead of horizontally, by which means a ball will strike, as it were, with the grain, and then be more readily deflected."[44]

The first gunboat launched at Carondelet on October 12, two days past the contractual deadline. Flag Officer Andrew H. Foote, naval commander in the Western Theater, named it *St. Louis*. Engineering and construction problems delayed the completion of the other craft, but by mid-November the *Carondelet*, *Cincinnati*, *Louisville*, *Mound City*, *Pittsburg*, and *Cairo* had been launched. The vessels were designated unofficially as City Class gunboats.[45]

The gunboats were sent to Cairo, Illinois, at the confluence of the Mississippi and Ohio rivers, where they received their cannon and underwent inspection by Foote and naval officers. Painted black, with a low and unique profile in the water, they appeared to one officer "like gigantic turtles." They soon were nicknamed "Pook's turtles" in honor of their designer.[46]

The inspections consumed weeks because design flaws and construction mistakes required attention and resolution. Foote informed Quartermaster General Meigs that he and Eads argued over numerous matters. "Mr. Eads also says," wrote Foote, "that while he had no part in the modeling of these boats [he] is therefore relieved of all responsibility as to their imperfections."[47]

Foote accepted the seven gunboats finally in January 1862 and commissioned and assigned them to the Western Gunboat Flotilla. Eads, meanwhile, delivered to Cairo two larger converted gunboats, *Benton* and *Essex*. The major shortcoming of all the gunboats was their slowness even when traveling with the current. Two inspectors recommended more powerful engines and larger steam boilers.[48]

Despite these problems, Pook's turtles, in the estimation of historians Williamson Murray and Wayne Hsieh, "were the perfect vessels to fight for and control the western waters." The construction of the gunboats underlined "the immense superiority the North enjoyed in manufacturing strength as well as the ingenuity and competence of its engineers."[49]

Although commanded by naval officers, the Western Gunboat Flotilla served under the authority of the War Department and army. Led by Foote, the *St. Louis, Cincinnati, Carondelet, Louisville, Pittsburg,* and *Essex* joined army units in the campaign against Confederate-held forts Henry and Donelson on the Tennessee and Cumberland rivers, respectively. The gunboats silenced the Rebel cannon at Fort Henry but performed less successfully in the bombardment against Fort Donelson. Nevertheless, the joint operation, commanded by Brigadier General Ulysses S. Grant, resulted in the capture of both forts.[50]

After the surrender of the forts, a Tennessee woman wrote: "Those hateful gunboats. They looked like they were from the lower regions," and a Nashville newspaper declared, "We have nothing to fear from a land attack, but the gunboats are the devil." Not long after the newspaper published those words, the *Cairo* and seven army transports arrived at the Tennessee capital and forced its surrender.[51]

After the victorious Union campaign, the Detroit *Free Press* observed, "Congratulations are being showered upon Mr. James B. Eads, the St. Louis contractor, for his success in the construction of the experimental gunboats, which so signally fulfilled the most sanguine expectations of the government." The newspaper listed the name of the seven gunboats, claiming that they "are now household words."[52]

Ironically, at this same time, Eads was embroiled in a dispute with Quartermaster General Montgomery Meigs over penalties and payments in the construction of the gunboats. Eads had missed the contractual deadline and had been forced to pay penalties. In turn, Meigs had delayed payments to Eads as stipulated in the contract. By its terms, Eads was to receive $627,000 and, when repairs and alterations were completed, Eads claimed the costs amounted to an additional $100,000.[53]

During the dispute, Eads wrote a lengthy letter to Meigs, reminding the quartermaster general of the difficulties in constructing the vessels, which should entitle "me to some consideration." "My proposition for building seven Gunboats contemplated their construction in an almost incredibly short period, much less, I believed, than any other bidder," Eads explained. "The specifications of the hulls and engines, with some general plans of the boats, were all the information I had to guide me in bidding, as to time and price."[54]

Eads argued further: "The contract stipulated that the boats were to be built according to the specifications and *the directions* of the Superintendents. It also stipulated that all extra work was to be estimated and paid for." In the end, the boat builder received the main contractual amount and some, if not most, of the repair request, but not before entangling Attorney General Edward Bates, Secretary of War Edwin Stanton, and Francis P. Blair Jr. of the powerful Missouri political family in the disagreement with Meigs.[55]

Pook's turtles served on the western waters during the 1862 and 1863 campaigns. The *Cairo*, *Cincinnati*, and *Baron De Kalb* (formerly *St. Louis*) were sunk, and the *Mound City* was struck by an artillery round that exploded her boilers, killing or maiming almost the entire crew.[56]

The Navy Department, meanwhile, awarded Eads a contract to build a pair of boats constructed entirely of iron. Each vessel had a revolving turret, one modeled on that of the famous *Monitor* and the second one "invented and patented" by Eads. He built the gunboats at his Union Iron Works in Saint Louis and received $320,000 for each one. By 1865, Eads had built four more iron turreted boats for the department.[57]

One of the monitors, *Winnebago*, had a turret unlike the others' "in all respects from any heretofore constructed," according to a navy inspector. For the first time, the cannon were operated entirely by steam. The naval officer was impressed, declaring, "The design, construction and arrangement of the details of the machinery [in the turret] is highly creditable to the ingenuity, mechanical skill and ability of the inventor."[58]

When the war ended, Eads journeyed to Europe, where he was honored for his inventive brilliance in Liverpool, London, Paris, and other continental cities. Andrew Carnegie met Eads during the postwar years and described him as "an original genius *minus* scientific knowledge to guide his erratic ideas of things mechanical. He was seemingly one of those who wished to have everything done upon his own original plans. That a thing had been done in one way before was sufficient to cause its rejection."[59]

Carnegie's assessment was, however, skewed. Eads's "erratic ideas of things mechanical" had resulted in a diving bell and a personal fortune. Although the gunboats were designed primarily by Samuel Pook, Eads oversaw their construction and alterations. He patented his design of a revolving turret and built six iron gunboats. More of "his own original plans" were to come and, once again, had to do with the Mississippi River.

BY 1860, THE BURDEN IRON WORKS OWED ITS PROFITABILITY MAINLY TO a horseshoe-making machine patented in 1835 by the company's owner, Henry Burden. The original machine required three movements to produce a horseshoe, but Burden refined it, securing new patents in 1843 and 1857. By the latter date, he had reduced the manufacturing to one movement, and as a newspaper reported, the machine "devours the heated bar, cuts, bends, and forges it into perfect shape with one movement, at the rate of sixty a minute."[60]

In an age of horsepower, the machine proved to be a marvel of the times. The settlement of Burden's legal squabbles in the 1840s over his hook-headed offset rail spike machine forbade the defendants from making horseshoes, giving Burden a corner on the market. A talented manager and shrewd businessman, he advertised his machine-made horseshoes extensively in the United States and Europe. He guaranteed the quality of the horseshoes and pledged to return customers' money if they were not satisfied with the product.[61]

Burden horseshoes dominated the market. In 1859, he traveled to Great Britain, where he sold the British rights to his machine. That same year, the federal government approved the purchase of his horseshoes, with Burden warranting the quality. When the war began two years later, however, government officials proposed taking control of the factory, but Burden assured them that his company could supply the army.[62]

But the demand was staggering and beyond the capacity of his factory. Shoes for horses came in eight sizes for fore and hind hooves; for mules, five sizes for fore and hind hooves. And a cavalry regiment at full strength comprised 1,200 horses, and a standard artillery battery included at least 110 horses. The hundreds of wagons in a supply train counted horses and mules into the thousands.[63]

With the Upper or Water Works at capacity, Burden purchased a forty-five-acre farm along the Hudson River downstream from the original factory and constructed a new complex of buildings known as the Lower or Steam Works. The blast furnaces and other ironworks were powered by large steam engines. He also bought tracts of land in Vermont that contained significant deposits of iron ore. He further refined his horseshoe-making machine and secured another patent in 1862.[64]

By 1864, the company employed fourteen hundred workers and consumed ninety thousand tons of coal yearly. Two other companies supplied horseshoes for the Union, but neither matched the output of the Burden Iron Works. Annual sales soared from $600,000 during the antebellum years to $1.3 million during the war years. In 1864, Burden officially brought his two surviving sons into the business, reorganizing it as Henry Burden & Sons.[65]

The quality of Burden horseshoes was well known in the South before the war. During Confederate mounted raids and attacks on Union wagon trains, the Rebels sought Burden horseshoes. Confederate spies operating from Canada tried to acquire the patterns used in the horseshoe-making machines. In fact, the scarcity of horseshoes in the Confederacy affected its cavalry units in the final year of the war.[66]

During the conflict's four years, the Troy, New York, company supplied the Union cause with seventy million horseshoes. The miles-long ranks of blue-jacketed cavalrymen, trailed by scores of wagons and artillery batteries, testified to the firm's contribution. Credit for it belonged to a Scottish immigrant who had come to the United States more than four decades earlier. A few years after the war, the Troy *Times* put it well: "Mr. Burden belongs in the front rank of American inventors."[67]

Chapter Five

THE IMPROVISERS

—w—

I T WAS JUNE 1862, AND PRESIDENT ABRAHAM LINCOLN, ESCAPING
  the nation's capital, traveled to New York City and then up the
Hudson River to the United States Military Academy at West Point.
The trip was timely because Union fortunes in the conflict seemed
ascendant. Since midwinter, federal arms had captured forts Henry
and Donelson, won the Battle of Shiloh in Tennessee, and seized New
Orleans in Louisiana and Roanoke Island in North Carolina. Most
importantly, perhaps, more than a hundred thousand officers and men
of the Army of the Potomac, under Major General George B. Mc-
Clellan, camped only miles from the Confederate capital, Richmond,
Virginia.[1]

Lincoln's rare excursion away from Washington City brought him
to the academy to seek advice from the army's former general in chief,
Winfield Scott, the "long ago soldier," as an enlisted man described the
old warrior. Upon his departure from the national capital in November
1861, Scott had been in retirement at the academy. Although plagued
with health problems, the general counseled the president, particularly
on affairs in Virginia. They would not meet again.[2]

Before the president returned to Washington, he crossed the Hudson and visited Cold Spring, site of the West Point Foundry. Led by
superintendent Robert P. Parrott, Lincoln toured the factory and
watched during a torrential rainstorm the firing of one-hundred- and

71

two-hundred-pounder cannon. Within days of Lincoln's visit, the foundry shipped guns to McClellan's army in Virginia.[3]

The foundry had been established in 1817 by brothers Gouverneur and William Kemble, wealthy New York merchants. After the War of 1812, President James Monroe advocated the construction of foundries and other factories that would strengthen the country economically and militarily. The Kembles purchased ninety acres from a large tract of land that had been seized from a Loyalist family after the Revolutionary War. The acres lay in a sheltered inlet on the east bank of the Hudson River upstream from West Point.[4]

The region provided sand for casting products, water from Margaret's Brook—renamed Foundry Brook—forests for charcoal, and local iron ore deposits. The foundry location, soon dubbed Foundry Cove, accorded immediate access to the river for the transportation of raw materials and finished products. The Kembles built two dams on the brook for power and created the village of Cold Spring by constructing houses for foundry workers. In 1831, the Kemble brothers, Brigadier General Joseph G. Swift, a munitions expert, and James Renwick Sr., a Columbia University engineer and professor, formed the West Point Foundry Associates.[5]

During the 1820s, the foundry supplied the federal government with 440 cannon. With the newly organized company, the product line expanded. Gouverneur Kemble directed operations, and Swift provided the primary technical knowledge. In 1831, for instance, the foundry cast the first locomotive in America for the South Carolina Canal and Railroad Company. The Cold Spring manufacturer delivered a second engine for the same railway a year later. The foundry also cast the largest Cornish-type steam engine in the United States for the Jersey City Water Works in Belleville, New Jersey.[6]

In 1836, the firm hired Captain Robert Parker Parrott as superintendent of the foundry. Born October 5, 1804, in Lee, New Hampshire, Parrott was an 1824 graduate of the military academy and was serving as the academy's inspector of ordnance. While on an inspection of the foundry, Parrott was offered the position by Kemble, accepted, and resigned his army commission. Three years later, Parrott married Kemble's forty-year-old sister Mary, and the couple had no children.[7]

Under Parrott's superintendency, the New York company became one of the country's foremost iron foundries. He imported skilled workers from the British Isles and continental Europe and instituted an apprenticeship program for teenagers. He had more houses built for laborers, knowing that the residences discouraged turnover in the workforce. The West Point Foundry cast steam engines for naval warships, engines and pumps for the Naval Dry Dock at the Brooklyn Naval Yard, and iron architectural components for buildings.[8]

The manufacture of ordnance and projectiles remained, however, the foundry's main business. Throughout the 1850s, it cast smoothbore cannon for the War and Navy departments. By 1860, the West Point Foundry complex contained six blast furnaces; molding, machine, and pattern shops; three blacksmith shops; an office building; and a dock on the cove. The entire set of structures covered nearly one hundred acres, employed about 350 men, and forged $240,000 worth of iron castings annually.[9]

Parrott, meanwhile, experimented with artillery design. He wanted to manufacture a cheaper cannon and tested a cast iron hollow gun tube. He controlled the cooling process to give the tube greater strength. Although he was not the first gunmaker to make a rifled cannon, he obtained a patent for a ten-pounder rifled cannon in early 1861. His major innovation in design was a wide wrought iron band coiled around the gun's breech, a distinctive feature of Parrott cannon.[10]

Kemble and Parrott had been experimenting with the wrought iron band for nearly two decades. In 1842, Kemble wrote to Colonel George Talcott, the army's chief of ordnance: "We are not fond of vague experiments, but we think that your field artillery might be lightened, if useful, below the weight of brass guns, and at the same time cheapened, by hooping a cast iron gun behind the reinforce with wrought iron hoops."

Kemble continued, describing the process of "hooping": "We should turn the gun, and bore the hoops, to a diameter something less than the piece, and after expanding them by heating, shrink them on. If you deem it of sufficient importance to subject a gun of this description to the proper tests and trials, we would make one at our cost and risk: in a caliber and weight of the army's choice."[11]

Talcott referred the letter to Secretary of War John C. Spencer. Within a fortnight, the War Department awarded the foundry a contract in the amount of $25,000 for cast howitzers. Spencer endorsed the letter, "I see no objection to his [Kemble's] making a gun at his cost hooped as proposed." There is no record that Kemble and Parrott cast any hooped cannon at that time, but Parrott obviously continued refining the work until 1861.[12]

For four decades, the West Point Foundry's major customer was the federal government. Interestingly, as the furor mounted in the Southern states over the election of Abraham Lincoln to the presidency and shouts of secession amplified, Parrott signed a contract with the state of Georgia on December 19, 1860. According to the terms, Parrott agreed to deliver sixteen rifled cannon of 3.3-inch caliber, various types of projectiles, and 100,000 pounds of lead in sixty days. Georgia seceded from the Union exactly one month later and whether the foundry fulfilled the contract remains uncertain.[13]

Parrott did, however, fulfill a contract with the state of Virginia in April 1861. The year before, the Virginia legislature appropriated $500,000 for arms for the state. A three-man commission traveled to Cold Spring and witnessed the test-firing of Parrott's new ten-pounder rifled cannon. The War Department's ordnance bureau had not approved the gun for purchase, but a member of the commission, Francis H. Smith, superintendent of the Virginia Military Institute, proposed a trial conducted by the institute's "first rate Instructor of Artillery." Parrott accepted and sent a ten-pounder to Lexington, Virginia.[14]

Major Thomas J. Jackson, the institute's artillery instructor, oversaw the trial, and, according to Smith, Jackson's "experiments" were "in the highest degree satisfactory." The state of Virginia agreed to purchase twelve cannon and one hundred shells for each gun. When Parrott had the guns loaded for shipping in New York City, Virginia voted to secede from the Union. The commanding army officer in the city halted the shipment. Parrott argued that he was "honor bound to forward the guns." The officer relented, and the dozen cannon arrived in Richmond. On June 10, Confederate gun crews manned some of the Parrotts in the battle of Big Bethel.[15]

IN THE SPRING OF 1861, JAMES W. RIPLEY HAD BEEN IN THE UNITED States army for nearly half a century. He had served as an artillery officer and, for more than a dozen years, as commander of the Springfield Armory in Massachusetts. With the war under way, Ripley was the army's chief of ordnance, whose duty entailed the approval or disapproval of new weapons.[16]

As an institution, the army was a reluctant adopter of new weapons. A change in a firearm required a change in production, a new supply of ammunition, and maintenance of the firearm. Prior to the conflict, however, the former secretary of war John B. Floyd predicted "surely will the breech-loading gun drive out of use those that load at the muzzle." Yet, even though Ripley preferred the muzzle-loading smoothbore to the more modern rifle musket, in 1860, the Springfield Armory produced 9,601 muzzle-loading rifle muskets, the army's standard shoulder weapon.[17]

Ironically, the government's Springfield Armory was directly and indirectly responsible for changes in American manufacturing during the antebellum decades. The United States military helped develop the concept of interchangeable parts. At the same time, armories adopted new methods of manufacture, which became known as "armory practice." Floyd's prediction had yet to come true when the attack on Fort Sumter occurred.[18]

Then, within weeks of the war's beginning, a Connecticut Yankee arrived at the War Department with a revolution in his hands. The

New England inventor was Christopher Miner Spencer, who brought with him to Washington, DC, his patented model breech-loading repeating rifle. Evidently, Ripley examined the firearm and argued that it was too heavy, too expensive, and required special ammunition. He or a subordinate officer informed the inventor that the ordnance bureau "would not approve the new-fangled jimcrack."[19]

Born June 20, 1833, in Manchester, Connecticut, Spencer had a natural talent for making things. He learned mechanics in general and gunsmithing in particular from his grandfather, Josiah Hollister, a Revolutionary War veteran and armorer. By the age of seventeen, Spencer had apprenticed in a Manchester machine shop and worked in the Cheney Brothers silk mill, earning the title of "journeyman machinist."[20]

During the next several years, Spencer worked as a machinist with companies in New York and Connecticut, including Colt's Firearm Company. In 1855, he rejoined the Cheneys as superintendent of the machine shop. At the encouragement of Frank Cheney, Spencer invented an automatic silk-winding machine, which allowed one worker to operate three machines simultaneously. It took Spencer a month to devise and to build the machine for which he received a patent. In time, he and a fellow inventor, Hezekiah Conant, refined it, and it was the first machine built by the firm of Pratt and Whitney.[21]

Later in life, Spencer spoke about his inventions, telling an acquaintance, "I go to sleep thinking about them, and often in the morning I have the solution." That acquaintance remarked that Spencer's "mind was always seeking new truth in every direction, and he took the attitude that the best was yet to come."[22]

It appears that Spencer conceived of the idea of a breech-loading repeating firearm in 1857. He likely discussed it with Frank Cheney, who allowed him to use the firm's machinery after his eleven-hour shift of work. According to family tradition, Spencer needed two years to build a wooden model of the rifle. He believed that his gun would be an improvement over the Sharps breech-loading rifle. Nevertheless, he approached Richard Lawrence, who was connected with the Sharps Rifle

Company, and received from Lawrence a barrel, locks, and other parts to make a working model.[23]

Spencer's wooden model intrigued Charles Cheney, who hired an expert gunmaker, Luke Wheelock of Worcester, Massachusetts, to help build the working model. Spencer and Wheelock finished the model in two weeks, often fashioning parts with a chisel and file. Spencer received a patent for the rifle on March 6, 1860.[24]

Scientific American described the "new-fangled jimcrack": "The Spencer Seven Shooter was a breech-loading and repeating rifle using metallic cartridges which were fed forward into the barrel from a magazine in the breech, by a forward and back motion of the trigger guard." Spencer drilled a channel the length of the stock and placed a tube with seven cartridges in it that fed each cartridge into the breech using the motion of the trigger guard. The design allowed a shooter to fire seven shots by repeating the procedure. It was like no other weapon at the time in the country.[25]

When Ripley and the army's ordnance bureau rejected Spencer's rifle, the inventor and Charles Cheney turned to the Navy Department. Cheney and Secretary of the Navy Gideon Welles were close friends, and the cabinet member agreed to a trial of the firearm at the Washington Navy Yard. Spencer demonstrated the rifle before the Navy Yard's commandant, John A. B. Dahlgren. Spencer fired a thousand rounds without cleaning the gun, with a rate of fire at one point of twenty-one shots in sixty-two seconds.[26]

Captain A. B. Dyer of the navy's ordnance bureau conducted his own test of the rifle. He fired it eighty times, and then, according to his report: "The loaded piece was laid on the ground and covered well with sand to see what would be the effect of getting sand into the joints. No clogging or other injurious effects appeared to have been produced. The lock and lower part of the barrel were then covered with salt water and left exposed for 24 hours. The rifle was then loaded and fired without difficulty. . . . I regard it as one of the very best breech loading arms that I have ever seen."[27]

The rifle was 47 inches in length, with a 30-inch barrel and a caliber of .552 inches. The gun weighed ten pounds. On June 22, the Navy Department ordered seven hundred rifles and seventy thousand cartridges. When Spencer and the Cheneys received the purchase letter, the inventor reportedly said, "The only things they lacked were a factory, machinery, and a workforce."[28]

A VISITOR TO THE WEST POINT FOUNDRY AT COLD SPRING, NEW YORK, in the autumn of 1861 described what he witnessed: "We could hear the deep breathing of furnaces, and the sullen monotonous pulsations of trip-hammers, busily at work at the West Point Foundry, the most extensive and complete of the iron-works of the United States."[29]

At this point in the war, the foundry was manufacturing ten-, twenty-, thirty-, and hundred-pounders for the federal government. Other foundries in Massachusetts, Connecticut, and Pennsylvania were casting cannon or heavy ordnance for the War and Navy departments, which relied entirely on private firms to produce these guns. No foundry, however, was forging more cannon than the Cold Spring firm.[30]

Not only did Parrott manufacture more guns but also he did so more cheaply than the other makers. Each Parrott cannon had that distinctive wrought iron band around its breech. In a report, "Remarks," dated June 4, 1861, Parrott explained that each gun had a "*cast iron body* . . . made of the best material," with "A *Wrought Iron* reinforce" around the breech. He admitted that iron bands had not originated with him, but "I do consider my plan to be attended with some points of positive & original value—and I also claim an important improvement in the process of shrinking on the Reinforce."[31]

Orders from the army and navy flooded into the foundry. Production rose from 230 cannon in 1861 to 580 in 1862. Each gun was test-fired, or proofed, and stamped with "WPF" (West Point Foundry) and "RPP" (Robert Parker Parrott) before delivery to the military. In April 1862, Parrott rifled guns and other artillery pieces battered down the allegedly impregnable masonry walls of Confederate-held Fort Pulaski outside of Savannah, Georgia, ensuring the acclaim of the West Point Foundry. An ordnance officer with the army reported that Parrott's low wrought iron carriages for heavy cannon exceeded others.[32]

By the summer of 1862, the foundry's workforce increased to several hundred men. A visitor to the complex at that time stated: "The Foundry is in full blast with everything in the ordnance line. One can hardly worm his way through the piles of shot and shell for rifles; and the machine shop, foundry, and boring mill contain nothing but rifled Parrotts of all sizes. Wonderful place."[33]

Controversy dogged Parrott, however, as fellow gunmakers and critics accused him of stealing others' designs. His success lay not in the original concepts of rifling or wrought iron bands but in the systematic production of a simple, basic gun design. He was able to cast in late 1862 and early 1863 a two-hundred-pounder and a three-hundred-pounder rifled cannon. The larger gun cost $4,500, with a carriage for an additional $1,400. In November 1862, he confided to an army officer, "Of course everything in these times is exceptional, and one hardly knows what turn things may take." He added, "Profits were larger than usual."[34]

Production continued to rise, nearly doubling from the previous years to 1,141 cannon in 1863. At the same time, the foundry manufactured approximately ten thousand shells each week. That spring, Parrott informed his brother Peter, "We continue very busy and likely to use all the iron you can make" at nearby Greenwood Furnace. He declared days later, "Guns are ordered by the fifties and all my efforts required to keep up supply." In June, he noted that orders for guns and projectiles were "increasing daily," while in August, he asserted, "I am over head and ears in business and demand for guns, etc."[35]

A newspaper correspondent toured the foundry in September and reported, "When I look round upon my country, I am struck with nothing more than the singular and persevering ingenuity with which our countrymen adapt themselves to all exigencies." He observed Parrott

and recorded, "He belongs to the class of quiet, working men, who ac-
complish most of what is done in the world, and of whom the world
knows little, because they don't blow their own trumpets."[36]

WHEN THE CIVIL WAR BEGAN IN 1861, 239 PRIVATE FIRMS MANUFAC-
tured firearms. The two major companies were the Colt's Patent Firearms Manufacturing Company and the Sharps Rifle Company, both
located in Hartford, Connecticut. As noted, in Massachusetts, the
Springfield Armory, owned by the federal government, produced the
standard muzzle-loading shoulder rifle for the army. But with the conflict's demand for rifles and revolvers, businesses that made kitchen
utensils, sewing machines, wagon axles, and textiles retooled their factories for guns.[37]

It was against this competition that the Spencer Rifle Manufacturing Company entered the gun-making business with its contract
with the Navy Department for seven hundred rifles. With the purchase
agreement secured, Charles and Frank Cheney and investors in Boston
raised $500,000 in capital to form the company. The Cheney brothers
owned four very profitable silk mills and were the primary financiers
of the enterprise. For the armory, they rented the second floor of the
Chickering Piano factory on Tremont Street in Boston, paid Spencer
$5,000 for the patent rights, and agreed to give him a royalty of $1 on
each sold gun.[38]

"It was the beginning of struggles and troubles," recalled Spencer,
who oversaw the establishment of the Boston factory, "the installation
of the machinery, building a forging shop, making of tools, fixtures,
gauges, and many special machines." A gun-making business needed
steam engines and boilers, reamers, milling and grinding machines,
lathes, drill presses, screw machines, polishing frames, furnaces, and
other devices along with the skilled labor to produce the firearms. Mark
Twain walked through the Colt factory after the war and described it as
"a dense wilderness of strange iron machines" on every floor. During the

conflict, it would have been, in Twain's words, more of "a tangled forest of . . . imaginable and unimaginable forms of mechanicism."[39]

The "struggles and troubles" continued for months as the company could neither purchase machinery nor hire skilled laborers. Spencer designed new machines and had them built. The Cheney brothers and James G. Blaine, a Republican supporter of Abraham Lincoln in 1860 and Speaker of the Maine House of Representatives, lobbied the War Department and evidently appealed directly to the president for an army contract. Secretary of War Simon Cameron agreed to the purchase of 10,000 rifles in December 1861, with delivery of 500 guns at $40 each in three months.[40]

The company could not fulfill the terms of the contract in the designated time. When Edwin Stanton succeeded Cameron as secretary, he reviewed contracts and reduced the Spencer rifle order to 7,500. It was not, however, until December 1862 that the War Department received its initial 500 rifles, and it was not until February 1863 that 600 rifles were delivered at the Boston Navy Yard.[41]

The War Department issued its initial delivery of rifles to the 5th Michigan Cavalry, following lobbying efforts by the regiment's Colonel Joseph T. Copeland. When more rifles reached Washington, companies of the 6th Michigan Cavalry received the guns. Both units carried the rifles during the Gettysburg campaign, fighting with them at Hanover, Pennsylvania, on June 30 and on July 3 in the cavalry action east of Gettysburg. The Michiganders were the only troops in the Army of the Potomac with repeaters in the three-day battle.[42]

Earlier in the spring of 1863, Spencer visited the Union Army of the Cumberland. The inventor had traveled to the West to demonstrate the rifle's capability to officers in the army. The firearm impressed Colonel John T. Wilder, commander of the Lightning Brigade of mounted infantry. Wilder had tried to purchase Oliver Winchester's Henry rifle, a sixteen-shot breech-loading repeater, but the company could not fulfill the order in a timely manner.[43]

Wilder was so enthusiastic about Spencer's seven-shot repeater that he negotiated a private purchase with Spencer, even securing a personal loan from a bank to expedite the sale to his men. Wilder did, however, then meet with the army commander, Major General William S. Rosecrans, and convinced him to order the rifles through the War Department. The Lightning Brigade members began receiving their rifles on May 15, 1863.[44]

Wilder's troops displayed the rifle's effectiveness in combat on June 24, during the Tullahoma campaign for control of Middle Tennessee. The Lightning Brigade spearheaded the Union attack on Confederate defenders in Hoover's Gap of the Highland Rim. The Yankees seized the defile, then repulsed a series of Rebel counterattacks with withering fire from their Spencer rifles. The victory at Hoover's Gap forced the Confederates to retreat into Georgia.[45]

Although Wilder's men at Hoover's Gap and the Michiganders at Gettysburg had demonstrated the rifle's effectiveness and firepower in combat, opposition to the gun persisted in the War Department. It appears that not only Ordnance Chief James Ripley but also Secretary of War Edwin Stanton did not approve of the purchase of additional rifles. It also appears that when army officers' requests for the rifle were rejected, the officers appealed directly to the president.[46]

From the war's earliest days, Lincoln welcomed new ideas and inventions that might aid the Union cause and possibly shorten the struggle. Even as a young man, he had a curiosity about how things worked. In fact, he received a patent in 1849 for a series of bellows placed in a boat's hold that when deployed would lift the vessel over obstructions in a river. Lincoln, however, could not find an investor to finance a working model.[47]

When proposals or models from inventors arrived at the White House, Lincoln's secretaries placed them on a table for the president to examine. He remarked that he "never assumed that an idea must be mad because madmen pursued it." One of his secretaries, William O. Stoddard, said of the president, "He takes a special interest in the new ideas of breech loaders and repeaters, but the Bureau officials are against him."[48]

It was the request from officers to arm their regiments with Spencer rifles that apparently led Lincoln to examine and personally to test the firearm. He received a pair of rifles from the navy's chief of ordnance. The president had difficulty removing the cartridge tube from one of the guns. Lincoln had the second rifle fired as he and Secretary of War Stanton witnessed the test. The gun jammed, however, when two cartridges were brought forward simultaneously.[49]

Major General Stephen Hurlbut had forwarded the request for the Spencer rifles to the president. In reply, on August 4, 1863, Lincoln wrote, "The result is that I have tried two of these guns; and each so got out of order as to have been entirely useless in battle." Stanton and General-in-Chief Henry Halleck opposed the purchase of more rifles, continued the president, "and my own discouragement, at the trials, I am sorry to disappoint you by saying I can not now order these guns for you."[50]

Less than two weeks after Lincoln's rejection of the rifle, Christopher Spencer went to the White House. He and the company's owners had learned of the failed trial and decided to send Spencer to the capital. The inventor carried with him a new rifle and a letter from the company's treasurer, Warren Fisher Jr. "It would give us much satisfaction," wrote Fisher, "if you allow Mr. Spencer to make a trial of the rifle in your presence, and we would suggest that as the Hon. Secretary of War, Gen. Halleck and others were knowing of the mishaps of our gun at its former trials before you, that it would be very desirable that they should be present if possible."[51]

When Spencer arrived, he was taken to Lincoln in his office on the second floor. "I found the President alone," recounted Spencer. "With brief introduction, I took the rifle from its case and presented to him." Lincoln handled the rifle, then asked Spencer to take it apart to show him the "inwardness of the thing." The president suggested that Spencer return the next day "at 2 o'clock and we will go out and see the thing shoot."[52]

The "shooting match," as Spencer called it, occurred in Treasury Park, south of the White House and near the unfinished Washington

Monument. Robert Lincoln, John Hay, and a naval officer accompanied the president and the inventor. Lincoln sent his son to the War Department to ask Stanton to witness the trial. While they waited, Lincoln told stories, and Spencer vented his frustration with the War Department. "That's not strange," rebutted Lincoln, "you ought to hear what I hear from them over there." Robert Lincoln returned, reporting that Stanton declined as too busy to leave the department.[53]

A wooden board three feet long and six inches wide, with a black circle near each end, served as a target. Lincoln shot first, hitting the dark spot once and putting the other six rounds into the board. Spencer went next and apparently hit the bull's-eye more times than the president. According to Spencer's recollection, Lincoln said to him, "Well, you are younger than I am and have a better eye and steadier nerve."[54]

John Hay witnessed the "shooting match" and described it the next evening in a letter: "A wonderful gun loading with absolutely contemptible simplicity and ease with seven balls & firing the whole readily & deliberately in less than half a minute. The President made some pretty good shots. Spencer[,] the inventor[,] a quiet little Yankee who sold himself in relentless slavery to his idea for six weary years before it was perfect[,] did some splendid shooting."[55]

Lincoln and Spencer returned to the White House, where they shook hands, wished each other well, and parted. The naval officer had cut off Lincoln's end of the board and gave it to the inventor as a memento of the event. The president and Hay went the next evening back to Treasury Park to shoot the rifle at a target.[56]

Within days, Lincoln instructed the War Department to purchase Spencer rifles and newly designed carbines. Weeks earlier, a commission in Massachusetts selected Spencer's firearms as the best breechloaders, and the state ordered two thousand of the rifles and carbines. The contract with the War Department saved the financially strapped company. By year's end, the Boston firm had delivered seven thousand carbines to the federal government.[57]

THE WEST POINT FOUNDRY CLANGED AND HUMMED WITH ACTIVITY IN the spring of 1864. Inside the sprawling landscape of shops, twelve hundred workers forged nearly a hundred cannon of various sizes and types monthly. A two-day strike by the workers over wages could not slow production because Union troops arrived and enforced martial law. Four strikers were imprisoned, and three other men reportedly fled Cold Spring.[58]

The ordnance firm extended beyond Cold Spring into the New York countryside. Robert Parrott and his brother Peter owned furnaces, and the foundry had contracted with three iron mines, an anthracite coal mine, and a charcoal business. The three iron mines had the capacity to produce twenty thousand tons of ore, and the foundry received more than nine thousand tons of coal and charcoal in a year. Parrott also opened an office for the business at 30 Broadway in New York City.[59]

Although the foundry produced first-rate guns and projectiles, prematurely exploding shells and bursting cannon brought Parrott before a Senate committee in 1864. In August 1863, an eight-ton, two-hundred-pounder siege gun, dubbed the "Swamp Angel" by its crew because of its location, was disabled after firing only three dozen shells in two days. The Union Navy had reported earlier of the bursting of hundred-pounders, and the army had abandoned the twenty-pounders because they were cumbersome and brittle.[60]

Parrott admitted to a Union general that the elongated shells, with a "quite large" charge of powder, sometimes wedged in the bore and gave the cannon "a violent strain." He had corrected the problem by varnishing the interior surfaces of the shells. He asserted, however, to another officer, "In designing these Guns, I have considered their safety & strength with reference to long continued use *in Service with the proper charge.*"[61]

The gunmaker learned subsequently that army officers had concluded, as Parrott put it, that "the premature explosion of shells" was related more to "the exposure of these guns to drifting sands" during the campaign against Confederate defenses around Charleston, South Carolina. In a letter to the War Department, Parrott argued further, "There are some singular discrepancies in the circumstances attending the failure of guns at Morris Island, which go far to prove the operation of causes of a peculiar and accidental character, rather than defects in the guns."[62]

Unknown to Parrott, a Confederate ordnance officer, Major John Barnwell, had endorsed the safety of Parrott cannon in 1863. Barnwell had inspected ruptured guns on James Island outside of Charleston and reported the problem was that the rifled artillery pieces had "acute or sharp-edged grooves" in the barrels. Parrott guns, however, reduced the chances of premature explosions by having "rather flattened curves." Barnwell believed that Confederate guns needed Parrott's type of rifling.[63]

In his appearance before the Senate committee, Parrott described the practicality and efficiency of his cannon. "As a new gun," he testified, "they were considered very successful indeed. At all events, they were looked upon as very much in advance of anything they [army and navy] then had. I do not profess to think they are the best gun in the world, but I think they were the best practical thing that could be got at the time, and I suppose that was the great reason for getting them."[64]

In November 1864, months after the testimony in the capital, Parrott wrote to the army's chief of ordnance: "My operations have necessarily been large. I never could have met the calls upon me without extending the works and from the nature of the calls for Rifled ordnance & projectiles have been obliged to do so in a particular way." He thought that his cost for wrought iron would exceed $100,000. By year's end, the foundry had cast 1,624 cannon, the most in a year during the war.[65]

The New York *Times* reported in March 1865 that Parrott "is lying dangerously ill" with pneumonia and typhoid fever. "But little is entertained of his recovery," continued the article. Parrott did recover and, with the surrender of the Confederacy's two major armies in April, demand for his guns and shells ceased.[66]

Artillery units in every federal army had Parrott guns and shells. The cannon were engaged on all the major battlefields and with the navy in operations along the coasts. During the conflict's three full years, 1862–1864, the foundry produced 3,345 guns. If 1861 and 1865 are included, the Cold Spring firm forged another 1,125 cannon. The company also manufactured 1.3 million projectiles.[67]

The West Point Foundry cast more guns than the second and third leading ordnance companies combined. In fact, the Cold Spring business was the North's largest munitions firm, with 2,332 contracts and sales of $4,733,059. Robert Parrott and his hundreds of workers could be rightly proud of their contribution to Union victory.[68]

COLONEL JOHN T. WILDER AND THE OFFICERS AND MEN OF THE LIGHTning Brigade manned a section of the Union line on the Chickamauga battlefield in northern Georgia. Before them, across an open field, came the ranks of veteran Confederate infantrymen. The Yankees began working their Spencer rifles and, as Wilder told it, "the head of the column, as it pushed on by those behind, appeared to melt away or sink into the earth, for, though continually moving, it got no nearer." Against the rapid fire from the seven-shot repeaters, the Rebels had no chance.[69]

Major General George H. Thomas, who commanded a Union corps at Chickamauga, declared later that the Spencer carbine was "the most effective weapon in use." In April 1864, the army's chief of ordnance, Brigadier General George D. Ramsay, stated about the carbine: "The demand for them is constant and for large quantities. It seems as if no soldier who had seen them used could be satisfied with any other."[70]

The production and delivery of the lighter, shorter barreled carbine far exceeded that of the rifle. By the late spring and summer of 1864, officers and men of the cavalry regiments in the Union armies carried the Spencer carbine. In Virginia, the horse soldiers fought with them in the Overland and Petersburg campaigns, and in Georgia they were engaged in Major General William T. Sherman's advance on Atlanta. Several Yankee infantry units possessed the Spencer rifle, but the mounted troopers with the carbine had a significant advantage in firepower against Confederate horsemen, decisively so in the Shenandoah Valley campaign in the late summer and early fall of 1864.[71]

Late in the year, a North Carolina newspaper observed, "The most formidable of the breech-loading small arms which have been employed in the present hostilities is the Spencer rifle." The same could have been stated about the carbine. A veteran of many actions with the rifle and carbine, Colonel James H. Kidd of the 6th Michigan Cavalry argued, "A better gun had not been issued," adding with exaggeration, "and if the entire army had been supplied with it the war would not have lasted ninety days."[72]

At war's end, among private gun-making firms, the Spencer Rifle Manufacturing Company ranked eighth in sales to the War and Navy departments, which amounted to $2,078,427. Owing to incomplete records, the precise number of carbines and rifles delivered to the Union military is unknown. It appears that the company sold roughly 94,200 carbines and 12,400 rifles. The Burnside Rifle Company manufactured another 30,000 Spencers for the government. Years later, Spencer claimed that the Boston firm produced approximately 200,000 of his model for the Union military, states, and private individuals. If a veteran trooper bought a Spencer carbine when he mustered out, it cost him ten dollars; all other carbines cost eight dollars.[73]

The "quiet little Yankee" from Connecticut had invented a weapon that contributed to Union fighting prowess, particularly of cavalry units. In specific engagements, its rate of fire and effectiveness proved decisive. It was the first repeater produced in America, portending a deadlier landscape of war in the future. Before the war ended, the War Department announced that a breech-loading rifle would be the standard arm of the infantry once a manufacturer was selected.[74]

Spencer left the company in 1866. He was not one of its investors and only received a royalty on each gun. An acquaintance in Spencer's later years put it this way: "He made other men rich out of the richness of his mind, but it did not seem to be a part of his plan to become rich himself." In 1869, the Winchester Repeating Arms Company purchased the assets of the Spencer Rifle Manufacturing Company.[75]

Chapter Six

THE PATRIOTS

—m—

Dr. Edward Robinson Squibb lay in bed, his eyes and hands covered in bandages. He had been injured in a fire at his laboratory, or "chemical factory," in Brooklyn, New York, on the evening of December 29, 1858. Although a newspaper reported that he had been "somewhat burned about the face and hands," attending physicians despaired over whether he would see again or regain full use of his fingers.[1]

The fire occurred when a young, inexperienced worker broke a small bottle of ether and a nearby candle ignited the vapor. The flames spread rapidly. Squibb rushed to the scene, trying vainly to extinguish the blaze. He managed to save his journals and papers, but his clothes were on fire as he ran out of the building. The back of his hands and face were severely burned. Weeks of painful recovery awaited, but he would heal, for Edward Squibb was on a crusade.[2]

Born into a Quaker family on July 5, 1819, in Wilmington, Delaware, he was thirty-nine years old at the time of the accident. His parents, James Robinson and Catherine Harrison Bonsall Squibb, had moved from Philadelphia not long before their first child's birth. Both branches of the family had lived in southeastern Pennsylvania among the Society of Friends communities for a century. Why the couple relocated is unknown. When Edward was twelve, tragedy struck the family and his mother and three sisters died, most likely from some type of fever.[3]

James Squibb, Edward, and another son, Robert, returned to Philadelphia. Edward was sent to live with his Grandmother Bonsall in Darby, outside of the city. He received some formal schooling until he apprenticed himself at the age of eighteen to Warder Morris, a Philadelphia pharmacist, in 1837. He learned the trade of grinding and mixing drugs and of compounding powders from Morris. Within a year or two, he hired on with the pharmaceutical firm of H. H. Sprague.[4]

According to a biographer, Squibb planned for years to enter the medical profession. In 1842, he gained admission to the prestigious Jefferson Medical College in Philadelphia. He graduated in a class of 116 members on March 20, 1845. He had written a required thesis on tetanus.[5]

Squibb opened a private practice in the city, and the medical college retained him as clerk of clinics, assistant demonstrator of anatomy, librarian, and curator of the medical specimens museum. Since his youth, however, the sea had appealed to his imagination. He decided in early 1847 to enlist as a surgeon in the United States Navy, a difficult choice because his Quaker heritage extended back to an ancestor who came to America with William Penn. Squibb was commissioned as an assistant surgeon on April 26, 1847. A pair of Quaker meetinghouses subsequently disowned him.[6]

The navy doctor served on three ships during the next four years. He maintained detailed logs of diseases and injuries suffered by crew members. He also began to notice the inconsistencies and impurities in the drugs he administered to patients. He was granted a six-month leave in 1851 to study, "rubbing up" as it was called then, at his alma mater. He studied chemistry and obstetrics and observed surgeries. In January 1852, he received orders to report to the Brooklyn Naval Hospital. He could not have known when he reported for duty, but his life's work had been redirected.[7]

Dr. Benjamin Franklin Bache, a professor at Jefferson Medical College, had been appointed commandant of the Brooklyn installation. Great-grandson of Benjamin Franklin, Bache likely requested Squibb's assignment to the hospital. Squibb studied under Bache, and both men shared concerns over the quality of drugs and opposed the government's policy of purchasing medicines from the lowest bidder and from foreign countries. The Navy Department authorized Bache and Squibb to establish a Naval Laboratory to produce quality drugs at the hospital's complex of white-washed brick buildings. They outfitted the laboratory on the upper floor of the installation's former smallpox ward.[8]

Squibb experimented to find a safer and cheaper method for purifying ether and chloroform. Doctors called both anesthetics "wild cards" during surgeries because impurities and inconsistencies in them caused patients to awaken from unconsciousness during operations. In 1846, Congress had enacted a law prohibiting the importation of impure drugs, but the measure was never enforced. By the time of Squibb's experiments, adulterated domestic and foreign drugs were common, if not predominant.[9]

The traditional method of producing ether was to heat a mixture of ethyl alcohol and sulfuric acid over an open flame. It was a dangerous procedure and one that resulted in the uneven quality of the drug. Squibb experimented by trial and error for two years before he succeeded in making ether by steam distillation. He refused to patent the process or apparatus in order to share it with other drugmakers. His work appeared with full text and detailed diagrams in the September 1856 issue of *American Journal of Pharmacy*. He had waited to further refine the process before publishing it.[10]

As he had done with ether, Squibb undertook numerous experiments and tests to produce chloroform, ultimately making an effective anesthetic by steam distillation in 1855. He also conducted experiments on other pharmaceuticals that led to the manufacture of more purified drugs. He, Bache, and others successfully petitioned Congress to enact a law requiring the federal government to purchase medical supplies and gunpowder on "quality first and price second."[11]

A disagreement over rank and pay with the navy caused Squibb to consider private enterprise. He had married Caroline Cook, Bache's sister-in-law, in 1852, and the couple had a son. When an offer came for a partnership in a commercial laboratory in Louisville, Kentucky, Squibb requested and was granted a year's furlough by the secretary of the navy. The Squibbs had barely relocated to Louisville when the secretary ordered Squibb to report for sea duty. Instead, he submitted his resignation, which was approved on December 5, 1857.[12]

The Louisville Chemical Works manufactured drugs and chemicals. There, Squibb continued his experiments on perfecting ether and chloroform. He stayed with the firm, however, less than a year. In July 1858, the War Department offered to purchase drugs for the army from him if Squibb would open his own laboratory. A month later, he dissolved his share of the partnership with the laboratory and returned to Brooklyn, where he planned to open his facility.[13]

Squibb rented a four-story brick building at 149 Furman Street for the laboratory. It took weeks to secure the necessary apparatus and furniture. He financed the business with a $1,300 loan from a wealthy Georgian and former classmate at Jefferson Medical College, Dr. Samuel White. Years earlier, White had urged his close friend to leave the navy and to open a private laboratory. Squibb began producing pharmaceuticals on December 1, 1858. Twenty-eight days later, the fire that severely injured Squibb gutted the building and destroyed the laboratory, darkening his future.[14]

ON DECEMBER 12, 1844, THE *ALABAMIAN* FLOUNDERED IN THE HEAVY surf off the New Jersey coast near Cape May. The crew and passengers— eighteen persons in all—abandoned the ship and piled into a surfboat and a longboat. Heavy swales pounded the vessels for more than seven hours until the sails of another ship were spotted. Another two hours passed before the ordeal ended, with all of them rescued by the *Atlanta*.[15]

Two of the surviving passengers were close friends and fellow Columbia College graduates, Abram Hewitt and Edward Cooper. The two young men were returning to America after a months-long tour of

Europe. All of the *Alabamian's* cargo and passengers' belongings were lost when the ship sank. All Hewitt possessed was the two dollars in his pocket. He stated later: "That accident was the turning point, of my life. It taught me for the first time that I could stand in the face of death without fear and without flinching." He added, "Self-help is the remedy for all of the evils of which men complain."[16]

To be sure, the twenty-two-year-old Abram Hewitt had done well for himself since his impoverished childhood. His father, John Hewitt, had emigrated from England to the United States in 1795 and worked as a machinist before opening a cabinetmaking shop in New York City. Unfortunately, he signed a note for a fellow Englishman who absconded with the money. When Hewitt could not repay the loan, he lost his business. By the time his and his wife's fifth child, Abram Stevens, was born on July 31, 1822, the family was surviving on a rented ten-acre farm near Haverstraw, New York.[17]

In 1824, the Hewitt family moved back to New York City, where John opened a bakery. For the next few years, the elder Hewitt changed occupations until he obtained a patent for a folding bedstead and began manufacturing it. But the business never flourished financially. Young Abram witnessed the family's struggles and came to possess an iron determination to succeed, a pragmatism, and an unblinking acceptance of life's difficulties.[18]

Abram proved to be a precocious child and an avid reader, who attended the Grammar School of Columbia College. Graduating in 1838, he received one of the college's two free annual public scholarships. Hewitt excelled at Columbia, winning a gold medal for scholarship and character each of his four years there. He was graduated first in his class in 1842. The next year, he studied law while teaching at the Grammar School and tutoring students privately.[19]

One of Hewitt's pupils was Edward Cooper. They had been classmates at Columbia until illness caused Cooper to fall behind in his studies. He did not withdraw from college, and with Hewitt's help, he graduated in 1843. They were an unlikely pair—Hewitt, forever restless, decisive, "high strung, and quick tempered," and Cooper, more restrained, less decisive, and with an affinity for making friends. When Cooper suggested a joint excursion to Europe, Hewitt agreed.[20]

Edward Cooper was the son of one of New York City's most innovative and wealthy businessmen, Peter Cooper. The elder Cooper had started out in 1808 at the age of seventeen as a coachmaker's apprentice. He spent four years learning the trade before pursuing various enterprises. He had written as a youth that he "was always fussing and contriving, and was never satisfied unless [he] was doing something difficult—something that had never been done before."[21]

During the 1820s and 1830s, Peter Cooper converted a factory into a furniture shop, opened a grocery, purchased a glue factory, and declared, "I determined to make the best glue that could be produced, and found out every method and ingredient to that end." He accomplished this and received a patent for his glue. He then manufactured isinglass from fish, undercutting the import market, and was the first to make table gelatin, which he sold in packets.[22]

The inventor and entrepreneur invested in New York City real estate and the Baltimore & Ohio Railroad. He designed and built "Tom Thumb," the country's first successful steam locomotive. He also constructed an iron foundry at Thirty-Third Street and Third Avenue. In 1837, he sold it to two wire manufacturers, but when the Panic of 1837 struck, the new owners defaulted on money owed to Cooper. He took possession of the foundry and continued its operations.[23]

By the time his son Edward and Hewitt returned from Europe, Peter Cooper had decided to relocate his foundry to Trenton, New Jersey. The state capital offered nearby iron ore deposits, anthracite coal mines across the Delaware River in Pennsylvania, and a direct route between New York City and Philadelphia. Cooper also planned to involve Edward in the business. His son, in turn, suggested that his father offer a position, even partnership, to his good friend Hewitt.[24]

Peter Cooper was reluctant, however, to agree to his son's proposal. He had known Hewitt's father for many years and Abram for the past few. He decided to send Hewitt to Boston to negotiate the purchase of a patent for a forging machine and a machine to make horseshoe nails. Hewitt succeeded, and Cooper supposedly said to the twenty-two-year-old, "I don't know that you can get books far enough out of your head to let even a little business in, but if you'd like to try, here's your chance."[25]

Work began on a wire and rod mill during the spring of 1845, and by October the establishment was completed. Peter Cooper was the president of the Trenton Iron Works, Edward Cooper served as super-intendent of the plant, and Hewitt, as secretary. Peter Cooper did not make either his son or Hewitt partners in the firm but in 1847 created a corporation and later a second company, Cooper & Hewitt, to manage Trenton Iron Company. The president held $151,000 of the initial stock issue, and Edward Cooper and Hewitt held the remaining $149,000.[26]

The ironworks began production at the end of 1845. A contract with the Camden & Amboy Railroad for two thousand tons of rails ensured the company's early profitably. The railroad had been buying T-rails from English firms, but workers at the Trenton Iron Works rolled the first American-made T-rails for it. Within a year, Cooper & Hewitt employed five hundred American, English, Irish, and German laborers and forged fifty tons of rail iron daily.[27]

Cooper and Hewitt proved to be astute ironmakers and business-men. Like his father, Edward Cooper had a mechanical aptitude, while Hewitt possessed financial acumen and entrepreneurial vision. In 1847, Cooper & Hewitt purchased Andover Mine in Sussex County for its quality iron ore; a firm in Trenton that manufactured iron spikes, nails, and wires, which they merged into their company; the Delaware & Raritan Canal; and the Philadelphia and Trenton Railroad. Hewitt was twenty-five years old; Cooper, twenty-three.[28]

Dr. Edward Squibb recovered slowly from the burns he suffered in the fire at his Brooklyn laboratory on December 29, 1858. The backs of his hands and face were scarred, and, more grievously, his eyelids had been so badly seared that for the rest of his life when he slept he would have to close them with adhesive strips. "His visage [was] permanently and sadly marred," reported a newspaper years later. He was very conscious of his disfigurement, which caused him to avoid public occasions when he could.[29]

While Squibb recovered from his injuries, the rebuilding of his laboratory at 149 Furman Street proceeded. Fellow scientists and physicians and friends paid for the restoration. "Their gift to him was a debt, they felt," observed Squibb, "not a gift and not a loan." He thought otherwise, however.[30]

Production resumed at the Furman Street facility later in the spring of 1859. Before the fire, Squibb had recorded in a journal, "Do not get to bed nowadays before 12." The extent of his injuries likely prevented him from undertaking such long workdays for some time after he returned to the laboratory.[31]

He never ceased, however, his crusade for the purification of drugs. "He is well known," stated a newspaper, "as the uncompromising enemy of adulterated drugs and chemicals, come they from whatever quarter they may." In 1860, for instance, he served on the Committee for the Revision of the US Pharmacopoeia, whose purpose was to create a register of approved drugs, chemicals, and pharmaceutical preparations. The committee's work laid the basis for safe drugs, which saved lives in the approaching conflict.[32]

Squibb's laboratory, meanwhile, manufactured a variety of pharmaceuticals. The company was noted for the consistent quality of its drugs. Although written decades after the Civil War, a newspaper's declaration about the firm is relevant to these antebellum years: "Every doctor knew that the Squibb preparations were exactly what the names on them indicated, and that they could be prescribed with perfect confidence that the patient would get what the prescription called for. There was never any question about this."[33]

Other laboratories began modeling their procedures on Squibb's. Once the war began, the federal government established a laboratory in Philadelphia and, according to an inspector, all methods of manufacture and apparatus used there were the same "as those then practiced and in use in the laboratory of Dr. E. R. Squibb."[34]

By 1861, sales of pharmaceuticals were so good that Squibb repaid his benefactors who had financed the rebuilding of his laboratory two years earlier. Most importantly, since he had established the business, the United States military bought large quantities of his drugs. The Medical Department of the army had given, in Squibb's judgment, "preference . . . to a good class of medicinal preparations."[35]

With the attack on Fort Sumter, Squibb prepared for the inevitable increase in demand for drugs and medicinal preparations. He leased additional buildings and hired more workers. His prior business relationship with the army's Medical Department assured his company of a stream of government contracts. He continued experimenting with different pharmaceuticals while sharing any discoveries and new techniques with other drug-making firms.[36]

By the spring of 1862, his laboratory and rented properties could no longer meet the demand for his products. On May 1, Squibb bought a property at 36 Doughty Street in Brooklyn and laid the new factory's cornerstone by month's end. He borrowed money from a bank for the construction, which was completed in seven months.[37]

The factory, consisting of two levels with a private and a public entrance, had massive concrete walls and six-inch-thick floors. One of his sons commented on the building's construction: "It was almost monolithic. To make any changes was a tough job, we could seldom get a whole brick out of the walls. The Big Boss was a stickler for pure cement." Squibb opened the facility for production on January 1, 1863.[38]

Pharmaceutical firms prospered during the conflict. In a span of about a year, Squibb received more than $286,000 from the Medical Department of the army. Wyeth & Brother in Philadelphia earned more than $657,000 during the same period. Squibb served on the board that revised the Medical Department's Supply Table. In May 1863, he rejected an offer from Surgeon General William A. Hammond for the government to lease his laboratory and for Squibb to be a surgeon of volunteers.[39]

Squibb's major contribution to medical service during the war was the design and construction of compact medicine chests, or panniers. Surgeon General Hammond specified the dimensions of the chests. Each one contained forty-nine pharmaceuticals packed in bottles and lacquer-coated boxes. A pannier was divided into two compartments and could also hold coffee, tea, sugar, whiskey, condensed milk, herbs, anesthetics, and surgical instruments. Squibb contracted with suppliers, such as Gail Borden with his condensed milk, for nondrug items.[40]

Squibb initially built the pannier as an iron frame covered with cowhide. He subsequently made the chest out of wood and reinforced its edges with black metal straps. On the inside of the hinged lid, a paper label showed the location of each drug. On the front of the pannier, stenciled in black, were the words: "This package contains / Medical Supplies only, / put up in glass bottles / and well packed." On the back: "U.S. Army / Medical Pannier No. . . . / Edward R. Squibb, M.D. Brooklyn, NY."[41]

The panniers first appeared in the spring of 1863, and from then until the war's end, Union surgeons throughout the armies carried them. Squibb sold each pannier for $111.00 on credit or $100.93 in cash. The Medical Department of the army initially purchased $40,000 worth of panniers. Before long, however, Surgeon General Hammond found a company that could sell a pannier "equal in all respects to those now furnished by" Squibb. Nevertheless, Squibb continued to sell his medicine chests, and other companies used his pattern for theirs.[42]

By war's end, Squibb's company had supplied roughly 12 percent or more of the drugs consumed by federal armies. Its panniers were highly regarded and apparently preferred by Union surgeons. Undoubtedly, however, Squibb's greatest contribution to the cause came before the war in his tireless, even selfless, efforts against adulterated drugs. The process he shared for the purification of ether and chloroform saved countless lives. Edward Squibb served his country patriotically both as a naval physician and as a scientist dedicated to the safety and efficacy of drugs. The quest continued.[43]

IN 1853, THE BRITISH GOVERNMENT PREPARED A REPORT ON AMERICAN ironmaking firms. The document described the Trenton Iron Works as "the leading establishment of the United States not only in regard to its production, but also in regard to its working arrangements."[44]

In the eight years since Peter Cooper founded the ironworks, he, his son Edward, and Abram Hewitt built it into one of the country's foremost producers of iron rails, wires, and nails. Cooper & Hewitt Company owned several iron ore mines, including the recently purchased Ringwood Manor, which had been in operation since the Revolutionary War. In fact, Hewitt called the Ringwood mines "the best I have seen." The firm also built three large blast furnaces—fifty-five feet high, twenty feet in diameter—at Phillipsburg, New Jersey. The furnaces produced twenty-five thousand tons of pig iron annually, the most in the country at the time.[45]

By the mid-1850s, then, the Trenton Iron Works had the capacity to forge thirty-five thousand tons of finished iron each year. "No pains or expenses have been spared to make the mill perfect in its arrangements," explained Hewitt. He contended that Trenton itself had a "great advantage" in its location between New York City and Philadelphia. "It is so happily placed, that it is as cheap to use bituminous coal as anthracite. . . . It is healthy, and has the choice of hands which were skilled in metalworking," he concluded.[46]

Although mills in Pennsylvania and Ohio led in annual tonnage, Cooper & Hewitt led in experimentation and innovation in iron products. It had a rolling machine that could form a railroad rail in one minute. It was the first American ironmaking business to roll I-beams for buildings. Soon, its I-beams were used in the construction of the

General Post Office and Capitol dome in Washington, DC; the Philadelphia Mint; Nassau Hall at Princeton, New Jersey; and other federal buildings in various states.[47]

Cooper & Hewitt's beams went into the construction of Cooper Union for the Advancement of Science and Art. Peter Cooper saved money to fulfill his dream of educating New York City's working folks in the natural and social sciences, "open and free to all." The cornerstone was laid in 1853, and construction took five years. Cooper Union opened formally on July 1, 1859. Less than nine months later, on February 27, 1860, Abraham Lincoln addressed a capacity crowd in the edifice.[48]

When Cooper Union opened, Peter Cooper removed himself almost entirely from the operations of the Trenton Iron Works. He had withdrawn gradually during the 1850s, relinquishing control to his son Edward and his son-in-law Hewitt, who had married Amelia Cooper on April 6, 1855. As the elder Cooper's role decreased, Hewitt's increased. Hewitt had negotiated the purchase of Ringwood Manor and advocated more innovations and expansion. He proved to be an able administrator and a visionary businessman.[49]

Hewitt and Peter Cooper invested in Cyrus Field's endeavor to lay a telegraph cable across the Atlantic Ocean. The younger men joined Samuel Morse and other investors in founding the American Telegraph Company. Hewitt and Edward Cooper were the first American ironmakers to test the Bessemer process, but it did not work because iron ore was "not being adapted to it." Hewitt wrote and published a book, *On the Statistics and Geography of the Production of Iron*. By the middle of the 1850s, he was, in the words of a historian, "already entrenched in the very highest echelons of New York City's financial and cultural elite."[50]

"The consumption of iron is the social barometer by which to estimate the relative height of civilization among nations," Hewitt asserted in 1856. A year later, however, the Panic of 1857 crippled the American economy. The deep recession cost Cooper & Hewitt tens of thousands of dollars, forcing the company to borrow $20,000 from Peter Cooper.

By the fall of 1857, more than half the iron furnaces and mills had closed, with companies in Pennsylvania hit particularly hard. The War Department in Washington, DC, increased orders to Cooper & Hewitt and other firms, helping them weather the economic storm.[51]

Recovery from the panic proved to be slow in coming. Nevertheless, by 1861, the Trenton firm was one of the largest corporations in the country. Edward Cooper and Hewitt were conservative Democrats and apparently sympathetic to Southerners' argument for secession. Rumors circulated that their company was making wrought iron gun carriages for the seceded state of Georgia. A New York City lawyer, George Templeton Strong, wrote in his diary that Hewitt had expressed "Southern and quasi-treasonable talk."[52]

Like many Northern Democrats, Cooper and Hewitt supported the Union cause after the attack on Fort Sumter. Strong recorded in his diary that the pair of ironmakers and fellow Democrats were now "denouncing rebellion and declaring themselves ready to go all lengths in upholding government. If this class of men had been secured and converted to loyalty, the gain to the country is worth ten Sumters."[53]

Hewitt's conversion to the Union cause was swift and complete. He hurried to Washington to secure government contracts and from there on April 23 wrote, "There is too much noise and too little system in public affairs, as at present conducted, to suit my taste." He continued: "I do not see how any incorporated company can be wanting in 'loyalty'— individuals may be. But inasmuch as all the owners and officers of this company are sacrificing time, money, and effort for the country, I should think there could not be much doubt as to the company."[54]

Three days later Hewitt assured his company's agent in London: "The issue is certain. The power of the general government will be asserted, and rebellion crushed once and forever, if it takes every man and dollar in the Northern States."[55]

Hewitt secured agreement from ordnance officers in the War Department that they would experiment with Cooper & Hewitt wrought iron for gun barrels. At the time, ironmakers in England and Germany produced the finest gunmetal, but in the spring of 1861 imported iron was scarce. Unfortunately for Cooper & Hewitt Company, gunsmiths at the government's Springfield Armory rejected its iron for gun barrels. The Trenton firm did sign a contract with the Whitney Arms Company in Connecticut, but further experiments with gunmetal at Trenton Iron Works resulted in more rejections by the armory. By the autumn of 1861, Cooper & Hewitt Company was experiencing financial difficulties.[56]

Before the year's end, however, the Navy Department ordered twenty-one mortar beds, which the company had never made and which were difficult to cast. The Trenton works obtained a one-and-a-half-ton model from the Watertown Arsenal, took it apart, made templates, and delivered the beds in early January 1862.[57]

On January 25, Chief of Ordnance James W. Ripley wired Cooper and Hewitt that the War Department needed thirty mortar beds as soon as possible for operations in the West. President Lincoln even sent an appeal to have the beds delivered to Brigadier General Ulysses S. Grant at Cairo, Illinois, within thirty days. Hewitt oversaw the work. He acquired additional iron bars from another firm and assigned the casting to four shops.[58]

The first four beds shipped on February 8, and Hewitt wrote to Ripley that same day: "We have redeemed the promise made by us at the outset, almost against hope, considering the delay in procuring some of the materials, but no effort has been spared." By February 14, the company had delivered twenty-one and had nine more beds ready for shipment. The ordnance bureau, however, took only the twenty-one but paid Cooper & Hewitt $21,000 for the full thirty beds. Even so, the company did not receive payment until Lincoln intervened upon a personal request from Hewitt.[59]

Hewitt described the completion of the contract as the "bringing to a close the most remarkable mechanical achievement, so far as time is concerned, that we have ever witnessed." He then declared to Assistant Secretary of War P. H. Watson, "To serve the country in its time of trial is the dearest wish of our hearts, and we hope that the Department will avail itself of our services at any and at all times when we can be useful; and we can promise fidelity, industry, and honesty in the execution of its behests." Grant, meanwhile, used mortars with the new beds in his bombardment of Confederate Fort Donelson.[60]

Although demand for rails for railroads made Cooper & Hewitt profitable again, the Trenton firm still could not make suitable gunmetal for the Springfield Armory. In March, Hewitt traveled to England, hoping to learn from English mills their methods for making gunmetal. He visited the Marshall & Mills and Whitworth companies, but they refused to disclose their secrets. Undeterred, Hewitt visited pubs near the mills, and the wealthy Yankee somehow extracted the secret formula from working men.[61]

Hewitt returned to the United States in July, and two months later, a newspaper reported that the tensile strength of the Trenton works' iron compared favorably to that of iron produced in England and Germany. More importantly, Secretary of War Edwin Stanton accepted Cooper & Hewitt's gunmetal for the Springfield Armory. The War Department ordered five thousand tons of it, enough for one million rifle muskets.[62]

At some point during 1862, Hewitt proposed to Secretary of the Navy Gideon Welles that the government assume operational control of the Trenton Iron Works to cast armor plates for the navy. Hewitt admitted to Welles that Cooper & Hewitt would lose considerable profits, "but in my judgment all private interests should in this crisis yield to the public welfare." The secretary rejected the offer.[63]

Still, the contract with the War Department for gunmetal adversely affected profits for the company. The ironworks had to purchase new equipment and to reconfigure production lines in part of the mill, both costly endeavors. Ripley offered to pay more for the gunmetal, but Hewitt replied on November 10, 1863: "But if I could consistently with my sense of right to the public have got enough money to have made good the actual loss to the Trenton Iron Company, you cannot appreciate the load of anxiety which would have been removed from my shoulders. The past year has been most painful to me, because by my action in the gun-barrel business the interests of my associates have suffered."[64]

The company, though, employing nearly five hundred workers in 1864, did earn modest profits from gun carriages, rails, and wires. There was some money to be made during the war: six newly built mills in Pittsburgh, Pennsylvania, produced $26 million worth of iron and steel in the final year and a half of the conflict. Yet the claim in a postwar newspaper seems accurate: "In fact the works of Cooper & Hewitt were for four years particularly devoted to the public service in the manufacture of gun-barrel metal and other munitions of war, without profit to the owners."[65]

The secretary of war praised the efforts of the Trenton ironmakers: "It is the purpose of this Department to acknowledge and place in its archives a memorial of all loyal and patriotic services of Cooper, Hewitt & Company of New York are publicly acknowledged. On the sudden call of the Department, and at no small sacrifice of their own interests, the energies of their establishment were devoted to the construction of mortar-carriages for the Western gunboats, which completed within a time unexampled in mechanical history, enabled the government to shell the rebels in their stronghold at Fort Donelson. They and the mechanics in their employment have well served their country."[66]

Staunch antebellum Democrats Edward Cooper and Abram Hewitt had indeed embraced the Union cause. When the War Department needed quality gunmetal, they delivered it, risking their company's financial well-being in the fulfillment of the contract. It can be argued that few, if any, major Northern industrial firms rendered a more patriotic contribution to the federal war effort than Cooper & Hewitt Company.

Chapter Seven

THE INVESTORS

———ᘏᘏᘏ———

I N THE LATE WINTER AND EARLY SPRING OF 1861, CYRUS HALL Mc-
Cormick watched events closely as the divide between North and
South appeared to grow irreconcilable. Like the country itself, the
wealthy inventor of a reaper and businessman was torn in his allegiance.
He had been born and lived most of his life in Virginia but now owned
a factory, investments, and a residence in Chicago, Illinois. With seven
Southern states withdrawn from the Union, he preferred a peaceful sep-
aration of the sections.[1]

A loyal Democrat, socially and politically conservative, McCormick
blamed Northern abolitionists for the portentous times. He still owned
a few slaves, whom he leased to former neighbors in Rockbridge County,
Virginia. In July 1860, he had purchased the Chicago *Times*, a Democratic newspaper that endorsed Northern Democrat Senator Stephen A.
Douglas in the presidential election. McCormick's personal sentiments
likely favored Southern Democrat John C. Breckinridge. With the conflict at hand, this transplanted Virginian's invention promised to con-
tribute to the Union war effort against his fellow Southerners.[2]

Cyrus McCormick belonged to the fourth generation of his Scots-
Irish family living in America. His great-grandfather, Thomas, had arrived
in the colonies in 1734, having been expelled from Ulster in Northern
Ireland. Thomas McCormick settled in Pennsylvania, but his son Robert relocated to the Shenandoah Valley of Virginia. Robert's namesake

son married Mary Ann Hall in 1808, and Cyrus was born on the family farm, Walnut Grove, in Rockbridge County on February 15, 1809.[3]

Cyrus's father was a tinkerer, building hydraulic, threshing, and hemp-breaking machines. According to family tradition, he failed in an attempt to make a mechanical reaper as early as 1816. Robert McCormick continued efforts to construct a workable reaper, even conducting a trial in a field of unripened wheat in May 1831. Cyrus, meanwhile, fabricated surveying instruments and invented a hillside plow. Unquestionably, he watched and probably assisted his father's work on a reaper.[4]

History resides in shadows. What transpired and who was responsible for it in a field near John Steele's Tavern in Rockbridge County on a day in July 1831 are disputed. There is, according to Cyrus McCormick's grandson and biographer, "no written record of what took place." What occurred there eventually made Cyrus McCormick rich and internationally famous.[5]

McCormick family oral history claims that two months after Robert McCormick's failure, Cyrus successfully tested the reaper he designed on six acres of oats. Cyrus and Jo Anderson, a family slave, had built the machine in a log-sided blacksmith shop on the farm. On the day of the demonstration, a slave boy rode a horse pulling the reaper, while Anderson walked beside it and McCormick behind it. How much grain it harvested on that day is unknown, but the trial revealed that the original reaper had design flaws.[6]

It remains undeniable that a member of the Rockbridge County, Virginia, McCormick family invented a mechanical reaper. Cyrus obtained a patent for such a machine in 1834. What seems more likely, however, is that Cyrus and his father, Robert, built the reaper based on the latter's design and experiments. Cyrus might have made changes between the failed tests in May and the successful demonstration in July. That Cyrus and Anderson constructed a newly designed reaper in two months strains credibility.[7]

McCormick tinkered with the reaper throughout the 1830s. He advertised in a nearby Lexington, Virginia, newspaper in 1833, but no

farmer bought a reaper. He started a pig iron business during that decade, but the Panic of 1837 closed it. The first sale of his reaper came in
1841. He priced the machine at $100, a considerable sum for most farm-
ers, but, in the next three years, he sold more than eighty. McCormick
noticed that sales had been primarily in the states north of the Ohio
River, among the grain farmers of Ohio, Indiana, and Illinois.[8]

By this time, the McCormick reaper business included his brothers
Leander and William. In 1845, he sent Leander to Cincinnati, Ohio,
to open a sales office. That same year he contracted with a factory in
Brockport, New York, to build reapers and to sell them to farmers in the
central section of the state. McCormick blanketed the states from New
York to Wisconsin with newspaper advertisements while dispatching
sales agents across the agricultural region.[9]

A Reverend Patrick Ball had built a reaper in 1826, and Obed Hussey received a patent for a machine in 1833. Ball's invention failed, but
Hussey opened a reaper manufacturing company in Cincinnati. The
arrival of the McCormicks in the city likely spurred Hussey to challenge
McCormick to a demonstration before judges of their respective machines. McCormick's reaper cut wet grain; Hussey's did not.[10]

Other individuals built reapers, but, as Cyrus McCormick's grandson noted, his grandfather "knew how to organize an invention into a
business and they did not." McCormick licensed a firm, Gray and War-
ner, in Chicago to manufacture reapers. When disagreements arose between them, the Chicago company sold out to William B. Ogden and
W. E. Jones. Ogden was wealthy and the city's mayor, and he offered
McCormick $50,000 to build a factory in the city. The inventor ac-
cepted and created McCormick, Ogden & Company.[11]

McCormick purchased three hundred feet of frontage on the north
bank of the Chicago River on North Water Street for $25,000. He then
constructed a three-story brick factory, with outbuildings for steam engines, lathes, and forges. He employed initially thirty-three workers to
produce the reapers. In 1849, the company manufactured fifteen hundred machines, earning enough profits for McCormick to buy out Ogden

and Jones for $65,000. Two years later, a fire destroyed the main section of the factory. McCormick rebuilt the interior, added new machinery, and erected a four-story wing on the building.[12]

The businessman continued making technical improvements to his invention, having secured new patents in 1845 and 1847. He changed the cutting bar; added a divider to separate the stalks as they entered the machine, reducing jams, a common problem; increased the width of the cut; and placed the driver and laborer on seats, lessening time for harvest and increasing production. The larger machines required pairs of animals, either horses or mules, to pull them.[13]

To be sure, the improvements made the reaper more efficient and more reliable, which convinced increasing numbers of farmers of its value, but it was McCormick's foresight and business acumen that bolstered sales. He attended, for instance, two Great International Exhibitions—London in 1851 and Paris in 1855. The British awarded his reaper the Great Council Medal; the French, the Grand Gold Medal of Honor. The awards brought the company prestige and promotional materials for its advertisements.[14]

In 1855, McCormick sued the John Manny Company of Rockford, Illinois, for patent infringement. George Harding, a patent law specialist, Ohioan Edwin McMaster Stanton, and Springfield, Illinois, attorney Abraham Lincoln comprised the original defense team for the Manny Company. When the case was transferred from Chicago to Cincinnati, Ohio, Harding and Stanton expected Lincoln, whom they had ignored in preparing the case, to remove himself from the team, which he did. In the trial of McCormick v. Manny, or the Reaper case, as it was known, the defendant's lawyers prevailed in the Ohio courtroom. The United States Supreme Court upheld the decision, validating the Manny patent.[15]

The McCormick company's marketing campaign relied again on many newspaper advertisements and a legion of salesmen, who tramped countless farm lanes. By the mid-1850s, a reaper cost a farmer $125, but McCormick extended credit: a farmer could pay $35 and the cost of freight at the time of purchase and the remainder by year's end at 6 percent interest. Unfortunately, as the decade lengthened, extending too much credit resulted in debts piling up for nonpayment. McCormick informed those in arrears, "I shall proceed to make you both trouble and expense if you don't pay the note at once." In 1858, he organized his own commission house to handle sales and finances.[16]

Sales of the reaper grew each successive year. The company sold 9,451 machines during the 1840s, 33,700 during the 1850s. It employed about two hundred men and boys in the factory. Profit in 1856 amounted to $300,000. In 1859, McCormick expanded the factory to cover 110,000 square feet. A year later, the plant manufactured 4,131 reapers and mowers. Perhaps more importantly, American farmers had come to accept the mechanical device as a necessity.[17]

The McCormick brothers comprised a team—Cyrus ran the company, William offered business and investment advice, and Leander served as plant superintendent. In 1859, Cyrus formed C. H. McCormick and Brothers, a firm to oversee the business. He supplied the capital at 8 percent interest and leased the factory for $10,000 annually. William and Leander each received a yearly salary of $5,000 and a fourth of net profits.[18]

They had been investing in Chicago real estate for several years. They began buying residential lots in 1854 and continued to do so throughout the decade. In 1860, they purchased the Revere House, a five-story brick hotel, for $60,000 and then leveled it, clearing space for what became known as the McCormick Block at Randolph and Dearborn streets. That same year, the factory site, with its buildings, was valued at $600,000 or more.[19]

Like their fellow Americans, North and South, the McCormick brothers awaited the seeming inevitability of civil war in the spring of 1861. Though their sympathies lay with their kindred in the South, their business fortunes lay in the rich soil of the Free States. They had five thousand reapers built and ready for sale. Ahead were unparalleled demand and a harvest of money.[20]

ANDREW CARNEGIE STOOD BARELY FIVE FEET TALL BUT ASPIRED TO BE
a giant. According to a friend, even as a teenager Carnegie was "hell
bent on improving himself." He stated later in life, "I have spoken of a
constant determination, from the first, to get on in the world."[21]

For Carnegie, getting on in the world began in impoverished circumstances in Dunfermline, Scotland. He was born on November 25,
1835, into a family of hand loom weavers. The Carnegies, including his
father and grandfather, wove damask cloth, and his maternal grandfather, Thomas Morrison, published a newspaper and was regarded as
the village radical. "Steam-loom weaving was disastrous to our family,"
he recounted later. It forced his father, William, out of the trade and to
sell his looms. In July 1848, when Andra, as his family called him, was
twelve years old, he, his parents William and Margaret, and his brother
Thomas left Scotland.[22]

The Carnegies joined Margaret's twin sister and family, who had
journeyed to America eight years earlier, in Allegheny City near Pittsburgh, Pennsylvania. William and Andra found work in a cotton mill,
where the youth stoked a boiler with wood chips and tended the steam
engine. The younger Carnegie could read and write—probably taught
primarily by his mother—and soon the mill owner made Andra a
clerk.[23]

While at the mill, he learned that the Atlantic & Ohio Telegraph
Company was seeking messenger boys at its office on Wood Street, adjacent to Market Square, in Pittsburgh. With the assistance of his uncle,
Carnegie got the job and earned $2.50 a week. "I knew nothing about
the streets of Pittsburgh, and the business houses to which I had to deliver messages," he remembered. "So I started in and learned all the addresses by heart, up one side of Wood street, and down the other. Then
I learned the other business streets in the same way. Then I felt safe."[24]

"The tick of the telegraph instruments fascinated me," wrote Carnegie. He arrived often at the office before others, "playing with the key."
James D. Reid, the office superintendent, agreed to help the inquisitive

messenger boy learn to be an operator. "I was soon able to receive any message by ear, alone, and at that time there were possibly only two other people in the country who could do this."[25]

Colonel James Anderson, a local gentleman, opened his private library to "working boys" on Saturday afternoons and allowed the boys to take home books. Carnegie visited often to borrow books. He viewed reading as a means to personal improvement, or, as he put it, "In this way I became acquainted with the world that lay behind the green curtain." He favored works on history and retained a fondness for books the rest of his life.[26]

The Scottish immigrant was effusive in his praise of his new home. Writing to friends in his native country, Carnegie exclaimed:

> Our public lands of almost unlimited extent are becoming settled with an enterprising people. Our dense forests are falling under the ax of hardy woodsmen. The Wolf and the Buffalo are startled by the shrill scream of the Iron Horse where a few years ago they roamed undisturbed. Towns and cities spring up as if by magic. . . . Our railroads extend 13,000 miles. You cannot supply iron fast enough to keep us going. This country is completely cut up with Railroad Tracks, Telegraphs, and Canals. . . . Pauperism is unknown. Hundreds of labor-saving devices are patented yearly. . . . Everything around us is in motion.[27]

Carnegie's prowess as a telegraph operator came to the notice of Thomas A. Scott, superintendent of the Western Division of the Pennsylvania Railroad. Scott hired the teenaged Scottish immigrant as his private telegraph operator in 1854. At some point, Scott made Carnegie his private secretary. "I went wherever he went," the assistant said of Scott, "traveled with him, slept in the same room with him." Carnegie also related: "Mr. Scott was one of the most delightful superiors that anybody could have and I soon became warmly attached to him. He was my great man."[28]

As Scott's private secretary, Carnegie met the railroad company's president, J. Edgar Thomson, whom Carnegie later described as "the greatest man of all on my horizon at this time." Thomson, thought Carnegie, "was the most reserved and silent of men, next to General [Ulysses S.] Grant, that I ever knew." Carnegie recounted that the railroad president "walked about as if he saw nobody when he made his periodical visits to Pittsburgh. This reserve I learned afterwards was purely the result of shyness." Thomson referred to the secretary at first as "Scott's Andy."[29]

Named general superintendent of the railroad in 1858, Scott relocated his office to Altoona, Pennsylvania. At the time, Altoona had a foundry building new locomotives, repair shops, huge roundhouses, and nearly thirty-five hundred employees of the railroad. Carnegie joined Scott, keeping the accounts and paying the workers monthly. He bought a house, and his mother and brother Tom joined him. His father had died.[30]

Thomson or Scott brokered a deal with the Adams Express Company granting that firm exclusive use of the railroad line for the transport of its packages. It seems that the railroad's executives could buy shares in the express company. Scott urged Carnegie to invest five hundred dollars in the enterprise. "I felt that this was the crisis in my life," Carnegie characterized it, "my chance to become independent, to get away from the slavery of salary to the independence of competence." Scott loaned him the money.[31]

Before long Carnegie received his first dividend check in the amount of ten dollars. He confided later: "I shall remember that check as long as I live. . . . It gave me the first penny of revenue from capital—something that I had not worked for with the sweat of my brow."[32]

Carnegie returned to Pittsburgh in 1860, having been promoted to superintendent of the railroad's Western Division. He was only twenty-five years old and responsible for all the rail traffic between the Allegheny Mountains to the east and Pittsburgh to the west. Scott, meanwhile, had assumed the vice presidency, with his office at the company's headquarters in Philadelphia.[33]

Carnegie was justly proud of his rapid rise in the railroad company and quite conscious of his new status. He dressed well and, perhaps at this time, began wearing high-heeled boots and a top hat to disguise his short stature. He had older ladies, probably friends of his mother, teach him manners. He was "vain, boastful, and cocksure." Behind his back, acquaintances and associates called him "dapper" and "trim." He was blond, fair complexioned, with narrow eyes and a rather flattened nose.[34]

The Civil War engulfed the divided nation within a year of Carnegie receiving the new position. When Secretary of War Simon Cameron summoned Thomas Scott to the capital to untangle the transportation problems, the railroad executive told Carnegie that he also had to come to Washington. Carnegie had been an abolitionist for several years, having an abiding hatred of slavery. He admitted later, "I didn't want to go much, for I had a most responsible position, attending to the moving of troops and stores, but he wouldn't hear of my staying behind." Simply put, Scott needed Carnegie for the difficulties that awaited them.[35]

Carnegie arrived in the capital in May, on board the first train over the reconstructed line from Annapolis, Maryland, to Washington. He brought with him four telegraphers from the company's Altoona office. While en route, he saw that the telegraph line had been torn down. He halted the train, stepped off, and pulled up a stake, which caused the line to snap back and to slash his face. He was "bleeding profusely," remarked an eyewitness, when he detrained in the capital.[36]

"The general confusion which reigned at Washington at this time," recalled Carnegie, "had to be seen to be understood. No description can convey my initial impression of it." Scott wanted him to act as his assistant in charge of telegraphs and military railroads. The railroad company's telegraphers went to work at the War Department.[37]

Once Virginians voted officially for secession on May 23, federal troops crossed the Potomac River and occupied Alexandria, Virginia. The War Department assigned Carnegie the duty of reopening the ferry to the Virginia town and of supervising the construction of a railroad trestle across the river beside Long Bridge. Carnegie established an office in Alexandria, and he and the crew of workmen completed the rail project in seven days, laboring day and night.[38]

"A dapper little flaxen-haired Scotchman," in the words of historian Margaret Leech, Carnegie remained in Washington until November 1861. He continued working for Scott, who had been appointed assistant secretary of war. After the Union defeat at the First Battle of Bull Run on July 21, Carnegie wrote in a letter: "Depend upon it the recent defeat is a blessing in disguise. We shall now begin in earnest. Knowing our foes, the necessary means will be applied to ensure their overthrow."[39]

Carnegie had not been impressed with General-in-Chief Winfield Scott, who at seventy-four years was older than the capital, overweight, a hulk of a man worn away by time and indulgences. Hero of the War of 1812 and the Mexican War, the native Virginian had towered over the army for nearly three decades. Carnegie described him, however, as "an old, decrepit man, paralyzed not only in body, but in mind . . . this noble relic of the past." It was an unfair characterization of a soldier whose intellect remained sharp and whose devotion to the Union was steadfast.[40]

The railroad man's remembrance of President Abraham Lincoln was altogether different than that of General Scott. "I never met a great man who so thoroughly made himself one with all men as Mr. Lincoln," declared Carnegie, adding, "He was certainly one of the most homely men I ever saw when his features were in repose; but when excited or telling a story, intellect shone through his eyes and illuminated his face to a degree which I have seldom or never seen in any other."[41]

Carnegie's direct role with the government ended that November when he returned to Pittsburgh. Thomas Scott had decided that the demands on the railroad with its increased volume of traffic required Carnegie's leadership. The Scottish immigrant had fulfilled a debt to his adopted country and now, for him, this terrible scourge of war offered opportunities.[42]

Cyrus, William, and Leander McCormick's sympathies lay with their Southern brethren from the conflict's outset. They advocated for compromise before and after the attack on Fort Sumter, believing that a negotiated peace could restore the Union. That idea died amid the carnage because neither side would or could compromise on the issue of slavery in a reunited nation.[43]

Like so many fellow Americans, the brothers' views deepened, even hardened, as the struggle reaped a harvest of the dead and the maimed and scarred the land. Perhaps William's words in a February 1863 letter to Cyrus expressed the three brothers' sentiments: "The Atrocities of the Federal Army in Va. have been inhuman, devilish, beastly, brutal, barbarous—I suppose no language could express it."[44]

However intense were the McCormick brothers' political views, they were, first and foremost, businessmen. Ironically, when the war began, farmers in slaveholding states owed the McCormick Patent Reaper Company $75,000 in unpaid debts. For weeks after Fort Sumter, the company endeavored to collect the monies and even tried to sell reapers in the South, which undoubtedly included states in the Confederacy. But ultimately their market lay solely in the loyal states.[45]

"The Civil War furnished supreme test of the worth of the reaper," contended Cyrus McCormick's grandson and early biographer. Indeed it did, and demand for reapers and rakes soared immediately after the first cannon shots arced over Charleston harbor. Sales of reapers and mowers rose from more than 10,000 in 1861 to 33,000 in 1862 and 80,000 in 1864. The number of patent applications for improvements in farm machinery more than doubled between 1862 and 1865.[46]

The commissioner of agriculture reported in 1862 that the year's wheat harvest would have been "impossible" without "horse-rakes, mowers and reaping machines, one half of the crop would have been left standing on fields." The commissioner estimated that every piece of farm machinery released five men for service in the Union army.[47]

Secretary of War Edwin Stanton declared: "The reaper is to the North what slavery is to the South. By taking the place of regiments of young men in the western [Ohio to Minnesota] harvest fields, it releases them to do battle for the Union at the front end at the same time keeps up the supply of bread for the Nation and the Nation's armies. Thus without McCormick's invention, I fear the North could not win and the Union would be dismembered."[48]

Although Stanton's words were indeed effusive praise for McCormick, his and the agriculture commissioner's assessments were not inaccurate. Machinery did replace gangs of laborers and reaped more acres in less time. Four manufacturers, including the McCormick brothers, dominated the production and sale of reapers and mowers.[49]

The McCormick factory in Chicago, with its two hundred workers, made 10,750 reapers in 1861 and 1862. The brothers charged $140 for a two-horse model and $155 for a four-horse machine, offering a $10 discount for cash payment. William McCormick claimed that they could even make a "first-rate" profit on a reaper at $125. In a six-month span from October 1861 through March 1862, the company's monthly income averaged slightly more than $66,000. Annual sales totaled $596,000 in 1861 and increased each year during the war.[50]

Cyrus McCormick traveled to Europe in the fall of 1862 and remained abroad for nearly two years. He entered a reaper in another international exhibition in Hamburg in the German Confederation. His machine won the Grand Gold Medal. While he was in Europe, brother Leander continued running the factory, and brother William oversaw sales, finances, and investments.[51]

Not long after Cyrus's departure for Europe, William wrote a letter to his brother informing him of the company's finances. "The importance of your business here involves *tens of thousands of dollars per day*." An accountant placed the company's assets at some $800,000 over liabilities. If they could sell six thousand reapers at $140 each, William noted, they could earn $840,000 in gross sales. "I suppose," William observed, "there has been no time in this world's history when events of *so great* importance had & were so *rapidly* transpiring."[52]

William wrote again to Cyrus two days later, relating that the company owned "*staple goods*"—pig iron, lumber, and other material—gold, and silver in the amount of $386,104. Their assets and liabilities totaled $2.5 million. Months later, William reported that collections for the year's final quarter had reached $233,000. He expected that sales for January and February 1863 should amount to $200,000.[53]

Inflationary prices for pig iron and lumber and demands by workers for higher wages affected profits. William warned Cyrus, "Just now our men with others are on a strike & our Foundry *stopped* & our work behind." He could not find capable workers and sales agents, complaining, "We are obliged to take 2nd or 3rd rate men into our employ." The company also had outstanding notes owed to it in the amount of $100,000. "There is in the whole *past* nothing to compare with the *business* & responsibilities."[54]

Nevertheless, by the spring of 1863, the brothers had purchased $455,500 worth of Chicago real estate, from residential lots to stores, a mill, a hotel, and farmland. William informed Cyrus and Leander, "I think it is most important that nearly all of our property is paying something & the average *well* in view of the now abundance of money." He stated elsewhere, "Farmers are 'paying us without mercy,'" and called their company "this tremendous business."[55]

Cyrus McCormick returned to the United States in the spring of 1864. That fall, he ran for the House of Representatives in the state's First Congressional District but was defeated. In his lengthy absence, William and Leander had manufactured the machines, handled labor difficulties, managed the finances, and overseen the investments. By the war's end, the McCormick brothers were the largest landowners in Chicago, with properties valued at about $1 million and annual rents of $100,000.[56]

The four-year struggle had tested the loyalties of these native Virginians. They sympathized with Southerners, but their business materially benefited the Union cause and its final victory. William McCormick,

more than his brothers, quietly hoped for a Confederate victory. Tragi-
cally for him, however, he suffered from "nervous dyspepsia" and admitted himself to the Illinois State Asylum in Jacksonville, where he died
on September 27, 1865. Perhaps the war ended the life of a Virginia son
in a Yankee asylum. Whatever or whoever it might have been, the inventor of the reaper lost his most trusted counselor.[57]

WITH HIS GOVERNMENT SERVICE ENDED AFTER SIX MONTHS, ANDREW
Carnegie returned to Pittsburgh, Pennsylvania, in November 1861, and
resumed his duties as superintendent of the Western Division of the
Pennsylvania Railroad. The heavy demands on rail traffic the war gen-
erated kept Carnegie busy during the next several months. Increasingly,
however, he searched for investment opportunities that would give him
a personal fortune and independence from a salaried position.[58]

By the end of 1861, his initial investment in the Adams Express
Company before the conflict had grown to shares in more than ten
companies. He owned stock in American Express Company and Western Union, in two coal companies, a pair of horsecar companies, the
Freedom Iron Company, and the Woodruff Sleeping Car Company. He
and his best friend from his teenage years in Allegheny City, Thomas
Miller, invested jointly in a number of these enterprises.[59]

For men seeking quick wealth in western Pennsylvania during the
1860s, nothing offered more allure than the nascent oil industry. "Pe-
troleum was a paradise for speculators," historian Allan Nevins writes.
Wells and refineries sprouted everywhere, and they reeked with the
pungency of oil. The region produced 1,200 barrels in 1860 and 5,000 in
1861. Oil camps resembled the gold rush mining sites in their roughness
and violence. An estimated $450 million was invested in western Penn-
sylvania oil fields.[60]

Carnegie owned stock in a small oil company, but, in the spring
of 1862, he, a wealthy neighbor named William Coleman, and other
associates bought a farm along Oil Creek for $40,000 and formed the

Columbia Oil Company. It proved to be a bonanza, paying a 30 percent dividend within a year. In a memoir, Carnegie claimed that eventually the company's stock was worth $5 million. Within two years, the oil venture made him a rich man. In another two years he sold his shares but continued investing in petroleum ventures.[61]

That same spring of 1862, Carnegie and two engineers with the Pennsylvania Railroad—John Piper and Aaron Shiffler—formed a partnership to build iron railroad bridges in Pittsburgh. J. Edgar Thomson and Thomas Scott also invested in Piper & Shiffler Company as silent partners. From Pittsburgh, Carnegie managed finances and operations; from Philadelphia, the two railroad executives guaranteed lucrative contracts with their firm. A year later the company was renamed the Keystone Bridge Company. Carnegie declared in his autobiography, "The Keystone Bridge have always been a source of satisfaction to me." He seemed to be never uncomfortable in such crony capitalistic enterprises of those times.[62]

As the conflict entered its second summer and Confederate fortunes began to rise, Carnegie, his mother, and Thomas Miller departed for the British Isles. The railroad superintendent had requested and was granted a three-month leave—he called it a "blessing"—for a vacation to the family's roots. From Liverpool, England, they journeyed to the Carnegie homestead in Dunfermline, Scotland. They had left as poor emigrants and returned now as wealthy Americans.[63]

His birthplace disappointed Carnegie. "Everything seemed so small, compared with what I imagined," he wrote. He called it "a city of Lilliputians. . . . Everywhere was there in miniature." They stayed with relatives and visited London. While in Dunfermline, Carnegie suffered an illness, and his mother and best friend nursed him through the sickness. The trio returned to Pittsburgh in the fall.[64]

The trip across the Atlantic Ocean reaffirmed his desire for wealth. Months later he told a cousin, "I am determined to expand as my means do." Although he possessed an enduring dislike of aristocrats, he wanted to become eventually "a British gentleman," with all the man-made and natural trappings of a landed estate. Perhaps to soothe his conscience, he planned, however, to labor "diligently to educate and improve the condition of his dependents."[65]

In the spring of 1864, Carnegie redirected his business interests. Like many manufacturers, ironmakers had witnessed unprecedented demand for their product during the conflict. He joined Miller in forming the Cyclops Iron Company, which constructed a rolling mill that was advanced for its time. "The surest foundation of a manufacturing concern is quality," professed Carnegie in his autobiography. "After that, and a long way after, comes cost."[66]

A year later, in May 1865, the new firm merged with a competitor, Kloman & Phipps. Thomas Carnegie owned shares in the latter company, which brought him into partnership with his older brother. They named the new company Union Iron Mills, and the Carnegie brothers, Andrew and Thomas, were installed as president and vice president, respectively.[67]

On March 28, 1865, before the merger, Carnegie had resigned his position with the Pennsylvania Railroad. He owed J. Edgar Thomson and Thomas Scott more than he could possibly quantify. They had taught him managerial and administrative skills and led him into the world of investment. He broke with the past in a way, or, as he put it, "Thenceforth I never worked for a salary." In a nation's blood-soaked plight, he had sought the stature of wealth.[68]

Chapter Eight

THE TINKERERS

—⁓⁓—

URING THE 1830s, LIFE LEANED HARD UPON FOLKS IN VER-
mont. The state's economy and its citizens' welfare relied
mostly on sheep raising. The market for wool was, however, saturated,
and prices spiraled downward. Beyond the state, conditions worsened as
the country's economy descended into the Panic of 1837.[1]

Poverty seemed to be a constant companion of many Vermonters.
In the village of Hancock, one particular citizen, an itinerant blacksmith, struggled to provide for his family and avoid debtors' prison. For
John Deere, poverty was never too far away for most of his life. Hard
times clung to him like a tattered coat.[2]

Deere had worn the old frayed garment for many years. Born February 7, 1804, in Rutland, Vermont, to William and Sarah Yates Deere,
he was the fifth of six children. His father had emigrated from the British Isles—he was probably Welsh—in the early 1790s. Deere's maternal
grandfather, James Yates, had served as a captain in the British army
during the Revolutionary War before settling after the conflict in New
Hampshire. William and Sarah married in 1793 and moved eventually
to Vermont.[3]

In 1806, the Deere family relocated to Middlebury, Vermont, where
John's father opened a tailor shop. For two years, William Deere prospered in the trade. Then, he received notification of a cousin's death accompanied with a summons for him to appear to receive an inheritance,

so he sailed for the British Isles in June 1808. Accounts claim that his trunk arrived in England, but he had disappeared and never was heard of again.[4]

Sarah Deere worked as a seamstress, but circumstances became hard for her and the six children. John received a rudimentary education, at best, before working for a local tanner in his teenage years. In 1821, he apprenticed to Benjamin Lawrence, a respected blacksmith in Middlebury. He spent four years under Lawrence's tutelage before hiring out as a journeyman blacksmith.[5]

In 1827, John Deere married Demarius Lamb of Hancock, Vermont. For the next two years, the couple moved from town to town as he worked as an itinerant tradesman. They settled finally in Hancock, where he opened his first blacksmith shop. Twice, however, the building burned down, forcing him to borrow money each time to rebuild. By 1836, Demarius was pregnant with their fifth child, and John was unable to pay a debt of $78.76 to a Jay Wright, who had funded his shop. Authorities arrested Deere for nonpayment.[6]

Vermonters had been fleeing the hard times in the state for several years; many traveled on the Erie Canal into the states of the old Northwest Territory. With the defeat of Sauk and Fox tribes in the Black Hawk War of 1832, the lands in western Illinois opened for settlement. One of Deere's friends, Leonard Andrus, had been the first resident of Grand Detour, Illinois, located on the Rock River, a hundred miles west of Chicago. Word filtered back to Hancock that a blacksmith could prosper there.[7]

Deere posted bail, sold his shop to his father-in-law, gathered his tools, and, in November 1836, headed for Grand Detour, leaving his family in Hancock. Arriving weeks later, he rented land along the Rock River and began constructing a blacksmith shop. The town amounted to a few homes and fewer businesses. Wolves could be heard in nearby woods. For Deere, however, it offered a new beginning.[8]

Work found the new blacksmith in Grand Detour. In late winter or early spring 1837, Deere heard local farmers complain about the difficulty of plowing through the thick, black prairie soil of Illinois. Soil in the East was lighter and sandier so that it fell away from an iron moldboard or blade as a plow cut through it. The heavier, gummier soil in the state—described as "rich black gumbo"—stuck to the plow blade, forcing a farmer to halt every few feet to clean the moldboard. Also, the prairie grasses were thick and matted, dulling the edges of iron plows.[9]

On a visit to his friend Leonard Andrus's sawmill, Deere noticed a broken steel circular saw and asked Andrus if he could have it. Returning with it to his shop, he cut off its teeth and began shaping it into a plow using a hand chisel, striker, and sledge. "Deere must have given a great deal of thought to the shape," historian Wayne Broehl Jr. observes, "to the special curve of the moldboard, for its exact contours would determine just how well the soil would be turned over after the share had made the cut."[10]

He hammered the moldboard into the shape of "a curving parallelogram" and attached it with a bar iron rod to a handle carved from a sapling. "The width of the moldboard for this plow was just twelve inches; it was a light plow, a small plow that could be pulled by one horse," adds Broehl. Accounts conflict, but either Deere or a local farmer tried it initially. The plow cut smoothly, scouring through the black soil. Those who witnessed it thought it made a "singing sound," leading some folks to call it "the singing plow." Deere forged two more plows in 1838, ten in 1839.[11]

Deere's wife and children joined him in Grand Detour in 1838. He continued blacksmithing and making plows. A report was published on this new farm implement:

A self-polishing steel plow fashioned by Vermont-born blacksmith John Deere, 32, at Grand Detour, Ill., can break the heavy sod of the Illinois and Iowa prairie. Deere chisels the teeth off a discarded circular saw block of Sheffield steel, creates a plow with the proper moldboard curve for breaking the sod, and saves farmers from having to pull their plows out of furrows for repeated cleaning with wooden paddles. The Deere plow will permit efficient farming in vast areas that have defied earlier efforts.[12]

Deere expanded the size of his blacksmith shop and, in 1842, produced a hundred plows. A year later, he and Andrus formed a partnership to manufacture plows. Two other investors joined the firm briefly, but, by 1847, it became Andrus & Deere. A dispute over money arose between the friends, causing them to hire bookkeepers, including Deere's eighteen-year-old son Francis Albert. When Francis Albert died unexpectedly—he was Deere's third child to die in Grand Detour—in January 1848, Deere dissolved his partnership with Andrus and relocated to Moline, Illinois, on the Mississippi River.[13]

Founded only five years earlier, Moline—French for "City of Mills"—in Rock Island County offered the plow maker river transportation, a skilled workforce of German and Irish immigrants, and nearby natural resources. A visitor to the town wrote that there was a "constant din of water wheels, steam works, saws, planes and hammers." There, in 1848 Deere formed a new company, partnering with fellow Grand Detour men Robert N. Tate and John M. Gould. Gould joined the firm later as its bookkeeper after Deere and Tate had built a three-story sixty-foot by twenty-four-foot factory along the river. Within a year, they had sold twenty-three hundred plows.[14]

Plow makers abounded in America during these years. In fact, John Lane, a blacksmith in Lockport, Illinois, had forged a steel plow from an old saw blade in 1831 or 1833, years before Deere fashioned his plow. Lane's plow worked effectively, but Deere's proved to be better at scouring a furrow. More importantly, with his new Moline factory in production, Deere undertook a marketing effort that exceeded those of his competitors and changed the farm implement business.[15]

Deere's campaign mirrored that of Cyrus McCormick's promotion of his reaper, using advertising in newspapers throughout the region. An early advertisement, placed in February 1852, stated: "As my Plows, &c.,

are warranted to be as represented. I would respectfully ask Farmers and others to give me a call before purchasing elsewhere. John Deere." He stated typically in the press, "The quality of the stock used in my plows is not equaled by any establishment in the West, and the plows are finished in a very superior style."[16]

The manufacturer headlined advertisements with "John Deere's Celebrated Moline Plow." He informed customers that his factory used the best German, English, and American iron and steel in its plows. A Kansas newspaper invited the "attention" of readers to the advertisement for "The Michigan Double Plow, which is claimed as the *ne plus ultra* of improvement in plows, is manufactured by Mr. Deere."[17]

Deere entered his plows in contests at annual state fairs in Illinois and Iowa. His plows earned numerous "premiums" in the competitions. A newspaper at the sixth annual Illinois fair reported in 1858, "No manufacturer is better represented than John Deere of Moline; and his plows are in such good repute that we are glad to see a fine display of his various patterns." The fair's judges removed Deere's plows from contests, stating that it was the plan of the agricultural society "to place such plows in competition with common old ground plows."[18]

In February 1859, the Chicago *Tribune* declared: "The double Michigan plow is so fully perfected that it cannot fail of attracting the attention of all who wish deep cutting. At our State Fair at Centralia it exceeded all others in deep tillage and perfect work." The article noted further that Deere plows "are household words" in Illinois, Iowa, and Wisconsin. To be sure, newspapers of the era openly practiced boosterism of their region's and state's businesses, but in the quality and performance of Deere's plows, their praise rang true.[19]

At the Moline factory, meanwhile, a steady and increasing stream of plows left the building en route to farm implement dealers. Production rose from seventy plows per week in 1851 to four hundred weekly in 1859. At its peak of sales during the decade, the firm employed sixty workers and made roughly ten thousand plows annually. In 1854, a branch of the Illinois Central Railroad reached Moline, providing more rapid delivery of products for Deere and other manufacturers, particularly to markets in the East.[20]

Yet, Deere and Tate clashed frequently during their nine-year partnership. Deere harped about making improvements to the plow, which cost the company money and hinted at the possible need to retool the factory. Each time the partners argued about improvements, Tate allegedly replied to Deere's request, "Damn the odds, they have got to take what we make." Deere would counter, "They haven't got to take what we make and somebody else will beat us, and we will lose our trade. . . . If we don't improve our product, somebody else will," Deere asserted."[21]

Consequently, he continued to refine his designs throughout the 1850s. An advertisement in 1857 offered eight variations of plows, with some described as "universally esteemed for plowing in heavy stubble" or for "old ground plowing." Deere noted their differences in the type of steel used and the width of the cut, either fourteen inches or twelve.[22]

In January 1855, a local newspaper proclaimed, "JOHn DEERE, THE PLOW KING." An Iowa paper stated that the Moline factory "is the largest establishment of the kind, we believe, that there is in the United States—the largest in the world." The factory consumed in a typical year during the 1850s, 100 tons of steel, 200 tons of iron, and 200,000 oak planks, while burning 575 tons of coal for the steam engines.[23]

In the spring of 1858, Deere informed the Chicago *Press* of his company's work on a steam engine to pull his plow. "It will be a great day," Deere stated in the letter to the newspaper, "when Illinois can show a steam engine taking along a breaking plow, turning over a furrow ten or twelve feet in width as it goes. I think we shall be able to see it before June passes away." It was not to be, however.[24]

Financial difficulties plagued the company despite the increase in production and sales. Partner and bookkeeper John Gould confided about the early years in Moline: "Many nights I have gotten out of bed and walked the floor knowing that I had some money to pay in a few days and did not know where I could get it. My brain felt as though I had a swarm of bees in it." Dealers held back payment because farmers owed them money. The company owed considerable sums to its steel suppliers, Naylor & Company of Sheffield, England, and Singer, Hartman of Pittsburgh, Pennsylvania.[25]

By the spring of 1857, the company's financial situation reached a crisis point, with Deere facing personal bankruptcy. He had never been skillful in handling the firm's money and investments. On July 1, Deere dissolved the current partnership and promoted three bookkeepers, including his twenty-year-old son Charles, as partners. The new arrangement brought in capital and ensured credits, and the business was renamed John Deere & Company.[26]

The new reorganization lasted, however, less than ten months. A college graduate, Charles Deere had been with the company for four years and, with the changes, he assumed an increasing role in management. On March 13, 1858, "It is agreed by the partners that John Deere shall take all the stock on hand & property of every kind as his own; & shall pay all the debts of the Company." The firm then became what it had been when Deere fashioned his first plow from a discarded mill saw—a sole proprietorship. As Charles Deere wrote, "The business fell back into jno [John] Deere's hands."[27]

Undoubtedly, the Panic of 1857 contributed to the company's financial woes as it did for uncounted thousands of firms across the country. The renowned plow maker relinquished operational control to his talented son, who guided the company through three years of monetary storms. In November 1860, Charles Deere once again changed the business's name to the Moline Plow Manufacturing Company.[28]

Two years before the beginning of the Civil War, the Chicago *Tribune* observed, "Plow-making has gone out of the hands of the common blacksmith and has become an institution by itself." By 1860, twenty-one hundred companies manufactured plows. The size of grain and livestock farms had grown during these years from the common forty acres to sixty or eighty or even more. Plows sang through the rich sod, portending bountiful harvests for a Union in peril.[29]

WINTERS IN NORTHERN INDIANA COULD CHILL A MAN'S SOUL WHEN ICY winds blew south across a frozen Lake Michigan. February 16, 1852, might have been such a day in South Bend, Indiana, where two brothers opened a blacksmith and wagonmaking shop for business. A customer stopped, had a pair of his horse's hooves shod, and paid the owners twenty-five cents. It was a beginning in a family of new beginnings.[30]

Decades earlier and far to the east, in 1736, three brothers—Peter, Heimich, and Clement Stutenbecker—and two wives arrived in Philadelphia from a Germanic state. Members of the German Baptist Brethren Church, commonly referred to as Dunkers, the family was part of that tidal wave of immigrants from central Europe that flooded the colony founded by Quaker William Penn. According to family lore, the Stutenbecker brothers were skilled craftsmen who forged swords and tools in their homeland.[31]

The Stutenbecker brothers settled at first in Germantown, outside of Philadelphia, plying the trade of blacksmithing. From there, the direct line to their descendants in South Bend becomes murky. Family tradition holds that Clement headed west, likely moving to Lancaster County. His son, Peter, relocated to York County, where he and his wife had a son, Peter Jr. By that time, the family name had been Anglicized to Studebaker.[32]

Like his father, Peter Studebaker Jr. worked as a blacksmith and built wagons. A son, John, born in 1799, followed the trade of his father and grandfather. In 1820, John married Rebecca Mohler, an eighteen-year-old German woman from Lancaster County. For the next ten years, John did blacksmithing, and he and Rebecca raised two sons and two daughters. In 1830, John, Rebecca, and the children moved to a farm a few miles outside of the small, southcentral Pennsylvania village of

Gettysburg. John evidently prospered there, not as a farmer but in his trade as a blacksmith and wagonmaker.[33]

According to a family story, John Studebaker signed notes for friends who could not pay their debts. Unable himself to cover them, John, Rebecca, and their family that had grown to six children departed for the West, traveling in three wagons, one a Conestoga-style built by John. The Pennsylvania Germans, or Deutsch, had originated the heavy, broad-wheeled freight wagons for transporting goods between Philadelphia and Lancaster.[34]

The Studebakers halted their journey in northcentral Ohio, five miles east of the town of Ashland. John built a small house and a blacksmith and wagonmaking shop. The family struggled financially, however. He had work, but few customers could pay him. The Panic of 1837 struck hard, not only nationally but also locally, drying up specie and bankrupting businesses and financial institutions. Four more children were born to the couple in Ohio, making a dozen in the household who needed to be fed and clothed.[35]

Above his shop door, Studebaker hung a sign: "Owe no man anything, but to love one another." Unfortunately for him, according to an acquaintance: "He was a good old man who worked pretty hard at his anvil, but for all that had a constitutional tendency to financial prostration. . . . It was understood in the neighborhood that the old gentleman Studebaker owed nearly everyone in that part of the country and every merchant in the county seat whom he could induce to trust him."[36]

The blacksmith's money problems were not entirely of his own making. The farmers who brought him their business "were too poor to pay and Studebaker was therefore unable to pay the merchants who had sold him supplies." The hope of a new beginning in Ohio free of debts and prosperity eluded the family.[37]

Another decade passed, another ten years of shaping iron, framing wagons, scraping by. The Studebakers' oldest sons Henry and Clement— Clem, to the family—hired on as farmhands and brought home needed money. In 1850, twenty-four-year-old Henry and nineteen-year-old Clem followed a family tradition, going elsewhere to begin again, this time seeking a new start in South Bend, Indiana. Located south of Lake Michigan's tip, the town boasted mills, a small college, ample water power from the Saint Joseph River, forests of hardwood trees nearby, and a community of Dunkers.[38]

Clem Studebaker taught school in South Bend and worked as a blacksmith for fifty cents a day. His brother Henry likely did blacksmithing and perhaps odd jobs. After nearly two years in the town and with $68 in capital—$40 allegedly borrowed from Henry's wife—and two sets of tools, the brothers formed H. & C. Studebaker as a wagonmaking business. They planned, according to a reminiscence, "to produce the best vehicle that it is possible to make for the use for which it is intended."[39]

The brothers struggled during the first year, building two or three wagons while relying on blacksmith work for income. In the spring of 1853, a third brother, twenty-year-old John Mohler, arrived in South Bend. The younger brother had come not to enter the business but to secure one of his brothers' wagons. He was headed for the California gold fields and needed a wagon for the journey across the plains and mountains. Henry and Clem built a covered wagon for him, and in August, John Mohler joined a party of gold seekers and pioneers.[40]

The passage took five months and ended at gold camps outside of Hangtown, also called Placerville, California. "I had but fifty cents in my pocket," recounted John Mohler Studebaker. "Although that was my only earthly possession, my spirit was not daunted, for we were all led to believe that all we had to do was to go out on the morrow and dig up all the gold that the heart could desire."[41]

Joe Hines, a local wagonmaker, met the newcomers and inquired if any of them had experience building wagons and wanted work. Studebaker said he did but rejected the job offer, replying, "I came to California to mine gold." Another man, probably a down-on-his-luck prospector, advised Studebaker to take the job and to do so quickly. Hines hired Studebaker at ten dollars weekly. "I had strong arms," he wrote in a letter many years later, "sense enough to stick to my trade, at which I luckily got work at once."[42]

Hines built wheelbarrows, and demand for them was brisk. (Studebaker family lore maintains that the three brothers from Germany built wheelbarrows initially in colonial Pennsylvania.) John Mohler became so efficient in constructing them that miners called him "wheelbarrow Johnny." He and Hines worked "many a night all night." In three years, Studebaker amassed $3,000. By 1858, his stash had grown to $8,000.[43]

John Mohler corresponded with his brothers in South Bend, describing life in Hangtown and offering suggestions for improving wagons. Henry and Clem, meanwhile, had acquired a reputation for constructing wagons of quality and durability. They had devised kilns for drying lumber and had begun building carriages. Yet, with money scarce, they lacked capital to expand the business.[44]

Their fortunes changed temporarily in 1857, when George Milburn, owner of a wagon factory in nearby Mishawaka, Indiana, approached the Studebakers. Milburn had contracted with the army for wagons but could not fill the entire agreement. He subcontracted with the brothers to construct one hundred wagons. The army wanted the wagons for an expedition against Mormon settlers in Utah Territory. President James Buchanan had declared the members of the Church of Jesus Christ of Latter-Day Saints in rebellion against federal authority. The result was a clash of arms in the so-called Mormon War.[45]

Although H. & C. Studebaker needed the business, the contract presented challenges, financially and spiritually. To that point, the brothers were able to build about a dozen wagons a year. One hundred vehicles required far more lumber, more workers, and more indebtedness. Furthermore, the army's use of the wagons troubled Henry because it conflicted with his Dunker pacifism. In turn, elders of the Brethren church met with the Studebakers, stating their opposition to the army contract. Clem lacked the fervency of Henry's beliefs and refused to accede to the elders' wishes. To Clem, the agreement opened possibilities for growing their company and marketing their wagons beyond northern Indiana. But to Henry, faith overrode profits, and he expressed a desire to leave the firm.[46]

When they began constructing the wagons, the brothers turned to John Mohler Studebaker in California, appealing in a letter for him to return to South Bend and to purchase Henry's share of the partnership. With more capital, they could construct a hundred, if not two hundred, wagons annually. John Mohler did not decide immediately, but finally, in April 1858, he boarded a ship at San Francisco and arrived in South Bend two months later. He paid Henry $3,000 for his share and then invested much of his remaining $5,000 in the business. Henry bought a farm.[47]

The new partnership retained the H. &. C. Studebaker company name, but John Mohler's money and talent for business revitalized the enterprise. Probably at his suggestion, they adopted a slogan, "Always give a little more than you promise." The brothers increased their advertising and allegedly promoted the business by changing the lyrics of a song called "Wait for the Wagon":

"Wait for the wagon, wait for the wagon,
Studebaker's wagon, and we'll all take a ride."[48]

By the end of 1860, H. & C. Studebaker employed fourteen workers and had a manufacturing shop, a paint room, a lumber yard, a storeroom, and an office at its location in South Bend. Years before, another brother, Peter, had moved to Goshen, Indiana, where he worked as a dry goods clerk and an itinerant salesman before opening his own retail store that sold Studebaker wagons. John Mohler and Clem placed the value of their business at $10,000.[49]

In the spring of 1861, H. & C. Studebaker was but one—a small one, certainly—of the three thousand wagon manufacturers in the country.

The South Bend firm had become a thriving local enterprise, with a well-earned reputation for solidly built wagons and carriages. Before long an all-encompassing conflict would challenge the pacifist brothers, and their company's reputation would extend far beyond a swath of the old Northwest Territory.[50]

WHEN THE CIVIL WAR BEGAN IN APRIL 1861, JOHN DEERE MUST HAVE thought of himself as a businessman, a Republican, an abolitionist, but likely not a revolutionary. He stood with others, however, at the forward edge of an upheaval that had started nearly three full decades earlier. The profound change—the mechanization of agriculture—proceeded slowly, yet always along an ever-widening path. By the time cannon fire battered Fort Sumter's masonry walls, the revolution had altered the agricultural landscape, particularly in the Free States.[51]

Deere was a leader, an inventor at the forefront, his "singing plow" scouring furrows in the fertile, dark farmland north of the Ohio River. During the 1850s, Indiana, Illinois, and Wisconsin witnessed the creation of more than 150,000 new farms and the improvement of an additional nearly fourteen million acres. Ohio and Iowa were not far behind in new farmsteads and tillable acreage. In fact, the mechanization of farm work embraced the whole swath of the Free States, from the Atlantic coast to the Great Lakes.[52]

When the conflict began, barns in the North brimmed with grains and hay from bountiful harvests in 1860. The demand for wheat, corn, and hay soared at once to feed the floodtide of volunteers and horses and mules. Unfavorable weather limited the 1861 harvests, but, in the spring of 1862, farmers plowed furrows and planted crops in numbers never before witnessed.[53]

By the conflict's second summer, then, farm machinery factories hummed from orders brought by Union armies' insatiable appetite. In Moline, Illinois, Charles Deere oversaw the company's operations and handled the finances while managers supervised production in the factory. Before the war, he had renamed the business the Moline Plow Manufacturing Company. Although his father had withdrawn from daily operations, the elder Deere tinkered with improvements to the plow and the design of new machines.[54]

In 1863, the company began manufacturing a new product, the Hawkeye Corn Cultivator. It was Deere's first riding machine, designed to loosen soil and to destroy weeds. A year later, John Deere obtained his first patent for a "new and useful Improvement in Molds for Casting Steel Plows and other Articles." Two more patents followed, each related to the casting of or parts of a plow.[55]

The firm's profits mounted as the bloody struggle lengthened. With demand unabated and a seller's market, Charles Deere demanded cash from customers. In January 1864, fifteen of the major plow makers, including the Deeres, met and formed a "plow makers' society." Wartime inflation had raised the price of iron and steel and eroded the manufacturers' profits. To ensure net gains, members of the society agreed on prices for their plows.[56]

Six months later, on July 1, Charles Deere reorganized the company once again. He and his father each contributed $70,000 in stock, machinery, buildings, and debt and became equal partners in the newly named Deere & Company. The Deeres also invested in an insurance business and the First National Bank of Moline, for which they served on the boards of directors. The conflict had made the Deeres "Rich," in the words of a newspaper correspondent.[57]

Three years after the Civil War, a Chicago newspaper reporter toured the Moline factory of Deere & Company. Afterward, he wrote, "John Deere may be called a pioneer, if not the pioneer, plow manufacturer of Illinois," adding that "all plow makers respect and honor him for his skill and success, and conceded the service he has rendered Western agriculture by his efforts." Indeed, when his steel plow "sang" through the prairie sod, it opened a vast breadbasket for the nation and eventually the world.[58]

John Deere was, however, only one of hundreds of American farm machinery manufacturers. Cyrus McCormick's grandson drew an apt comparison in his biography of the reaper maker: "John Deere's steel plow was not the very first; but, like McCormick, he had organizing ability enough to build a great business." And like McCormick, who had a pair of brothers to help build a business, Deere benefited from able partners early on and from a talented son in Charles Deere. Working with a discarded mill saw blade, a tinkerer invented a company.[59]

Union military strategy of making offensive campaigns into the Confederacy posed enormous supply problems for the quartermaster and commissary bureaus. Railroads could haul rations, ammunition, animal forage, and other materiel to a large supply base, but an army on the march, striking into the Rebel heartland on bad roads, required a tether to the supply depot. Miles of white, canvas-covered wagons, stretching far beyond sight, must trail the advancing troops to carry the vital supplies.[60]

Nothing in the army's past, not even in the recent Mexican War, equaled the scope of this conflict, from the size of federal forces to the distances to be covered and the massive piles of supplies and ordnance needed to undertake offensive operations against the Confederates. The War Department had calculated needs at 1 wagon for 50 men, 20 wagons for 1,000 men, and 2,000 wagons for an army of 100,000 officers and men.[61]

The War Department issued specifications for the wagons. A regulation model was to be of the Conestoga type, with a canvas cover. Hardwood lumber would form the bed and sides, and the bed would carry a tool box in front, a feed trough in back, and a "slush bucket" for grease on the rear axle. A wagon should be able to haul roughly from twenty-five hundred pounds to four thousand pounds, depending on the number of mules and horses in a team and the weather and road conditions.[62]

When the war began, the Union military turned to private wagon and carriage makers for the vehicles. The largest manufacturers were located in Pennsylvania and Ohio. Eventually, five contractors supplied the War Department with seven of every ten wagons purchased by federal officials.[63]

The South Bend, Indiana, firm of H. & C. Studebaker did not receive a government contract until 1862. Once more, the brothers' pacifist beliefs conflicted with the wagons' use in a war. John Mohler Studebaker had forbidden the family's youngest brother, Jacob, from enlisting in the army. But John Mohler and Clem Studebaker signed the contract and began production. Peter Studebaker joined the company in 1863 to sell wagons and carriages to civilian customers.[64]

The army contract required the brothers hire more workers and expand the factory. Within weeks of signing, a fire destroyed the frame building. The brothers replaced it with a brick structure, but a second fire gutted that. The embers still smoldered when workmen began construction of another one. As production increased, the company acquired more land and added new structures.[65]

The Studebakers' wagon complied with army regulations. They used seasoned hickory and ash for the planking in the bed and on the sides of the frame. They innovated by putting smaller front wheels on the vehicle, which gave the teamster more play and the ability to turn more sharply. With a four-mule team, the wagon, known as a "Studie," could haul twenty-five hundred pounds of cargo.[66]

Studebaker wagons and ambulances formed part of the supply trains for the major Union armies. They followed the troops in campaigns in Tennessee and Virginia. They rolled through Georgia and the Carolinas with Major General William T. Sherman's armies. The Studie acquired a reputation for durability and quality that extended beyond Union lines. During the Gettysburg campaign, Confederates captured wagons in Chambersburg, Pennsylvania, and a Rebel soldier identified sixteen as Studebakers.[67]

During the war, the wagonmakers changed the company's name to Studebaker Brothers. The firm could not, however, supply enough wagons for the army. War Department orders slowed in 1864, but by war's end, the government had purchased about forty thousand wagons from contractors. Federal authorities bought a carriage for President Abraham Lincoln from the Studebakers. He and Mrs. Mary Lincoln rode in it to Ford's Theater on the night of April 14, 1865.[68]

During the conflict's final year, the Studebakers shifted production and sales to civilians. In 1864, Peter Studebaker moved to Saint Joseph, Missouri, and opened a wagon depot, which brought a sales boom immediately after the war. By 1867, the South Bend company employed 140 workers and built six thousand vehicles that year. The value of the firm had risen from $10,000 seven years earlier to more than $220,000.[69]

The contract with the army, which allowed the Studebakers to expand their factory, enriched the company. Perhaps more importantly, the Civil War introduced Americans in the Mid-Atlantic and New England to the solidly built wagons of the Studebaker brothers. Their reputation rested in their simple creed: "An uncompromising good product. Built by a group of loyal employees. Sold at a fair price."[70]

Studebaker Brothers was the only Civil War wagonmaker that eventually built automobiles. In 1901, one year before the company offered a horseless carriage, John Mohler Studebaker explained the firm's decades-long existence as a profitable business: "Our history proves that father made no mistake. Through the lessons that we received from him and from our mother, with the strength and health which they transmitted to us, and with the unity of our forces as brothers, we have won success."[71]

Chapter Nine

THE DREAMERS

—⚏—

" "WAR IS OUR ONLY COURSE," READ THE PROCLAMATION OF the Committee of Safety. "There is no other remedy but to defend our rights, ourselves and our country by force of arms." It was September 1835, and the "country" was Texas, a colony of Mexico. Trouble had been simmering for several years between the government in Mexico City and the settlers in this land a thousand miles from the capital. But the proclamation's words were a declaration of war, a rebellion against national authority.[1]

The most respected man in Texas and its guiding spirit, Stephen F. Austin, chaired the committee. More than a decade earlier, Mexican officials had awarded him an *empresario* grant to bring Anglo-American families into Texas. By the 1830s, more than thirty thousand settlers, many lured by the promise of thousands of acres of cheap land, lived in the province. Inevitably, perhaps, trouble arose between the native Tejanos, Anglo-Americans, and the distant government. When the committee issued the proclamation, Mexican troops were on the march toward San Antonio de Béxar.[2]

Austin and the other five members of the Committee of Safety signed the document, publicly admitting to an act of rebellion. All of them, except one, had been among the three hundred original émigrés from the United States. The sixth member, Gail Borden Jr., had arrived in Texas on Christmas Eve 1829, coming from New York by way of Kentucky, Indiana, and Mississippi. Borden might not have thought of himself as a rebel before, but his family lineage traced back directly to Puritan Massachusetts and to another dissenter who also had espoused "new and dangerous ideas."[3]

Born November 9, 1801, in present-day Norwich, Chenango County, New York, Gail Borden Jr. was the first child of Gail Sr. and Philadelphia Wheeler Borden. Both parents' families had been in America since the 1630s. Philadelphia Borden was the great-great-great-granddaughter of Roger Williams. A Puritan minister, Williams had angered the theocratic leaders of Massachusetts Bay with his advocacy of religious toleration and the separation of church and state. Banished for his heresy, Williams found refuge among Native Americans along Narragansett Bay. Fellow dissenters followed, leading to the establishment of Rhode Island colony. One of the seekers of religious freedom who joined Williams was Richard Borden, the original member of the family in the colonies.[4]

Soon after their marriage in 1800, the Bordens moved to central New York, where Gail Sr. farmed and speculated in land, and Philadelphia gave birth to five sons. In 1814, the family journeyed west, down the Ohio River on a flatboat, and lived briefly in Kentucky before halting at New London, Indiana, on a U-shaped bend in the river. Tradition claims that at one time New London had served as a rendezvous site for river pirates and counterfeiters. When the Bordens arrived in 1816, the gangs of thieves had departed to ply their nefarious trade farther downstream and away from legal authorities. An early visitor to New London described it as "one of the most pleasant situations on that river," offering "a charming view of the broad expanse of the Ohio."[5]

The river town still had a roughness to it and consisted of about twenty cabins, a store, a warehouse, a pair of taverns, and evidently a schoolhouse. Philadelphia Borden probably had taught her children to read and to write. It is believed that fifteen-year-old Gail Jr. received his first formal schooling in New London. He left the school after only a year or so, seeking work. He hired on a flatboat and traveled down the

Ohio and Mississippi rivers with cargo to New Orleans. From there it was a long trek back home to New London.[6]

In May 1822, Gail Jr. bought a plot of two and a half acres with a tanyard on it for two hundred dollars. Whether he worked as a tanner is uncertain, but he had been doing some surveying in Jefferson County. Plagued for years by a persistent cough, he thought the hot, humid southern weather might cure it. In the spring of 1822, with his brother Thomas, Gail Jr. left New London—the town no longer exists, its site having been reclaimed by the Ohio River—and headed downriver toward New Orleans.[7]

Instead of making a new start in the Louisiana city, Borden settled in Amite County, Mississippi, where he spent the next seven years. He taught school and later received the appointment of county and deputy federal surveyor. His health improved, and he earned a steady income. On March 18, 1828, the twenty-two-year-old Borden married sixteen-year-old Penelope Mercer, a former student of his. She was, he said many years later, "the only woman I ever loved." Borden purchased two slaves, a man and a woman, to help Penelope.[8]

Borden's father and brothers Thomas, Paschal, and John, meanwhile, had joined Anglo-Americans in Texas. Philadelphia Borden and a daughter, Esther, died during the family's journey to Texas. To encourage more settlement in the distant province, Mexican officials granted 4,428 acres of land to heads of households at a cost of about four cents per acre. By the time of Gail Jr.'s marriage, his father and brothers were well established near San Felipe de Austin, farming, raising livestock, blacksmithing, and surveying.[9]

They wrote letters to Gail Jr. in Mississippi describing the cheap land and the prospects Texas offered ambitious men. Tempted by their words, Gail Jr. visited his father and brothers, liked what he saw, and returned home. Penelope was pregnant with their first child at the time and reluctant to leave her family to make the difficult trip despite her husband's glowing reports. In the end, she acceded to his requests.[10]

Penelope's consent might have been made easier by her parents' decision to emigrate to the Mexican province. In fact, the Mercers preceded their daughter and son-in-law, traveling overland through Louisiana. Because of the pregnancy, the Bordens went by boat and arrived at Galveston Island on December 24, 1829. From there, they rode in a wagon to San Felipe. Unknowingly, the couple had found some permanency.[11]

A fellow Anglo came to know the Borden men and said of them, "It appears to be a very clever family." Gail Jr. secured a land grant and began farming, growing crops, and raising livestock. He might have taught school briefly, but when Thomas returned to the United States on business for a few months, Gail Jr. assumed his surveying duties for Stephen Austin. It was important work with the need for defined boundaries between properties.[12]

Borden's association with the original *empresario* changed his life in ways he could not have predicted. For two years, Borden surveyed and tended his crops and cattle. In 1833, Austin appointed him to the land records office. The colonial secretary, Samuel M. Williams, was seldom in the office, so Borden handled most of the duties. He kept the records, approved titles, answered correspondence, mediated property disputes, and surveyed land. He could have speculated in land, like Williams, but it appears he did not. He wrote to Williams in March 1835: "Had I $5000 now, I would not fear but what I could make it $10000 in one year. More stir of Emigrants now than have ever seen all pushing for land."[13]

Borden worked in the land records office while Austin was in Mexico City trying to resolve differences between the Mexican government, under President Antonio López de Santa Anna, and the Anglo-American community. On April 6, 1830, the national legislature had passed a law forbidding further immigration from the United States into Texas. Although the measure proved ineffective, it brought protests from the Anglos. Austin appears to have resolved the issue, but as he headed home, Santa Anna had him arrested for allegedly inciting an insurrection. Austin was eventually released but spent twenty-eight months in Mexico before returning to Texas in the late summer of 1835.[14]

Borden had involved himself in the colony's political turmoil seemingly from the time of his arrival in Texas. He served as a member of the conventions in 1832 and 1833. In the first meeting, the attendees passed resolutions asking for repeal of the 1830 immigration act and the admission of Texas as a separate state. Mexican officials ignored them. A year later, however, the attendees filed petitions and, more ominously, framed their own state constitution. Santa Anna reacted by detaining Austin and sending more troops to the colony. Days after Austin's return, Austin, Borden, and four other members of the Committee of Safety issued their declaration of war against the Mexican government.[15]

Within weeks, the revolt in Texas went from words on a proclamation to armed resistance. The uprising needed a voice, and Borden, his brother Thomas, and a Joseph Baker began publishing a newspaper, the *Telegraph and Texas Register*, in San Felipe on October 10, 1835. The publishers explained their purpose in the first issue: "We shall therefore endeavor to make our paper what the title indicates, the organ by which the most important news is communicated to the people, and a faithful *register* of passing events."[16]

Borden believed that the newspaper could be "an indispensable tool" for the rebellion and "a unifying force" with Anglos and Tejanos. The paper chronicled the advance of Santa Anna's army, the thirteen-day siege at the Alamo in San Antonio, and the Mexicans' execution of Texan prisoners at Goliad. On March 2, delegates to a convention at Washington-on-the-Brazos declared Texas's independence and named Sam Houston commander of the army. "Texas Has Declared Her Independence" read the banner headline in the *Telegraph and Texas Register*.[17]

From San Antonio, Santa Anna marched his victorious army southeast, pursuing Houston's retreating force. The Mexicans entered San Felipe and burned and looted buildings. Meanwhile, the interim Texas government asked Gail Borden Jr.—Thomas and Baker had joined the army—to let his publication serve as its official newspaper and to relocate to the new capital at Harrisburg, present-day Houston. He agreed to move the heavy press, stating that he was "determined to spend the last dollar in the cause we had embarked: we believe the people must have information, without which no concert of action could be had."[18]

Though he had agreed to follow Houston's retreating army to Harrisburg, Borden did so reluctantly. He explained months later that by staying at San Felipe he believed "that so long as a paper should be printed *west* of the Brazos, the people *east* of it would not take the alarm. . . . We endeavored to cheer and encourage our countrymen to the contest."[19]

Everything that the Borden brothers possessed was in San Felipe. When Gail Jr. departed, he took his and Thomas's families with the fleeing Anglos to Harrisburg. Behind them came Santa Anna's troops, which burned the newspaper office, residences, and other businesses. With homes and furnishings in ashes, with no income from subscribers to the newspaper, "we felt for the moment," admitted the older brother, "discouraged in carrying on the further publication of the paper." He "could see nothing but ruin" for himself and Thomas.[20]

Upon reaching the rebellious capital, Borden readied the press and prepared an issue. Before it could be printed, however, Mexican soldiers approached Harrisburg. Borden fled the town, abandoning the press. When Santa Anna arrived, he had it dumped into Buffalo Bayou. The Mexicans continued their pursuit of Houston, halting only to camp along the San Jacinto River. Houston saw an opportunity, stopped the retreat, turned his nine-hundred-man army around, and attacked Santa Anna on April 21, 1836. Shouting "Remember the Alamo," "Remember Goliad," the Texans routed the Mexicans, killing and capturing hundreds of them, with a loss of fewer than fifty men. Santa Anna was found the next day, and he recognized Texas's independence in exchange for his freedom.[21]

The revolution financially broke Gail Jr. and Thomas Borden. The new Republican government owed them money for public printing but had no funds. The brothers wanted to resume publication of the newspaper, so Thomas traveled to Cincinnati, Ohio, where he purchased a printing press, ink, paper, and fonts using his and his brother's land as collateral for the debt. The *Telegraph and Texas Register* resumed publication in August 1836, in Columbia, the temporary capital of the Republic of Texas.[22]

Instead of profit, the newspaper incurred debt. Personal sufferings exacerbated its public difficulties—Thomas's wife died of fever, leaving him with two young sons, and Gail Jr. was plagued by illness. The brothers sought buyers for the newspaper. "We did not wish to toil so hard, & bear so much responsibility," explained Gail Jr. By June 1837, both had sold their interest in the newspaper.[23]

President Sam Houston appointed and the Senate confirmed Gail Jr. as the collector of customs at the fledgling settlement of Galveston on the Gulf of Mexico. The position was undoubtedly a reward for his devotion to and services for the revolution. The republic needed an intelligent, conscientious, and honest customs agent to collect the duties. Borden possessed all of the qualities and was steadfast in his loyalty to the new government.[24]

Galveston was to be Borden's home for the next fourteen years—a time marked by controversy, tragedy, and a new venture. His six-year term as collector of customs ended in a dispute over the value of the republic's paper currency. Borden refused to obey a law that required the collection of duties at market value, arguing that duties should be collected on a value closer to full value. When he believed that he knew better, he could be stubborn, self-righteous, even defiant. In the end, his stance resulted in his resignation and an irreparable break with Houston.[25]

The former customs official nevertheless became one of Galveston's foremost citizens. In the summer of 1839, he discovered a source of fresh water for the growing town, ensuring it a steady supply. He served a brief term as an alderman and surveyed lots as the general agent of the Galveston City Company. On September 5, 1844, however, Penelope Borden died of yellow fever. They had been married for sixteen years, and she had given birth to seven children, five of whom were alive.

Although he claimed many years later that she had been his only love, he married a widow in February 1845.[26]

Borden seemed to possess a restless energy, as if he needed to turn one more corner to finish something. A local minister, seeing him on a street in Galveston, described Borden as "quite a tall man, very shabbily dressed, with a singularly narrow but high forehead. He had . . . an unusually long nose. I never saw a person drive along at such a swift pace, his head bent forward, his eyes on the ground."[27]

Since he had arrived in Texas, Borden was always in a hurry, brimming with ideas and seeking opportunities. It was likely one of the reasons he embraced the revolution. While in Galveston fulfilling his official duties, he began experimenting with novel things. He evidently attached a sail to a wagon, hoping that it would roll across land like a ship glided across seas. An acquaintance said of him at the time, "He had dozens of inventions, and he is the most wonderful of all himself."[28]

Borden conceived of the idea of a "meat biscuit" probably in mid-1849. Whether he had thought of it when he witnessed soldiers passing through during the Mexican War or learned of Americans en route west to the California gold fields, he experimented with a nonperishable food for travelers. He boiled meat, filtered the broth by removing "solid innutritive portions," evaporated broth to a syrup-like consistency, added flour to the extract, and then baked it. His original idea was to add flour to the meat extract.[29]

Borden shared his plans for manufacturing the meat biscuit with Dr. Ashbel Smith, the former surgeon general of the Texas army. They formed an unofficial partnership, with Smith writing letters of endorsement to newspapers in the East. One newspaper described their invention as a "Portable Desiccated Soup Bread," claiming that a biscuit could be made from beef, veal, fowl's flesh, or oysters. Borden received a patent for it on February 5, 1850, and in May, after conducting tests, the army approved it for officers and men.[30]

Borden built a two-story brick factory and a one-story frame building, financing the construction by mortgaging some of his land

President Abraham Lincoln (Library of Congress)

Simon Cameron, Pennsylvania politician, candidate for president in 1860, and Lincoln's first Secretary of War. Cameron's nine-month tenure as secretary was plagued by poor administration and charges of corruption. (Library of Congress)

Gideon Welles, Secretary of the Navy throughout the war. Welles welcomed inventors with novel designs for gunboats and weapons. (Library of Congress)

Montgomery C. Meigs, a career army officer and a designer and prime engineer of the Capitol dome. As Quartermaster General of the United States, Meigs was a major architect of Union victory. (Library of Congress)

J. Edgar Thomson, the railroad engineer who designed a marvel of its day, the Horseshoe Curve outside Altoona, Pennsylvania. As president of the Pennsylvania Railroad, Thomson was one of the North's most important railroad executives during the war. Painting by S. B. Waugh, 1868. (Courtesy of the Railroad Museum of Pennsylvania, Strasburg, Pennsylvania)

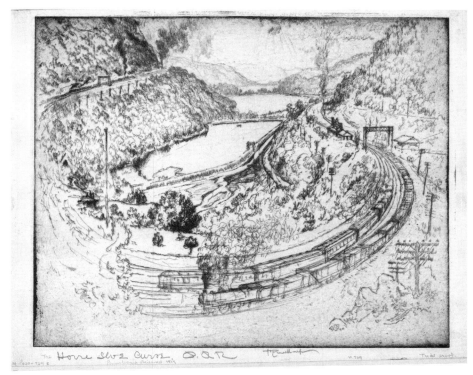

A drawing of the Horseshoe Curve as it appeared outside of Altoona, Pennsylvania, in the mid-1850s. A railroad engineering marvel of the time, it was designed and constructed by J. Edgar Thomson for the Pennsylvania Railroad. (Library of Congress)

Thomas A. Scott, a brilliant executive and vice president of the Pennsylvania Railroad. A political and business ally of Secretary of War Simon Cameron, Scott served as assistant Secretary of War during most of the war's initial year. (Library of Congress)

Edwin McMasters Stanton, Simon Cameron's successor as Secretary of War. Stanton proved to be a gifted and honest administrator and a bane to corrupt businessmen. (Library of Congress)

Jay Cooke, a banker and close associate of fellow Ohioan, Secretary of Treasury Salmon P. Chase. Cooke's sale of bonds to ordinary Americans revolutionized the nation's financing of wars. (Courtesy of Rutherford B. Hayes Presidential Center, Fremont, Ohio)

James Buchanan Eads, a self-taught engineer and salvager of sunken boats on the Ohio and Mississippi rivers. His ironclad gunboats proved vital in early Union operations on western rivers. (Library of Congress)

HENRY BURDEN.

Henry Burden, a Scottish immigrant and the inventor of a horseshoe making machine. His Burden Iron Company in Troy, New York, supplied the Union War Department with tens of millions of horseshoes. (Library of Congress)

Henry Burden's water wheel was called by folks in Troy, New York, the "Niagara of water wheels." With a diameter of 62 feet, it could produce between 500 and 600 horsepower a minute for his iron works. (Library of Congress)

USS *Louisville*, one of Eads's first seven ironclad gunboats, or "Pook's turtles," during operations on the Red River in Louisiana. (Library of Congress)

A battery of 100-pounder Parrott cannons with their distinctive wrought iron band around the breech. Photograph dates from late 1864 or early 1865 at Union Fort Brady on the James River in Virginia. (Library of Congress)

Robert P. Parrott, a graduate of the U. S. Military Academy and superintendent of the West Point Foundry. His firm in Cold Spring, New York, was the largest munitions supplier to the Union military during the Civil War. (Jack W. Melton, Jr. Collection)

Christopher Miner Spencer, "a quiet little Yankee" inventor. His breechloading, repeating Spencer rifle and carbine revolutionized American firearms and was desired by Union troops. (Courtesy of Windsor Historical Society, Windsor, Connecticut)

Edward R. Squibb, a Navy doctor, pharmacist, and idealist. His experiments on the purification of ether and chloroform saved the lives of countless Civil War soldiers. (Courtesy of the National Museum of Civil War Medicine, Frederick, Maryland [NMCWM])

Edward R. Squibb's pannier, or medicine chest, carried by Union surgeons during the war. (NMCWM)

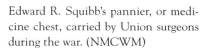

Contents of a Squibb medicine pannier, listed on the inside lid of the chest. Each pannier or chest held forty-nine pharmaceuticals and a number of other items, as shown. (NMCWM)

Abram S. Hewitt, a brilliant businessman and loyal Union patriot. He believed that "all private interests should in this crisis yield to the public welfare." (Library of Congress)

Cyrus McCormick, a Virginian and purported inventor of the first successful reaper. "Thus without McCormick's reaper," declared Secretary of War Edwin Stanton, "I fear the North could not win and the Union would be dismembered." (Library of Congress)

CYRUS M^cCORMICK'S REAPER

A drawing of Cyrus McCormick's original reaper as it appeared on a Virginia farm in the summer of 1831. (Library of Congress)

Andrew Carnegie, a Scottish immigrant and executive with the Pennsylvania Railroad during the Civil War. He amassed a modest fortune for the times through shrewd investments, including one in the iron and steel making business. (Library of Congress)

John Deere fashioned a plow from a discarded sawmill blade, which "sang" through the thick, black soil of the Midwest. Unknown photographer, John Deere (1804–1886), c. 1851–1856, daguerreotype, quarter-plate. (Collection of Middlebury College, Museum of Art, Vermont, purchased with funds provided by the Electra Havemeyer Webb Memorial Fund)

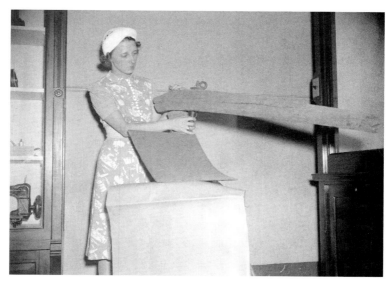

John Deere's original plow that proved to be able to cut cleanly through the thick, matted soil of the states in the Midwest. (Library of Congress)

The Studebaker wagon-making brothers, from left to right, Clement, Henry, John Mohler, Peter, and Jacob. All of them were partners at one time or another in the H. & C. Studebaker Company in South Bend, Indiana. (Courtesy of the Studebaker National Museum, South Bend, Indiana)

An 1858 artist rendering of the H. & C. Studebaker wagon-making shop in South Bend, Indiana. (Courtesy of the Studebaker National Museum, South Bend, Indiana)

The Studebaker state carriage purchased by the federal government in which President and Mrs. Lincoln rode to Ford's Theater on the night of April 14, 1865. (Courtesy of the Studebaker National Museum, South Bend, Indiana)

Gale Borden Jr., a leader of the Texas Revolution and an inventor. Union soldiers praised his condensed milk for its "sweetness," with an officer calling it "one of the luxuries." (Wikimedia Commons, accessed November 15, 2017)

Gordon McKay, a self-taught Massachusetts engineer who saw the "possibility of" a machine invented to sew uppers to the soles of shoes. His McKay Stitcher produced millions of pairs of boots and shoes for Union troops during the war. (Portrait by Hubert von Herkomer, titled Gordon McKay [1821–1903], Courtesy of Harvard University Portrait Collection, Gift to the University)

Three typical Union supply wagons without their canvas covers. Studebaker wagons were built on a similar design. (Library of Congress)

Philip D. Armour, a Milwaukee, Wisconsin, meat packer during the Civil War. He explained his business model, "Anybody can cut prices, but it takes brains to make a better article." (Library of Congress)

Frederick Weyerhaeuser, a German immigrant and partner in a lumber business in Rock Island, Illinois. Wartime demand for lumber brought profits to Weyerhaeuser, who began investing the money in large tracts of woodland in Michigan and Wisconsin. (Library of Congress)

Cornelius Vanderbilt, one the country's wealthiest citizens, at the age of fifty or fifty-one in 1845. Vanderbilt sold a fleet of ships to the War Department and invested heavily in railroad companies. (Library of Congress)

The *Vanderbilt*, the largest steamship of the era. Its builder and namesake, Cornelius Vanderbilt, presented it as a gift, valued at $1 million, to the Union War Department during the conflict. (Library of Congress)

Collis P. Huntington, a member and leader of the Associates, who formed the Central Pacific Railroad Company. Huntington helped secure passage of the 1862 Pacific Railway Act, which created the transcontinental railroad. (Library of Congress)

holdings. He equipped them with an engine, furnace, oven, grist mill, large kettles, and machine to slice meat into small pieces. When he finished, production of meat biscuits began. He invested $10,000 in the undertaking.[31]

Borden promoted the meat biscuit for the next five years. He hired sales agents, spent most of those years in the eastern United States, and sailed to London, where he received a medal at the Great Council Exhibition in 1851. The meat biscuit earned a second medal from the Metropolitan Mechanics' Institute two years later.[32]

Unfortunately, an army report filed June 21, 1851, opposed the adoption of the meat biscuit as a substitute for army rations. Private sales could not compensate for the loss of an army contract. The meat biscuit was simply not palatable—folks did not like it. Borden fought on, but by 1855, he had amassed tens of thousands of dollars in debt and then abandoned the enterprise. Gail Borden was virtually penniless, but his dreams would not die there in Texas.[33]

RESIDENTS OF ABINGTON, MASSACHUSETTS, MIGHT HAVE HEARD RUMORS; a few might have known the facts. It was 1857, and one of their own, Lyman Blake, had invented a machine to sew shoes' uppers to the soles. Blake's thing "was crude and would not work," according to talk, but a man had paid thousands of dollars for it. It was said that he saw the "possibility of it." Before long, town folks called him "a crank and a fool."[34]

The buyer of the machine and its rights was a fellow native of Massachusetts and a self-taught engineer, Gordon McKay. He was thirty-seven years old at the time, born on May 4, 1821, in Pittsfield. His father, Samuel, died when McKay was only twelve, and that's when he began studying civil engineering on his own. As a young man, he worked as a laborer on a railroad and on the Erie Canal. By the early 1850s, he had returned to his native state, serving as manager and treasurer of the Lawrence Machine Company. He also had become a specialist in the maintenance of factory equipment and machinery.[35]

McKay likely encountered Blake and his "makeshift machine" about the time the inventor had secured Patent No. 20,775 on July 6, 1858. The twenty-two-year-old Blake had worked at the Singer Sewing Machine Company before he began making shoes. Footwear was crafted individually by hand, piecemeal work, by either pegging or nailing a welt or strip of leather or other material to an upper and a sole. In a sworn statement years later, Blake testified, "It was not until some time after I made my invention that I ever saw a shoe sewed by hand [again]."[36]

Blake worked on his invention while he was a partner in the shoe-making firm of Gurney, Means & Blake. Years later he recalled:

> To increase the business of my firm . . . it was desirable to manufacture sewed shoes, and as there were no workmen in and about Abington skilled in such work, I began to consider whether or not I could devise machinery for sewing soles to boots and shoes. When I had clearly in mind a concept of my invention, which was afterwards patented by me, I went to my partners for consent to build a machine. At first they objected, but afterwards consented that I might build it with my own money, provided the firm should have use of the machine.[37]

When he had it built, he granted an option on the machine to a Lynn, Massachusetts, company for $50,000. Before the deal could be finalized, McKay approached Blake, having decided that the shoemaking industry held promise. He offered the inventor $8,000 in cash and $62,000 in future profits. Blake accepted, giving McKay the machine and rights to the patent. The firm in Lynn sued but lost the case.[38]

Blake's machine eliminated the use of a welt. It had an arm that worked inside the shoe, sewing the upper directly to the sole. When McKay obtained the invention, it did not function well, however. As a newspaper noted, McKay spent "long months" trying to perfect it. Blake worked with him for a while before moving for health reasons to Staunton, Virginia, where he opened a boot and shoe store. McKay took as a partner Blake's brother-in-law, Robert H. Mathias, who was described as "a practical man of inventive genius."[39]

McKay borrowed money to finish the work, but it was another four years, in 1862, until he received a patent for the redesigned McKay Stitcher. Like Blake, he had grasped how such a machine could revolutionize the shoemaking industry and dreamed of its possibilities. McKay lived and worked in the center of the country's boot and shoe manufacturing area—Massachusetts and the surrounding New England states.[40]

By the mid-1850s, the shoemaking industry had begun to adopt the factory system. In 1855 in Massachusetts alone, boot and shoemakers produced forty-five million pairs of footwear. Sales spread worldwide, even to Europe and Australia. Profits rose, and owners built factories to increase production. The Panic of 1857, however, affected the industry, slowing the growth of factory buildings.[41]

By 1860, 12,500 businesses made shoes and boots. Most were small firms, their employees likely working out of a shop or converted house. New England producers dominated the industry: three counties in Massachusetts made in value more than one-third of the total number of shoes and boots in the country. The construction of a shoe or boot had not fundamentally changed from pegging and nailing a welt into an upper and a sole.[42]

McKay kept promoting his stitching machine to shoemakers, offering them the use of it on a trial basis. Lyman Blake returned from Virginia and rejoined McKay's firm. Blake visited factories to demonstrate how the machine sewed uppers to soles. Part of his effort, wrote Blake, was "to remove from the public mind all prejudice concerning the machines." Some factory owners experimented with McKay's stitcher, but there was no wide-scale adoption of it. McKay had a dream and a machine, but he and Blake needed a major increase in the demand for shoes and boots.[43]

By the winter of 1853, Gail Borden Jr. should have abandoned the enterprise. A man of lesser faith or more sense would have done so, but not Borden. His factory in Galveston, Texas, kept making meat biscuits, and he kept losing money. His company had never recovered from the army's rejection of a contract nearly two years earlier. He admitted in a letter about this time, "I have spent all my money and my friends . . . will not lend me any."[44]

If nothing else, Borden persevered. The man seemed to relish the challenge of leaning into strong winds. He remarked once, "I never drop an idea except for a better one—never." So even while he tried to salvage the old idea of meat biscuits, he turned to a new idea, "to keep milk sweet for a very long time," as he put it. When and where he conceived of condensing milk remains uncertain because of conflicting accounts. Unquestionably, he worked months, if not years, on it, conducting daily experiments and consulting with scientists.[45]

For decades, others had tried unsuccessfully to condense or to preserve milk while keeping its "sweetness" and taste. Borden allegedly decided to experiment with a vacuum pan after watching Shakers preserve fruit with such a method. He reasoned that milk was 97 percent water, which could be evaporated over high heat. In May 1853, he applied for patents on "evaporation in vacuo process" in the United States and Great Britain. (Borden's original product was, in today's designation, evaporated milk, not the thick, sweetened condensed milk of Eagle Brand.)[46]

Scientific American endorsed Borden's product two months later, reporting in its July 2 issue, "For domestic use it will be the means of saving much in families, especially in warm weather, and at no time need there be any necessity for a person taking a cup of milkless coffee, even after a thunder storm, or a week of hot weather."[47]

It took Borden, however, three years of lobbying efforts in both Washington, DC, and London before he obtained patents in August 1856. By then, his meat biscuit factory had closed, his second wife had died, and he lacked any funds to begin production. He convinced two men, Thomas Green of Virginia and James Bridge of Maine, to invest in his idea in return for shares in patent rights and profits. The partners rented an abandoned carriage factory in Wolcottville—present-day Torrington—Connecticut in October 1856. They had chosen the village in the Berkshire Mountains because of an abundant supply of wholesome milk from nearby farms.[48]

The endeavor failed within a few months. Green and Bridge quit temporarily, and Borden returned to Texas, where he sold more of his acres of land. Returning to Connecticut with only one good shirt and one presentable suit, he rented half of a building from Milo Burr in Burrville, five miles north of Wolcottville. He transferred the equipment, furniture, and coal from his former factory and renegotiated his partnership agreement with Green and Bridge. His new factory opened on May 11, 1857.[49]

The public remained unconvinced of condensed milk's purity and safety. Borden advertised in newspapers, but sales lagged, affected like so many businesses by the Panic of 1857. The company was failing until he met Jeremiah Milbank, a New York City wholesale grocer and banker, in a chance encounter on a train. Milbank believed in Borden's condensed milk, paid his debts of $6,000, invested money in the Burrville factory, and settled the patent rights held by the partners.[50]

Borden and Milbank formed the New York Condensed Milk Company. Milbank knew the market, so they opened sales offices in New York City and established delivery routes in Manhattan and across the Hudson River in Jersey City, New Jersey. They placed advertisements in major newspapers, claiming that doctors approved their condensed milk. When *Leslie's Illustrated Newspaper* ran a story about infant deaths due to contaminated milk from dairies, the partners had an advertisement in the issue. By 1860, the company was prospering, but when Milo Burr raised the rent, Borden and Milbank refused to pay and began building a new factory in upstate New York at Wassaic on a branch of the New York Central Railroad. They transferred the equipment from Burrville to Wassaic and began production in June 1861.[51]

Four months after the Wassaic plant opened, the War Department offered the company a contract for five hundred pounds of condensed milk. A decade earlier, Borden had believed that he had what the army needed with his meat biscuit, but a board of officers rejected it. Now, he had a nutritious product that kept safe for long periods of time and that was easily handled and transported in supply wagons. Perhaps he reflected on the irony, but the contract was providential, fulfilling an inventor's dream and ensuring his company's continuation.[52]

Demand soon outpaced production, a supply issue the company could not fill throughout the conflict. Borden and Milbank hired more workers and expanded facilities in Wassaic. During a three-month period in 1862, the business sold 50,000 quarts of condensed milk. A year later, the factory produced 50,000 quarts in three days. In 1863, to meet the increasing demand of both the military and the public, the partners licensed two firms—one in York, Pennsylvania, and one in Livermore Falls, Maine—to use the patent and mark the cans with "Borden's." They also purchased and equipped a third factory in Winsted, Connecticut, a few miles north of the former plant in Burrville.[53]

In 1864, a reporter for *Scientific American* described a tour of the Wassaic factory. He had never visited a plant where "so much order, cleanliness, and comfort were combined." Everything in the process was done "with such scrupulous regard to cleanliness, that the result is irreproachable." Young women made eight thousand cans each day in a tin shop. The reporter noted that the company's primary customer was "the army, where it is a great blessing as you will readily believe."[54]

Soldier wits called it "consecrated milk," but it was evidently liked by many Union officers and men. A colonel remembered it as "one of the luxuries." Sutlers sold the condensed milk for fifty to eighty cents a can, a steep price for most army privates. The War Department placed Borden's milk on an official list of medical supplies. Surgeon General William A. Hammond praised it in an 1863 report, noting its "extensive use in our armies and hospitals . . . as a source of nutriment for the wounded." Doctors prescribed "milk punch," a blend of condensed milk and whiskey or brandy, for low-grade fevers.[55]

As for millions of fathers, the war was personal for Borden. His son John Gail served in two New York infantry regiments, and son Lee rode with the Thirty-Fifth Texas Cavalry. Because of his years in Texas, Borden had to justify his allegiance to the Union war effort. In 1864, Horace Greeley declared in his New York *Daily Tribune,* "To all rebels, Gail Borden's opposed, heart and soul, and his greatest anxiety appears to be to live to work for the Union army." Borden's father died that year, and for a third time he married, another widow, Mrs. Emeline Eunice Church.[56]

For the penniless inventor, Borden, and the shrewd investor, Milbank, the conflict brought wealth perhaps beyond their most sanguine expectations. According to one account, the company earned $145,275.32 in 1864, which the partners shared. Throughout the four years of war, Borden worked on improving his condensed milk, garnering three more patents. A fourth patent for "Improvement in Concentrating and Preserving for use, Cider, and other Juices of Fruits" resulted in the sales of concentrates of cider, fruit, and even coffee.[57]

During the war's final year, Borden began construction of two new, modern factories—one in Brewster, New York, fifty-five miles upstate from New York City, and a second one in Illinois west of Chicago. Ironically, near the struggle's end, the War Department reconsidered adoption of his meat biscuit. In January 1866, he changed his condensed milk's name to Eagle Brand. Later that year, the former Texas revolutionary moved back to the Lone Star State and settled in a town that in time was named Borden.[58]

BY 1863, IT WAS THERE FOR ALL TO SEE IN LYNN, MASSACHUSETTS. A major antebellum center for the manufacture of shoes and boots, the city was in the midst of profound change in its leading industry. A correspondent for a local newspaper described it:

> Of course the system is yet in its infancy—the business is yet in a transition state; but the wheels of revolution are moving rapidly, and

they never turn backward. Operatives are pouring in as fast as room can be made for them, buildings for "shoe factories" are going up in every direction, the hum of machinery is heard on every hand, old things are passing away and all things are becoming new.[59]

By the Civil War's third year, "new" extended far beyond Lynn, Massachusetts, in the North. The massive struggle had ignited the novel in businesses and industries from Maine's coast to Wisconsin's farmland. No industry arguably underwent more dramatic transformation than shoe and boot manufacturing. It had begun in the years just before Fort Sumter with the introduction of the factory system. The conflict's demand was met by "the hum of machinery," most likely caused by a McKay Stitcher.[60]

The War Department initially rejected machine-sewn shoes or brogans. But, in early 1862, Seth Bryant, a shoe manufacturer from East Bridgewater, Massachusetts, brought samples of shoes sewn by McKay's machine to Secretary of War Edwin Stanton. The army tested the shoes in the field, and Stanton awarded Bryant a contract for twenty-five thousand pairs. The agreement stipulated that a maker's name must be stamped on all shoes. The army also required that shoes be made of oak-tanned leather.[61]

Bryant and many other businessmen acted as middlemen between the War Department and shoe manufacturers. In time, Bryant became a major government supplier of shoes and boots he received primarily from Massachusetts firms. Bryant's agreements with the shoemakers relied on the McKay Stitcher.[62]

McKay not only revolutionized the shoemaking industry with his machine but also originated "the royalty system of manufacture." He formed a company to secure separate contracts with shoemaking firms. He sold them his machine, taught workers how to use it, and in turn, the businesses agreed to pay him a royalty on each pair of shoes and boots made. Each machine kept a tally of its output. In 1861, the government paid $1.75 for brogans and $3.25 for cavalry boots; by 1865, the prices rose to \$3.20 and \$4.75, respectively. McKay's fee amounted to several cents per shoe and boot.[63]

McKay opened two factories and made footwear for the army. His impact on the entire industry and its material contribution to the Union war effort cannot be overstated. It has been estimated that during the war the government purchased ten million pairs of boots and shoes at a cost of \$25 million. McKay's stitcher provided approximately one-half of all the shoes and boots supplied to the Union military. His machine could make a pair a hundred times faster than by the peg and nail method, and each pair lasted eight times longer than handmade shoes. In 1864, for instance, McKay's stitcher produced five million pairs.[64]

A well-shod Union soldier owed much to a Yankee cobbler, Lyman Blake, and to a man of vision, Gordon McKay. They had revolutionized an industry with an invention and supplied the North with a vital product in a time of crisis. In turn, McKay also introduced a new kind of financial transaction in business. It was reported "that Gordon McKay never turned a dollar that was tainted." A newspaper correspondent observed, "Old things" had given way to "all things" new. Gordon McKay fostered such a passing.[65]

Chapter Ten

THE OPPORTUNISTS

—⁓〰⁓—

PHILIP DANFORTH ARMOUR WENT WITH AN AMERICAN TIDE, A westering in quest of riches. It was 1852, and with companions and some money, he left the family farm near Stockbridge, Madison County, New York, and followed sunsets. The journey took six months, most of the miles covered on foot. Like thousands of others, he was drawn across stark plains and lofty mountains by a hankering.[1]

For thousands like him, however, California refused to yield its gold. Armour discovered what he had known for years—hard, physical labor. But in it lay a beginning, a stake to be carried elsewhere, east toward sunrises. This new journey passed through Milwaukee, Wisconsin, and Saint Paul, Minnesota, before ending in Chicago, Illinois. Along the way, amid a national tragedy, he fulfilled his hankering and laid the foundation of a business empire.[2]

Born May 16, 1832, in Madison County, Philip Armour was the fourth of eight children of Danforth and Juliana Brooks Armour. The first Armours and Brookses in the colonies had settled in Connecticut. When the Revolutionary War began, members of both families fought for the Patriot cause. Danforth Armour might have come to New York for work on the construction of the Erie Canal, but eventually he and Juliana purchased a farm outside Stockbridge in the Mohawk River Valley. There, the children were born, from 1828 to 1842.[3]

Both Danforth and Juliana appear to have been strong-willed

individuals. A townsman in Stockbridge came to know them and said of the couple: "The children got studious habits from their mother. She knew how to get and Danford [sic] knew how to keep. And in the church, she was a regular politician. She could swing the female side of that Methodist meeting house any way she wanted to, but she was not as 'sot in her ways' as Danford. One time Danford took to lawin' one of the neighbors over a fence. It took a long time to settle that, but it was settled Danford's way."[4]

The Armours prospered as farmers on the rich soil of the Mohawk River Valley. They purchased a nearby small brick house and brick barn. They stored hay in the barn and likely rented the house to tenants. As the children matured, the sons worked the fields with their father and the daughters helped their mother with household chores. Life was good for the family in central New York during the 1830s and 1840s.[5]

Philip Armour has been described as having a "restless brain" and being "a regular dynamo of energy" as a child. He was auburn-haired and grew into a stocky, broad-shouldered, and physically strong young man. He declared later, "I think the old Armours were born as tough as mules."[6]

As a youth, Armour possessed an independent bent, an unwillingness at times to obey rules—"a colorful figure," according to a newspaper account. He attended a local school, Cazenovia Academy, until he was expelled for taking a female student on a buggy ride at night. He continued working on the family farm, hired on with other farmers, and, for a while, clerked in the village dry goods store before gold fever drew him westward.[7]

Armour left Stockbridge with three companions and one hundred dollars that he had saved or had been given by his parents. A biography of him claims that his parents gave him a wagon and a team of horses for the difficult trek across the continent. He stated years later that he walked to California, and other evidence seems to support his assertion. When he and his fellow travelers reached Independence, Missouri, they joined a wagon train that had gathered to follow the Oregon Trail.[8]

Like other men with the wagons, Armour must have driven oxen teams during the day and stood guard duty during the night. On the plains a typical wagon train managed about twenty miles a day; through the mountains, much fewer. Days lengthened into weeks; weeks, into months. Finally, after a half year on the crossing from New York to California, the twenty-year-old Armour arrived in Placerville in the Sacramento River Valley barefoot, ragged, and gaunt.[9]

Placerville was emblematic of rough, lawless gold rush towns. It had that haphazard, thrown-together look about it, with prospectors' tents and wooden shacks, frame buildings, saloons, shops, and a boardinghouse. Vigilantes meted out justice to the nests of thieves and murderers, earning Placerville the nickname of "Hangtown" for the many criminals who were strung up from an oak tree on Main Street.[10]

Like the other gold seekers there, Armour panned for the metal but came up empty. In time, he and a luckless fellow from Vermont saw an opportunity to supply miners with running water for sifting gold pieces from dirt and began constructing wooden sluices and sluice gates for the miners to channel and to control the flow of water. The partners were not alone in Placerville; other former gold seekers sought to make money in other endeavors there, too—Leland Stanford and Mark Hopkins went to storekeeping, John Mohler Studebaker built wheelbarrows, and Levi Strauss made denim jeans.[11]

Building sluices was hard, exhausting labor for five dollars a day. Armour claimed that it suited him physically and mentally, writing long afterward: "Work is the greatest blessing that ever was handed down to a man or boy. If a fellow is only busy, he never will be in mischief. Hard work never killed anybody but, of course, there is such a thing as working too hard. . . . I throw off cares easily. Give me plenty of work and that is about all the tonic I want."[12]

The "tonic" proved financially rewarding. Eventually, Armour and his partner hired workers to meet the demand for sluices and gates. After four years in the mining camps around Placerville, the New Yorker decided to return to Stockbridge and marry the young woman he had taken on the carriage ride. He had saved a considerable sum of money, perhaps as much as $8,000, which he brought with him to his family's farm in New York.[13]

The young woman had not waited on him, however, and had married another. Armour's younger brother Herman, meanwhile, had moved to Milwaukee and extolled the business opportunities in the growing city. While en route to join Herman, Armour stopped for some time in Cincinnati, Ohio. At the Ohio River city, known commonly as "Porkopolis," he learned about the wholesale butchering and processing of animals and met his future wife, Malvina Belle Ogden. By the end of 1856, Armour had arrived in Milwaukee, where he would spend much of the next two decades.[14]

By the mid-1850s, Milwaukee bustled with an influx of immigrants and businesses. It had earned a reputation as a "boom town." Newcomers from the German states poured in, giving the city a distinctive culture and a dozen breweries. Farmers from throughout Wisconsin marketed their grains in Milwaukee. Beer and wheat appeared to dominate enterprises there, and the population passed thirty thousand residents.[15]

Herman Armour was engaged in the wholesale grain business when Philip joined him in Milwaukee. It seems, however, that the older brother sought his own opportunities, investing initially in a wholesale grocery firm. Before long, he put more of his California savings into a soap-making enterprise. He either leased or purchased a factory, where he rendered pig fat from pork packers into lard, added it to water and lye, and cooked the mixture into soap. Customers bought the crude bars of soap, giving him a return on his money, until some sort of an accident caused a fire, which destroyed the factory. Armour had been in the city less than a year and had been drained of much of his California earnings.[16]

Armour left Milwaukee and traveled west to Saint Paul, Minnesota. There he sold animal hides to tanneries in the region. He met and became close friends with Canadian-born James J. Hill, an employee of a steamboat company at the time and the future railroad baron.

Altogether, Armour spent two years in Saint Paul, recouping some of his losses, before returning to Milwaukee in late winter of 1859.[17]

On March 1, 1859, Armour and Frederick B. Miles formed a partnership, with each man investing five hundred dollars in a commission business that would deal in grain and meat sales. The firm primarily sold pickled and salted pork to settlers who passed through Milwaukee on their trek westward. Armour and Miles bought pork from butchers and then processed, packed, and marketed it. Armour witnessed firsthand the reality of profits in the assembly and distribution of meat products in the packing industry. He learned the trade well.[18]

For many years, meat packers worked only in the winter months from their flatboats on a river. They bought dressed hogs from farmers in December and January, cut the carcasses into pieces, and cured the meat. When the ice thawed on the river, the packers sold the meat in cities on the Ohio and Mississippi rivers. By the time Armour and Mills opened their business, the industry was well established in Cincinnati, Chicago, and Milwaukee in the western part of the country.[19]

For the twenty-seven-year-old native New Yorker, his story was not untypical story for the times. Since he left the family farm near Stockbridge, he had walked most of the way across a continent, obtained modest riches not in gold but in the sale of sluices to miners, lost much if not nearly all of his savings to misfortune, and managed to recover a stake in the future. If hard work was indeed a tonic for him, he had drunk deeply of it.[20]

THE ATLANTIC VOYAGE FROM LONDON TO NEW YORK CITY TOOK SIX weeks, from late May to early July 1852. On board the sailing ship were Irish, Welsh, English, and German emigrants. Since the revolutionary turmoil in 1848, an outward stream of Germans was fleeing their homeland. Among the German passengers were members of the Weyerhaeuser family from the village of Nieder Saulheim near the city of Mainz in the province of Rhenish-Hesse. Relatives of the Weyerhaeusers had preceded them to the United States, and letters from these earlier arrivals praised their new country and encouraged others to follow them.[21] When financial obligations forced the sale of the family farm, the Weyerhaeuser family decided to embark for America and traveled by boat down the Rhine River to Rotterdam and then across the Channel to London, where they embarked on the Atlantic crossing.[22]

Seventeen-year-old Frederick Weyerhaeuser recounted the journey:

> For the voyage we had to provide our own food. No one would be received on board ships who did not have supplies for fifty days. We baked a lot of bread, baking it twice [Zwieback], and laid in a store of flour, ham, beans, rice, sugar, molasses, and a few potatoes. We took a few household articles, and [brother-in-law] Koch took his nail-making tools. This latter proved a mistake, for better and cheaper tools were to be had in the United States. . . .
>
> The voyage occupied about six weeks, and was somewhat rough at times; but I enjoyed every hour of it; and the harder the wind blew the happier was I.[23]

The teenaged Frederick, born on November 21, 1834, in Nieder Saulheim, was one of eleven children. The Weyerhaeusers were a close-knit family, and he emigrated to America with his widowed mother, brothers, sisters, and in-laws. He later described the passage from their Palatinate homeland to the United States as "a great event." When the family arrived in New York, they joined kinfolk in northwestern Pennsylvania, south of Lake Erie, where a large contingent of German immigrants had settled.[24]

For the next four years, Frederick worked at different times in a brewery, on a farm, and for a blacksmith, John Philip Bloedel, whose daughter, Sarah Elizabeth, he would later marry. There was a reserve to him, a quietness that hid a burning within. His new home offered possibilities that neither Nieder Saulheim nor Mainz could offer. They were there for the taking for opportunistic, ambitious, and hardworking folk, and he was one of them. When he turned twenty-one years old, he received his share of the farm's sale and, leaving his family, started west to Illinois.[25]

Weyerhaeuser arrived at Rock Island, Illinois, on the Mississippi River in early 1856. He found employment on a railroad construction crew and then for a German brewer before the Mead, Smith, and Marsh sawmill firm hired him as a night watchman. Soon after he began at the sawmill, he was there alone when buyers came to purchase lumber. He had no authority to sell lumber, but he did so for sixty dollars in gold. The owners were quite pleased with the sale.[26]

Weyerhaeuser remembered: "Marsh took a liking to me, and it was not long, before I had charge of the yard and the sales and presently was looking after all the business. My wages were raised from time to time." He attributed his increasing duties and income to "my readiness to work. I never counted the hours, or stopped until I had finished what I had in hand."[27]

In late 1857, the sawmill owners transferred Weyerhaeuser to their extensive lumber yard in Coal Valley on the railroad east of Rock Island. He had barely assumed his new position when Mead, Smith, and Marsh declared bankruptcy. The Panic of 1857 had caused a severe recession throughout the country, but an unscrupulous businessman had cashed their note as payment for a load of logs but never delivered the material. It ruined the company financially. Weyerhaeuser managed to keep the lumber yard open for a few months until the sheriff took possession of it.[28]

A local businessman who had loaned the sawmill owners money suggested that Weyerhaeuser purchase the lumber yard and assume its debts. The young man had saved money, but this was a risky venture. It offered an opportunity, however, to own a business, and after securing credit, he began selling lumber. Few folks had specie to pay him, so he bartered. "I went round among the farmers," he recounted, "exchanging lumber for horses, oxen, hogs, eggs, anything they had. This country produce I traded to raftsmen for logs or to merchants for stoves, tinware, and logging kits."[29]

The hard times lingered for months, allowing Weyerhaeuser to purchase timber at depressed prices. He leased his former company's sawmill in Rock Island and hired a sawyer to run it. He purchased wheat from farmers on commission for a company and established a construction business, building residences, outbuildings, even schoolhouses. He worked tirelessly from before dawn to after sunset.[30]

Despite his personal reserve, he wheeled and dealed, earning a reputation as an astute and honest businessman. He asserted once that work could be "a source of real gratification." It could also reap a net profit, $3,000 in his first year in business and $5,000 in the second year. By the winter of 1860, Weyerhaeuser wanted to purchase the sawmill in Rock Island, but he needed someone to run it and a partner with capital. He approached his brother-in-law, Frederick Charles Augustus Denkmann.[31]

Weyerhaeuser and Denkmann were married to sisters. In the spring of 1857, Sarah Elizabeth Bloedel had traveled from Pennsylvania to Rock Island to assist her older sister, Mrs. Denkmann, through childbirth. Known as both Sarah and Elizabeth in her family, she was eighteen years old, five years younger than Weyerhaeuser. They renewed their acquaintance from Pennsylvania, courted for six months, and were married on October 11, 1857. Together they would have seven children— four sons and three daughters—and she would offer advice and assist with clerical work for the expanding enterprise.[32]

The brothers-in-law signed Articles of Agreement on May 1, 1860, forming "copartners in business" under the name "Weyerhaeuser and Denkmann." The partners were, according to the agreement, "in the business of lumber and in the buying and Selling and Vending all sorts of wares to the said business." They owned the Rock Island sawmill and the Coal Valley lumber yard.[33]

Weyerhaeuser contributed $4,616.51 to the new firm—$3,212.80 in cash, and the remainder in a wagon, buggy, two horses, two cows, seven hogs, and "one brass collar." Denkmann invested only $1,607.03— $400.00 in cash, $810.00 in groceries, and the rest in other items. He agreed, in turn, that the difference between his outlay and Weyerhaeuser's was $3,009.48, for which he gave Weyerhaeuser a promissory note for $1,504.78 at 10 percent interest.[34]

They bought the sawmill from Mead, Smith, and Marsh for $5,100, paying $2,100 in cash and signing a note for the remainder. Under the terms of the agreement, they would divide costs and profits equally, even though Weyerhaeuser had invested more in the company. He brought his business acumen to the firm; Denkmann, a talent for mechanics. While Weyerhaeuser bought logs and sold lumber, Denkmann operated the sawmill.[35]

Weyerhaeuser and Denkmann established the company at a fortuitous time. The nation's economy was emerging from the depths of the Panic of 1857, and the demand for lumber was rising. In 1860, Rock Island had a population of fifty-one hundred persons, with thousands more in Moline, Illinois, and across the Mississippi River in Davenport, Iowa. Moline boasted John Deere's plow factory, and Davenport had flour mills and businesses devoted to farming. Rock Island possessed an arsenal, a saw works that made mill saws, and a railroad. The new lumber company had a local market for its product. And within a year, it had a market far beyond its immediate vicinity.[36]

UNION SOLDIERS' DIET CONSISTED PRIMARILY OF HARDTACK, A FLOUR-and-water cracker or biscuit, and salt pork, which the rank and file called "sowbelly." At times soft bread, fresh or pickled beef, and desiccated vegetables supplemented the standard fare. The Yankees fried, broiled on a stick, or baked with beans their ration of salt pork, while often making a soup by mixing the meat with the hardtack in water. The favorite drink with meals, coffee, washed down the various, if not ingenious, concoctions prepared around a campfire.[37]

From the conflict's outset, the demand for pork and beef immediately affected the meatpacking industry. In 1860, 259 companies, with roughly five thousand employees, cut, cured, and processed meat.

Traditionally, the animals were slaughtered in the winter months in the North and then delivered to meatpacking firms. Only since 1857 did companies first in Chicago and then in Milwaukee begin killing pigs in the summer months, using ice from frozen streams that they had stored to preserve the meat. Salt pork and cured bacon and ham did not require ice.[38]

Mechanization was introduced to the meatpacking industry during the antebellum years. It was the use of machines that proved critical in meeting the escalating demands of the Union military. A British visitor to a plant during the war described its operation: "At Chicago a million pigs die every year for the benefit of the public. They are killed by machinery in the quickest and most scientific way. Within twenty minutes of the time of your hearing a pig squeal, he is killed, cut up, packed in barrels, and on his way to Europe."[39]

This rapid processing of a pig produced a staggering amount of salt pork, bacon, hams, and salt beef for the Union armies. It has been calculated that the military received nearly 670 million pounds of processed pork and beef and another 161 million pounds of fresh beef during the war years. Meatpacking companies in Chicago, Cincinnati, Louisville, Saint Louis, and Milwaukee dominated the industry. The firms were, as a rule, well financed and efficient.[40]

During the conflict, the major meatpacking company in Milwaukee was Plankinton & Armour. In the spring of 1861, Philip Armour and Frederick Miles were still in the grain commission business and the sale of salted and pickled pork to travelers and local residents. They had prospered and owned a warehouse with increasing production. Armour married Malvina Belle Ogden of Cincinnati in 1862. Less than a year later, in May 1863, he dissolved his partnership with Miles after receiving an offer of a partnership with John Plankinton.[41]

John Plankinton and Frederick Layton had owned a meatpacking company for a decade. The two men had built it into the leading packing firm in the city. In 1863, Layton quit the business, and Plankinton approached Armour. Twelve years older than his new partner,

Plankinton was a skilled butcher and a shrewd businessman. Armour was a man driven by ambition and an equally astute businessman.[42]

With his new partner, Armour began work at the plant at four o'clock in the morning and stayed until late at night. He and Plankinton discovered how to make a dressed pig yield four hams. "Anybody can cut prices," Armour declared, "but it takes brains to make a better article." Within a year, Plankinton & Armour was booming in sales to the Union army. The firm combined with Herman Armour's grain commission company in Chicago and bought the largest grain elevator in Milwaukee. The firm also constructed a new three-story plant along the Menominee River.[43]

The Milwaukee partners adopted methods and machinery that improved efficiency and production. The creation of a better business drove Armour as much, if not more so, as increasing profits. "Ambition and pride keep a man at work when money is merely a by-product," he proclaimed. He believed that "close application" or constant management "accomplishes the best results." Once later in life when questioned about his faith, Armour, who belonged to the Congregational Church, replied: "I have a little religion, but no politics. I am simply a business man."[44]

By the early winter of 1865, Armour concluded that the war was nearly at an end with a Northern victory. He saw an opportunity in the market and approached his partner, proposing that they "ought to sell short." He reportedly said to Plankinton: "I am a bull on the Union and Grant and a bear on pork. It's $40 a barrel now, but with peace, it's going to break." Armour boarded a train soon afterward for New York City.[45]

In New York City, dealers in pork futures were trying to create a bull market by raising the price of a barrel above $40. When Armour arrived, his agents in the city endeavored to dissuade him from selling at the current price. Instead, Armour sold all of their pork at $40 and purchased pork futures at $18 per barrel. When the war ended, the market collapsed, as he expected, and Plankinton & Armour netted a profit believed to be $1.8 million. Armour's bold, risky, but farsighted transaction ensured the company's financial future.[46]

"Everyday in every way that war was a help to P. D. Armour," according to his biographers. In fact, the entire meatpacking industry, like other large businesses, underwent a transformation because of the four-year struggle. "Civil War years marked a turning point" with meatpacking in America, historian Margaret Walsh states. Before the war, a typical Chicago firm slaughtered 270,000 pigs annually, but by 1865 the number rose to 900,000. Innovations marked the postwar years, and Philip Danforth Armour, relocating to Chicago, emerged as one of the country's premier meat packers. His daring market coup underwrote an enduring enterprise.[47]

FREDERICK WEYERHAEUSER HAD AN ORDERED LIFE. HE HAD HIS WIFE, children, Dutch Reformed Church, and the lumber business. He used neither alcohol nor tobacco and had no time for distractions. Beside family and faith, work dominated his routine, for it could be, as he said, "a source of real gratification." Ironically, this modest, reserved, methodical individual was a risk-taking, gambling businessman.[48]

Weyerhaeuser and his brother-in-law Frederick Denkmann had been in the lumber business less than a year when the Civil War began. In those eleven months, they had made a profit and hired workers at the sawmill in Rock Island and at the lumber yard in Coal Valley, while gaining a reputation for square dealing. By the spring of 1861, the partners were regarded as "thrifty, industrious, honest and obliging."[49]

Like many other businesses, lumber companies endeavored from the conflict's outbreak to meet the soaring demands. Wagon and ambulance makers, gun manufacturers, and the Union army and navy soon clamored for more of their products. New lumber camps pockmarked the vast stretches of forest from Maine to Minnesota. As the war progressed, railroads became the major users of timber, needing stacks of ties to accommodate the heavy rail traffic and construction of new lines. Only grain surpassed timber in the quantities being hauled on the Great Lakes and canals. The price of wood rose from three dollars a cord to seven dollars.[50]

Production at the Weyerhaeuser & Denkmann Mill accelerated during the war's first year. In 1861, the firm made 6,000 to 10,000 board feet of lumber daily; within a year 20,000 board feet were sawed each day. Annual outlay grew from nearly 1 million board feet to 3 million. Production swamped the lumber yard in Coal Valley, so the partners secured a wholesale license on December 1, 1862, allowing them to purchase timber in western Illinois and across the Mississippi River in Iowa.[51]

Denkmann increased the production by adding new machinery, such as edgers, trimmers, lathes, and a shingle-making machine. As profits grew, the partners rewarded their skilled and unskilled workers. Among a majority of the employees, the wages at least doubled during the war years. When one worker received higher pay, he exclaimed, "It took my breath to get so much." The lowest daily wage was seventy-five cents for twelve hours of work; the highest reached three dollars for head sawyers.[52]

The partners bought a second sawmill and continued reinvesting in the company. Both men lived modestly, saving their shares of the profits. Weyerhaeuser declared once that the "surest way" to make money was to save it. He managed sales and purchased the logs for the mills, the business's "outside man."[53]

As the war continued, Weyerhaeuser found it increasingly difficult to purchase an adequate supply of logs. At some point, he concluded that they needed to acquire timber land and have the trees logged for the company. While his biographers argue that the firm's first documented land transaction occurred on December 14, 1870, postwar newspaper accounts, written while Weyerhaeuser was still alive, claim that he bought standing white pine along the Chippewa and Black rivers in Wisconsin.[54]

One account alleged that when Weyerhaeuser first traveled into Wisconsin seeking logs, he "saw all around him the lavish waste of

timber, and it struck to his saving soul." If and when this happened remains unclear, but he must have also seen opportunity. He reportedly
contended, "The only time I lost was when I did not invest." The Civil
War provided his firm with needed capital and profits, which Weyerhaeuser used to buy thousands of acres of trees, if not the forest land.[55]

Not surprisingly, a silent man, a modest man, a careful man imposed order on a disorderly industry. He integrated the parts of his business into a whole, from felling the trees to selling the planed lumber.
The waste that he had witnessed might have stirred his soul, but his
response became the foundation of a fortune.[56]

Chapter Eleven

THE BUILDERS

A CROWD OF THOUSANDS OF SPECTATORS FILLED BOTH BANKS OF East River on the New York City waterfront. The cold winter air of December 10, 1855, braced the onlookers as they watched a marvel of the times, a mammoth steamship, slip into the waters. It was the largest vessel of its kind ever built, "a leviathan of the deep," according to *Scientific American*.[1]

Many in the crowd probably gasped at the sight as four tug boats, looking "like dog-fish beside a whale," towed her into the river. A New York *Times* reporter called the ship simply a "monster." It measured 335 feet in length, had five decks, sidewheels of 42 feet in diameter, and could move more than 5,000 tons of cargo. No other steamship afloat compared to it. When outfitted with large twin engines, boilers, equipment, and furnishings, the cost of the ship exceeded $900,000.[2]

The *Vanderbilt*, as it was christened, symbolized and affirmed the wealth and commercial power of its owner and namesake, Cornelius Vanderbilt. Like his five-deck "leviathan," he towered over his business rivals. With arrogance and ruthlessness, he had destroyed competitors; sought favor from legislatures, Congress, even foreign governments; built a fleet of ships; and invested in railroads. The sixty-one-year-old Vanderbilt had amassed a fortune equaled or exceeded by few fellow Americans.[3]

It had been a half century since a barefooted eleven-year-old

Cornele, to his family, began working the waters of New York harbor. Born May 27, 1794, to Cornelius and Phoebe Hand Vanderbilt, Cornele was the fourth child in the family, whose Dutch ancestor had arrived in the colony of New Netherlands in 1650. The elder Vanderbilt farmed and ferried cargo and passengers from the family's home on Staten Island across the bay to Manhattan, Brooklyn, and New Jersey. After Cornele's older brother Jacob died in 1805, the boy helped his father on their periauger, a large, two-masted barge developed by the Dutch. Cornele received reportedly only a few months of formal schooling. His "handwriting was virtually illegible, his grammar atrocious."[4]

Legends—fueled by him and his early biographers—abound about his initial years in the ferry business. What has been reasonably established is that at the age of sixteen Vanderbilt operated the periauger and shared the profits with his parents. He saved money and, three years later, purchased his own boat. He increased his earnings by hauling troops during the War of 1812. On December 19, 1813, he married his cousin, Sophia Johnson, and months later, the couple moved to New York City.[5]

A burly, dark-eyed, six-footer, Vanderbilt acted with astonishing swiftness. He had larger boats built, known soon as "Vanderbilt models," for both ferry and short trips along the Atlantic coast. His father invested in the new schooners, but of greater import, Vanderbilt agreed to operate *Mouse of the Mountain*, a steam-driven boat owned by Thomas Gibbons. A wealthy rice planter from Georgia, Gibbons had moved to Elizabethtown, New Jersey, where he had opened his own ferry business. Before long, Vanderbilt was in the employ of the Georgian.[6]

The Vanderbilt-Gibbons association changed American commerce. Gibbons, Vanderbilt later said, "was a man that could not be led." The rich, transplanted Southerner could be tyrannical, foul tempered, self-righteous, and combative. In a complex and fiercely contentious dispute over a New York steamboat monopoly, Gibbons sued his former partner and New Jersey governor, Aaron Ogden. The ensuing case, *Gibbons v. Ogden*, ended up in Chief Justice John Marshall's Supreme

Court. Marshall and the associate justices ruled against the monopoly and in favor of commercial "intercourse" on March 2, 1824.[7]

During these years of personal feuds and legal maneuvers, Vanderbilt worked for Gibbons while running his own ferry business and buying more vessels, including steamboats. He also learned cold, unflinching business practices from Gibbons. Much of Gibbons's temperamental and arrogant personality was mirrored in Vanderbilt's own disposition. The lessons went deep into the younger man. After prolonged bouts of ill health, Thomas Gibbons died on May 16, 1826.[8]

For the next three decades Vanderbilt created a business empire whose reach extended from New York City to Le Havre, France, and Managua, Nicaragua. He constructed steamships, established his own oceanic route, operated a stagecoach line, invested in railroads, and sought partners and financial backers. He achieved all of this in a rapacious quest for wealth, using soulless business practices to achieve his goals. Given the honorary title of commodore, Vanderbilt squeezed bribes from competitors, purchased politicians, fashioned monopolies, and manipulated stock prices. At the same time, he improved services to customers, adopted new technologies, increased productivity, and welcomed change.[9]

To be sure, the commodore had setbacks and failures. Ships wrecked, losing cargoes; his steamship line to France amassed losses, and his heavy investment in a canal and railroad in Nicaragua never became a reality. When a dock or bridge collapsed at Vanderbilt Landing in New York City, drowning seventeen, mostly women, departing passengers, a grand jury on Staten Island indicted him for manslaughter. Several months later, however, the indictment was voided, likely because of his unrivaled influence on the island.[10]

By the 1850s, Vanderbilt's fleet of steamships numbered more than one hundred vessels, earning a reported monthly income of $100,000. He claimed in 1853 that his personal fortune amounted to $11 million. Seven years later, however, a newspaper estimated his worth at perhaps $6 million.[11]

From the first time he raised a sail on the periauger, ferrying and shipping had been the major source of his accumulating wealth. But as railroads expanded their web across the country, he increasingly invested in rail companies. In 1844, he made his initial expenditure, quietly buying shares of the New York & New Haven Railroad. Five years later, he acquired stock in the New York & Harlem Railroad, which ran from lower Manhattan through Harlem to Chatham in Columbia County.[12]

His involvement with the railroad industry accelerated during the final antebellum decade. He acquired stock in or served on the board of directors of the Hartford & New Haven Railroad; the Delaware, Lackawanna & Western Railroad; and the New York & Erie Railroad, for which he secured a loan of $400,000. Vanderbilt sold ships from his fleet to purchase railroad shares.[13]

Self-assured, even imperious, Vanderbilt broached little opposition from fellow directors. A contemporary said of him, "He held himself answerable to no one, least of all the public and minority stockholders. . . . He was the directorate—the law, he was Dictator." Continuing, he described the commodore as "the most conspicuous and terrifying exponent of his era."[14]

Another acquaintance remarked that Vanderbilt possessed a "dignified reserve" and "dignified self-control" in public. The wealth brought a lifestyle he coveted. Though he would never be a member of New York's old, aristocratic elite, his money opened doors to some of the city's first families. The Vanderbilts did the Grand Tour of Europe in 1853, and he kept a stable of blooded horses, which he drove in harness races. He helped establish a club "of many of the best people of the city" for the races. The Elm Park Pleasure Ground Association had four hundred members.[15]

When a son, George, died in 1846 and Vanderbilt's mother in 1854, Vanderbilt turned to spiritualism, a phenomenon of the times. He attended séances to communicate with them. His interest in it deepened later when his wife, Sophia, died. It was alleged that he inquired of a

Staten Island seeress the future of the stock market. Whether she fore-warned the rich commercial giant of his country's descent into a slaugh-terhouse remains unknown.[16]

"AN OLD-FASHIONED, DILAPIDATED HOUSE" TEETERED ON A HILL ABOVE Poverty Hollow in Harwinton Township, Connecticut. There, on October 22, 1821, Collis P. Huntington was born, the sixth of the nine children of William H. and Elizabeth Vincent Huntington. Many years later on one of his return visits to Poverty Hollow, Huntington stated that he had "been made glad that this was the place where I was born, and that I was born poor, for I think that was the reason, at least in part, of such success in life as I have been able to achieve."[17]

The Huntington family experienced a poverty that indeed ground down body and soul. William Huntington farmed and owned a "decrepit" fulling mill and shingle mill. A newspaper described the mother as "a hard working Christian woman, but the father was a man in whose makeup ambition had no part." William tried to earn extra money by mending umbrellas and sharpening razors, but his income was "far too meager" to support his large family.[18]

The children helped on the farm and in the mills. They received little formal schooling, and a teacher recalled them as "very poorly clothed, and not well cared for." In 1834, with the family destitute, town selectmen removed Collis and his older brother Solon from the family and placed them in separate homes of local farmers. Collis remembered it bitterly, declaring years later: "The Harwinton selectmen did not consult Solon or myself or our parents about taking us away from our home. . . . We were rudely moved and had to like it."[19]

Collis lived with the Orson Barbier family. Mrs. Barbier allegedly kindled a desire to succeed in the thirteen-year-old boarder. A tall, strapping fellow, Collis worked on the Barbier farm for only a year, earning seven dollars a month and room and board. He then clerked in Phineas Noble's store in Harwinton and sold wares door to door throughout northwestern Connecticut. Evidently with Noble's support, he ventured into New York City to hawk goods on the streets. For the next few years, he traveled through the South, a "Yankee peddler" with his merchandise.[20]

Solon Huntington, meanwhile, moved to Oneonta, New York, where he opened a dry goods store. Collis joined his brother in Oneonta in 1844, contributing his savings of $1,318 to the business. The S. & C. P. Huntington enterprise soon became the most successful store in the town and surrounding Otsego County. On September 18, 1844, Collis married a distant cousin he had been courting, Elizabeth Stoddard, in her hometown of Cornwall, Connecticut. The union endured until Elizabeth's death in 1883.[21]

Collis and Elizabeth lived in Oneonta for the next four years. He traveled often to New York City to buy goods for the store. He stated years later, "From the time I was a child until the present I can hardly remember a time when I was not doing something." Seemingly never quite satisfied with the present, he sought business opportunities. Huntington was a man "who seized the main chance before others even knew it was there," in the estimation of historian Stephen E. Ambrose. After four years, then, in central New York, he thought he saw "the main chance" far from Oneonta.[22]

News of the gold strike at Sutter's Mill in California prompted Collis to join the westward stream of seekers, not to pan or to mine for gold but to sell merchandise to the miners. Solon would send the goods to California, and the brothers would share the profits. Collis left on a ship bound to Panama on March 15, 1849. After an arduous trek across the isthmus, Huntington and companions missed a ship for California. Detained in Panama for nearly two months, he bought and sold scarce medicines and provisions.[23]

He estimated later that he crisscrossed the jungle at least twenty times, buying from farmers and selling in the town of Gorgona. When he discovered a creaky old schooner, he filled it, in his words, "with jerked beef, potatoes, rice, sugar and syrup in great bags and brought everything up to Panama and sold them." He had departed New York with $1,200 and made a profit of $3,000 or more while stranded along the Pacific Coast.[24]

In June, Huntington and the other passengers departed Panama on a Dutch ship and arrived in San Francisco at the end of August. Huntington continued on to Sacramento, a booming gold town that soon had ten thousand residents, forty gambling houses, and only a handful of churches. Unfortunately for the newcomer, he became seriously ill, perhaps with typhus, and his weight fell from 200 to 125 pounds. He was bedridden for weeks and did not fully recover until after the new year. He had managed, however, to store the wares that he had brought with him.[25]

When he recovered, Huntington opened a general merchandise store with partners Daniel Hammond and Edward Schultz. Hammond had no money to invest, so he agreed to work without pay for a year. Schultz contributed $5,000; Huntington, his stock of goods and cash. They built a store, primarily made of canvas, on K Street.[26]

Huntington's "Yankee shrewdness" served the partnership well. They and other merchants were at the mercy of sporadic shipments of goods from the East, which caused prices to fluctuate wildly in the gold camps. When scarcities mounted, Huntington exploited the situation; according to a newspaper account, "At such times he had the market in his hands and advanced prices accordingly."[27]

Although the partners managed to make a profit despite the difficulties, Huntington wrote a letter to Solon filled with phonetic spellings, complaints, and self-pity in the spring of 1850:

> I should hav bin to home long eare this if I had come alone and on my own act [account] for I hav Suffered mutch in this Country, mutch in Sickness and mutch in helth and how could it be otherwise how can one leave for som of the best yeares of his life his nearest and deares frends and a quiate Home and loving Wife Without looking back With bitter Regret. . . .

> I shall Stay until I have Sattisfied my Self and all others conserned that I hav don the best I Could under the Sircumstances. . . . God Speed the time of my return.[28]

Huntington returned to New York in the fall of 1850, retracing the route that had brought him to California. He made the journey to discuss business with Solon and their wholesalers. Most importantly, however, he wanted to bring his wife Elizabeth back with him to the newly admitted state. The couple was in Sacramento by May 1851. They settled into a cottage that he had purchased, but Huntington spent weekdays in San Francisco selling the firm's goods.[29]

In early 1852, the partners ended their agreement. The $5,000 investment returned $18,000 to each man in cash and goods. Huntington bought the lot that they had rented and built a new brick store on it. "We shall not have enny more Rent to pay," he informed his brother, "and Shall not hav danger of Burning up as we was in the old Store."[30]

On November 2, 1851, election day in Sacramento, arsonists ignited fires in the city. Fires were a constant menace to the ramshackle, mostly wooden buildings there and in San Francisco. The flames, reaching Huntington's store, came through windows and doors. He, Elizabeth, and clerks tried vainly to save the $5,000 stockpile of merchandise that had arrived the day before. The blaze consumed all of it and destroyed a store next door owned by Mark Hopkins and E. H. Miller Jr. On the other side of Huntington's lot, Leland Stanford and his brothers' brick warehouse and store were spared.[31]

The next thirty-six months proved to be difficult for Huntington. He scraped together enough money to restock his store, took on a new partner, and returned to New York to settle his and Solon's debts to wholesalers. His interests and fortunes changed dramatically, however, when he partnered with Mark Hopkins and Charles Crocker in 1854 in a scheme to construct a railroad from Sacramento east to the Sierra Nevada Mountains. Hopkins and Crocker, having come with the floodtide of forty-niners to California, were also merchants. Crocker, born in 1814, was the oldest of the trio; Hopkins, born in 1822, the youngest.[32]

Two years earlier, others had broached the idea for a railroad. A company had been organized, an engineer hired, and a survey undertaken before the three storekeepers invested in the risky project. Vice president of the Sacramento Valley Railroad was a former army captain, William T. Sherman. Investors in the enterprise secured shares at a 10 percent down payment.[33]

Construction of the sixty-mile track at a cost of $60,000 a mile began on August 9, 1855. The rail line reached Folsom, California, by February 22, 1856, when the company held a ball in celebration. Unfortunately for the investors, the Sacramento Valley Railroad never realized a profit. Losses for stockholders have not been substantiated.[34]

Huntington, Hopkins, and Crocker, meanwhile, continued operating their stores. All three men were abolitionists and, when Californians began organizing a Republican Party in the spring of 1856, they joined it. Crocker's brother, Edward, was one of the founders, and, soon afterward, Leland Stanford signed on. They campaigned vigorously for the party's presidential candidate, John C. Fremont, but Democrat James Buchanan won the state's four electoral votes.[35]

An issue during the presidential campaign of particular interest to Californians was a transcontinental railroad. Like nearly all disputes of the times, sectionalism framed the arguments. During President Franklin Pierce's administration, Secretary of War Jefferson Davis had ordered a study of possible routes. A Mississippian, Davis recommended a southern route from New Orleans to Los Angeles in the twelve-volume report.[36]

In California, the foremost advocate of a transcontinental railroad was Theodore Judah, the former engineer of the Sacramento Valley Railroad. Thirty years old in 1856 and a college graduate, Judah was obsessed with the idea. "Everything he did from the time he went to California to the day of his death was for the great continental Pacific railway," remembered his wife Anna. "Time, money, brains, strength, body and soul were absorbed." Three times he and Anna returned to the East, where he lobbied Congress for funds for the massive project.[37]

In November 1860, Judah gave a lecture on the railroad in Saint Charles Hotel in Sacramento. Huntington attended the event, having likely met the engineer or undoubtedly known of him. Judah presented a detailed description of a possible route, appealing at the end for funds for the organization of a company. Afterward, Huntington approached Judah because the project had a great appeal for him, and he had fellow storekeepers who would invest in it.[38]

Judah had been unsuccessful in his efforts in Congress, and now the country appeared to be facing the greatest crisis in its history. Huntington would not be dissuaded, however. As historian Richard White writes, Huntington "always had an eye for the main chance. He combined bulldog tenacity, which he demonstrated when necessary, with a shrewd sense that few fights were worth fighting to the finish." Judah's dream and the chance for great wealth had become one of those "few fights."[39]

PRESIDENT ABRAHAM LINCOLN HASTILY CALLED A CABINET MEETING on Sunday, March 9, 1862. Reports had reached Washington, DC, earlier in the morning of a naval disaster at Hampton Roads, Virginia. An ironclad Confederate warship, CSS *Virginia*, had sailed down the James River and attacked the blockading Union squadron, sinking the USS *Cumberland* and USS *Congress* and running aground the USS *Minnesota*. The *Virginia* had been built from the salvaged hull of the USS *Merrimack*, a frigate the navy had scuttled at Norfolk when it abandoned the naval yard on April 20, 1861.[40]

At the meeting in the Executive Mansion, Secretary of War Edwin Stanton "was at times almost frantic," wrote Secretary of the Navy Gideon Welles. Stanton paced back and forth, looking out windows at the Potomac River seemingly expecting the *Virginia* to be churning upriver toward the capital. He proclaimed that the Confederate ironclad would destroy every Union ship, prevent the offensive movement of the

Army of the Potomac to the Virginia Peninsula, and batter the public buildings in the city with cannon fire. Stanton was, declared Welles, "the most frightened man on that gloomy day, the most so I think of any during the Rebellion."[41]

For months, Welles had known from spies about the Confederate work on the *Virginia*. He had contracted with John Ericsson to build an ironclad vessel. Even as the president and cabinet met, Ericsson's creation, USS *Monitor*, was dueling with the *Virginia* at Hampton Roads. The confrontation ended in a stalemate, but the *Virginia* remained a formidable threat to the Union navy's wooden-hulled warships.[42]

Six days later, on March 15, Stanton telegraphed Cornelius Vanderbilt, inquiring whether he had an idea how they could prevent the *Merrimack*—the government kept using the warship's original name—from "coming out of Norfolk." Vanderbilt boarded a train and arrived in the capital on March 17. "I called at the War Department, where I saw for the first time Mr. Stanton, the Secretary of War," he recounted years later. "He requested me to accompany him to the Executive Mansion." At the White House, "I was introduced to Mr. Lincoln, to whom I was then personally a stranger."[43]

Like Stanton, the president asked if the wealthy shipowner "could do anything to keep the enemy vessel from steaming out of Norfolk once more." Vanderbilt stated that his massive steamship *Vanderbilt*, if properly manned, could "sink and destroy" the Confederate ironclad. When the war had begun, Vanderbilt had offered to sell the *Vanderbilt* and other steamships to the navy, but the idea was rejected. Lincoln inquired what the price for the ship would be at this time. According to Vanderbilt, he replied that he did not want to be "ranked with the herd of thieves and vampires who were fattening off the Government by means of army contracts." He offered the ship as a gift to the War Department if he could direct its preparations. Lincoln accepted the generous proposal.[44]

The commodore hurried back to New York City, where he soon received a telegram from Stanton thanking him for his "patriotic and generous gift to the Government." It read further, "Full discretion and authority are conferred upon you to arm, equip, navigate, use, manage, and employ the said steamship Vanderbilt, with such commander and crew and under such instructions as you may deem fit for the purposes hereinbefore expressed." Stanton noted that the Union quartermaster would supply the ship and recognize the crew as in government service.[45]

Preparations had been nearly completed when Stanton's telegram arrived. The Vanderbilt departed the city on March 21, with the commodore in command. The vessel arrived opposite Fort Monroe at the tip of the Virginia Peninsula. It never confronted the Virginia but transported troops and equipment during the army's movement from Alexandria, Virginia, to the tip of the peninsula, east of Richmond, which was the Confederate capital.[46]

The Vanderbilt was transferred subsequently to the Navy Department and outfitted for searching for Confederate privateers in the West Indies. In fact, the Vanderbilt sought a grand prize, the Confederate raider CSS Alabama, under Captain Raphael Semmes. As it had been with the Virginia, the duel never occurred. The steamship remained in naval service until 1873.[47]

Vanderbilt's gift of his namesake ship "was an unprecedented act of patriotic charity, worth nearly $1 million," a biographer, T. J. Stiles, argues. Another biographer claims that the commodore only meant it as a gift for the duration of the war. In 1864, Congress thanked him for the "free gift" and awarded him a medal. When he learned of it, he allegedly exclaimed: "Congress be damned. I never gave that ship to Congress. When the Government was in great straits for a suitable vessel of war, I offered to give the ship if they did not care to buy it, however, Mr. Lincoln and Mr. Welles think it was a gift, and I suppose I shall have to let her go." He received his medal two years later.[48]

Stanton, meanwhile, sought the services of Vanderbilt a second time in the fall of 1862. Secret preparations for an expedition, under Major General Nathaniel Banks, to New Orleans were under way. Stanton needed ships and approached the wealthy businessman. Eventually,

Vanderbilt chartered twenty-seven vessels for Banks, but it ignited a scandal.[49]

It was alleged that Vanderbilt chartered ships from his fleet that were "rotten and unfit for ocean duty." One of the steamers, the *Niagara*, had new planking, which concealed rotten timbers underneath. The Senate ordered an investigation that resulted in a motion to censure Vanderbilt. The motion never came up for a vote, and the alleged scandal faded away. Congress determined later that the outfitting of the military operation had been financially sound.[50]

When the war began, the value of Vanderbilt's fleet was estimated at more than $20 million (roughly $545 million today). Ships were the foundation of his wealth from his first periauger. Prior to the conflict, he had directed increasingly more of his investments into railroads. In 1862, Vanderbilt began buying a large amount of shares in the New York & Harlem Railroad. "It is not so big a road," he remarked about the rail line. Twice he had saved it from bankruptcy, and now he was amassing stocks in it.[51]

Vanderbilt kept purchasing stock and, in May 1863, he and his supporters on the railroad's board of directions won control of the line in an election. He accepted the presidency, refusing compensation for the office. Share prices in the railroad soared because it appeared that the New York City Council would grant it exclusive rights to a horse-drawn streetcar line down Broadway from Forty-Second Street to the Battery.[52]

Corrupt members of the council plotted to sell New York & Harlem short, rescind the railroad's streetcar franchise, and then buy in again at a profit as the stock prices plummeted. And so it began on June 25, when orders poured into Wall Street to sell the stock. At four P.M. the council revoked the contract, and shares tumbled from 83¼ to 72½. What the officials at City Hall did not know was that Vanderbilt had plotted to corner the market by buying all the shares on credit. Risks abounded in the bold scheme.[53]

The next day, June 26, the price of shares rose instead of declining, and short-sellers panicked. They sold more shares, and Vanderbilt's brokers bought the offers. Some sellers even borrowed shares with a promise to deliver, seeking to plunge the price down. Unknowingly, the shares belonged to Vanderbilt, who had indeed cornered the market. When the sellers could not deliver the promised stock, they had to pay him a daily interest charge. The price of a share peaked at 106 on June 28.[54]

City Council restored the railroad's streetcar franchise. A biographer of Vanderbilt estimates that he realized a profit of $5 million ($99 million today). Nearly eleven months later, a Cleveland, Ohio, newspaper recounted the Wall Street affair, concluding: "Vanderbilt is the most dangerous man in New York to meet in any moneyed strategy. He always wins, and he scoops up his profits by the hundreds of thousands."[55]

Vanderbilt's machinations continued during the war. In 1863, he also began purchasing shares of the Hudson River Railroad, which ran along the east side of the river from Manhattan to East Albany. A year later, he secured several thousand shares of the New York Central Railroad, from Albany to Buffalo, and supported Erastus Corning for its presidency. The two rail lines agreed on permitting through travel on their tracks. The commodore had maneuvered so effectively that he stood on the verge of controlling one of the country's most important postwar railroads.[56]

After the 1864 presidential election, speculation arose about changes in the cabinet. Newspaper publisher Horace Greeley wrote to Lincoln, recommending Vanderbilt for Treasury secretary. The New York businessman, stated Greeley, "has the largest private fortune in America" and was "thoroughly familiar with Stock Operations." His appointment would assure investors here and in Europe. "He is utterly and notoriously unconnected with any clique, faction, or feud among the Unionists of our state or of any other." Lincoln kept William P. Fessenden, whom he had appointed in July when Salmon P. Chase resigned, in the post.[57]

Cornelius Vanderbilt materially and financially aided the Union war effort. The gift of the *Vanderbilt* was arguably the largest monetary contribution of a single American to the cause. Unquestionably, during the four-year struggle, he was a calculating, intimidating businessman, who added millions in personal wealth. He plied the country's waterways for more than half a century and then, at the age of seventy-one, he sought a larger empire on land.[58]

ON APRIL 30, 1861, COLLIS P. HUNTINGTON GATHERED TOGETHER FELlow Associates, as they called their group, at the Saint Charles Hotel in Sacramento, California. The purpose of the meeting was to organize officially and to elect a board of directors of the Central Pacific Railroad Company. Present were Huntington's storekeeper partner, Mark Hopkins; another storeowner, Charles Crocker; the Republican candidate for governor, Leland Stanford; James Bailey, an importer of watches, clocks, and jewelry; and Theodore D. Judah, an engineer. While they met, news arrived from the East of the attack on Fort Sumter and the beginning of civil war.[59]

Since the discovery of gold, politicians, business leaders, and the military had advocated for a railroad that linked California to the Union. Difficulties with Native American tribes on the Great Plains and in Oregon Territory, the so-called Mormon War, the opening of the silver-rich Comstock Lode in Nevada, and the prospects for trade with Japan and China raised the clamor for such a project. During the 1850s, sectionalism prevented an agreement on the route. If a transcontinental railroad were to be built, it was, noted William T. Sherman in a letter to his congressman brother John, "a work of giants. And Uncle Sam is the only giant I know who can grapple the subject."[60]

Convinced by Judah that a feasible route existed across the Sierra Nevada and a lucrative return on investment, Huntington was the primary booster of the Associates and a railroad company. At the meeting at the Saint Charles Hotel, however, the newly constituted board of directors elected Stanford president and Huntington vice president. The outcome displeased Huntington, who soon represented himself as head of the company. The directors chose Hopkins as treasurer, Bailey as secretary, and Judah as chief engineer.[61]

When news of the organization of the Central Pacific Railroad Company became public, the directors "were laughed at for their hairbrained scheme." A California historian, Hubert Howe Bancroft, writing a few decades later, observed that for so "stupendous and hazardous an enterprise it appears an act of madness or of inspiration. . . . Many said that those Sacramento merchants who had ventured upon it would sink their personal fortunes in the canyons of the Sierra."[62]

Huntington claimed that the Associates had a combined wealth of $159,000. Each director contributed initially $1,500 to the company, or 10 percent down on 150 shares. When efforts to secure more investors failed at first, each member bought an additional 345 shares, for a total personal investment of $13,800. The cost of a railroad across the Sierras had been projected at $100,000 a mile. The Central Pacific Railroad Company needed a "giant."[63]

During the spring and summer of 1861, Judah prepared an extensive and detailed report on the proposed route of the railroad tracks. When the engineer presented his findings to the directors, they ordered him to proceed to the nation's capital "as the accredited agent of the Central Pacific Railroad Company of California, for the purpose of procuring appropriations of land and U.S. bonds from Government, to aid in the construction of this Road." Judah departed for Washington on October 11.[64]

Collis and Elizabeth Huntington followed Judah to the East weeks later, arriving in New York City on Christmas Eve 1861. Before he left California, Huntington and Crocker and governor-elect Stanford had secured a franchise for their railroad company from Nevada's territorial legislature and governor. The Associates now had control of a route on both sides of the Sierras.[65]

Huntington joined Judah in Washington, representing himself as the head of the Central Pacific Railroad Company, with capital of $8.5 million. Although Huntington could assert fairly that he and Judah were the guiding spirits in the company's formation, his claim about the railroad's financial reserve existed only on paper at best. Ahead of him lay the possibility of unimagined wealth, and at such times it was said of Huntington that he could be "as ruthless as a crocodile."[66]

On the surface, engineer Judah did the necessary dirty work with members of Congress. The House of Representatives Select Committee on the Pacific Railroad was chaired by California representative Aaron Sargent, who named Judah its clerk. Judah then managed to be appointed secretary of the Senate Committee on Pacific Railroads, whose chairman was Democratic senator James McDougall of California.[67]

Huntington worked evidently behind the scenes. He surely sought the favor of an old friend from Oneonta, New York, Congressman Richard Frachot, who served on Sargent's committee, and Senator Benjamin Wade of Ohio, a distant relative of his. Whether Huntington authorized it or knew of it, Judah disbursed $66,000 of nominal, not actual, value of Central Pacific stocks to unidentified persons. It would have been highly unlikely that Huntington was unaware or not countenanced in Judah's dealings.[68]

Collis and Elizabeth Huntington returned to California in early April 1862. Judah remained in the capital, working assiduously for passage of Pacific railroad legislation. Debate in both houses of Congress raged at times into the early summer. The Senate approved the measure first, then the House. President Lincoln signed the Pacific Railway Act into law on July 1.[69]

The legislation created complex financial awards of acreage and bonds for the construction of the transcontinental railroad. The Central Pacific, building from the west, was granted a contract, and the act established the Union Pacific to construct tracks from the east. Months later Lincoln designated Omaha, Nebraska, as its eastern terminus.[70]

The Pacific Railway Act awarded the Central Pacific nine million acres of land and $24 million in bonds. Huntington, Stanford, Hopkins, and Crocker formed a separate construction company, the Credit & Finance Corporation, which began construction on January 8, 1863. Final figures conflict, but when the golden spike united the Union Pacific and Central Pacific at Promontory, Utah, on May 10, 1869, the Associates had parlayed an estimated $275,000 into a corporation that would be valued four years later at $135,346,964 ($2.7 billion today). Leland Stanford tapped in the spike symbolically, but history would have been better served had it been Collis P. Huntington, a storekeeper originally from Poverty Hollow.[71]

Epilogue

AWAKENED GIANT

—《Ⅲ》—

ASHINGTONIANS AND VISITORS AROSE TO THE PROMISE OF A bright, warm spring day on Tuesday, May 23, 1865. It had been thirty-eight days since President Abraham Lincoln had died from an assassin's bullet. The tragedy had stunned the nation. Between then and now, "insignia of sorrow," in a diarist's words, had enveloped the capital as black folds of mourning hung from private and public buildings.[1]

On this day, with black replaced by colorful flowers, with flags at full staff, official and unofficial Washington gathered to honor veterans of the Union armies. It had been decided to hold a grand review, to have those who had fought the battles to pass in review before a crowd of grateful fellow citizens. May 23 was for the veterans of the Army of the Potomac, whose officers and men had defeated General Robert E. Lee's redoubtable Confederate Army of Northern Virginia; May 24, for Major General William T. Sherman's Army of the Tennessee and Army of the Cumberland, who had carried the war into the enemy's heartland with its March to the Sea.[2]

Newspapers estimated the throngs from fifty thousand to a hundred thousand spectators on both days. "On the steps of the treasury," reported a correspondent, "on the stoops of houses, on roofs, on balconies, at windows, on stationary carts, on tree tops, telegraph poles and lamp posts, anywhere and everywhere that would raise one above the level, were expectant waiters long before the pageant moved." On the imposing

Capitol, with its finished dome, a huge banner hung, "THE ONLY NA-
TIoNAL DEBT WE CAN NEVER PAY IS THE DEBT TO THE
VICTORIoUS SOLDIERS." Nearby an estimated two thousand school-
children—girls in white dresses, boys in white shirts and black pants—
sang "The Battle Cry of Freedom," "When Johnnie Comes Marching
Home," and "Victory at Last," welcoming the soldiers each day.[3]

For two days, then, May 23 and 24, the victorious armies marched
down Pennsylvania Avenue before the onlookers and past three review-
ing stands in front of the Executive Mansion, where government, military, and diplomatic officials watched. "Hour after hour until it seemed
that the peoples of the earth were marching by" wrote a reporter. It took
six hours or so each day for the two armies to pass in review—eighty
thousand veterans with Meade, sixty-five thousand with Sherman.[4]

"On the whole," wrote Sherman, "the grand review was a splendid
success, and was a fitting conclusion to the campaign and the war." John
Hay thought "no such touching pageant was ever seen." Describing the
two-day review years later, another newspaper offered its perspective: "It
took our peaceful nation, when rudely awakened in 1861, a long time to
learn the whole art of war. But when the lesson had been finally mastered, it was mastered thoroughly."[5]

The real and symbolic passage of 145,000 Union veterans on Pennsylvania Avenue was a powerful manifestation of how Northern society
in four years of civil conflict had "mastered thoroughly" the art of war.
That mastery stretched far to the rear of the marching ranks in the
capital to the cities, villages, and farmland from Maine to Minnesota
and beyond. One society had waged a terrible war against another society. The result, as Walt Whitman stated, a far-flung country had been
"condensed" into a nation and was "ratified" by the blood of hundreds of
thousands of Americans.[6]

⌐∽

THE CIVIL WAR WAS BARELY A YEAR OLD WHEN THE CHICAGO *TRIBUNE*
boasted: "On every street and avenue one sees new building going up:

immense stone, brick, and iron business blocks, marble palaces and new residences everywhere. . . . The unmistakable signs of active, thriving trade are everywhere manifest." Grain elevators and meatpacking houses signified the flow of agricultural wealth into the "queen of the West."[7]

In January 1863, *Scientific American* boasted: "It may well surprise ourselves and all other nations that, during a year of the greatest civil war on record, our country in her productive and commercial interests has been wonderfully prosperous. There has been no commercial suffering and want has been unfelt in the land."[8]

A month later the *American Railroad Journal* proclaimed: "The magnitude of the contest can scarcely be realized by us in the North, because the peculiar horrors of war have never reached our homes and firesides, little have they affected our comforts, or diminished our personal security. Our Northern cities are full of life and activity instead of death and decay; all our material interests appear to be thriving; we hear debt and taxation, but . . . they are scarcely felt beyond the anxiety which attends a perusal of . . . statements of our indebtedness."[9]

Before the year's end, Walt Whitman traveled by train from Washington to New York City and noted what he observed: "It looks anything else but war, everybody well dressed, plenty of money, markets boundless & the best, factories all busy." Had the poet been able to see farther, he would have seen ships laden with grains and meats for export and an ongoing tide of immigrants—about eight hundred thousand during the war—flowing into the North.[10]

In April 1861, as the national flag was lowered at Fort Sumter, few, if any, persons in government or in business, however, foresaw the ensuing struggle's impact on the North's society. Ohio senator John Sherman recalled, "None of us appreciated the magnitude of the contest—the enormous armies demanded and the vast sums required." When Fort Sumter fell and Lincoln called for volunteers, the president also summoned the section's entire population. "For the first time," historian Melinda Lawson writes, "the federal government confronted the need for widespread, protracted support and sacrifice from a voting citizenry."[11]

The resultant, unprecedented mobilization created ultimately a national economy. The federal government's demands for materiel to wage an encompassing struggle fueled the North's capitalist markets and industrial production, which emerged during the 1840s and 1850s. Northern businessmen waged their type of warfare against the Confederacy as surely did the Union's army and naval commanders.[12]

Numbers can reveal, in part, the extent of the conflict's reach into the social and economic fabric of the North. The national government spent $66.5 million in 1860. Two years later, it expended $474.8 million and, in 1865, $1.297 billion. Although precise figures conflict, the cost of the four-year struggle amounted to at least $3.2 billion. By August 1865, the wartime debt had reached $2.8 billion.[13]

This river of federal monies and the military's vast needs vitalized an unimagined degree of productivity and expansion. In Philadelphia, for instance, 180 new factories opened during the conflict's main three years. To the west in Pittsburgh, six iron mills were constructed in one year. Factory workers used machinery increasingly to make goods swiftly and in large amounts. By 1864, the North's overall manufacturing had risen 13 percent from 1861. Iron production had grown 29 percent, and more vessels filled shipyards in unparalleled numbers. The railroads in the North were in better shape than before the war.[14]

During the antebellum decades, Southern politicians derisively called working-class Northerners "mudsills," men trapped in "wage slavery" without the benevolent support of masters. In the war, these same "grubby mechanics" served in Union forces and manned the machines that produced cannon, rifles, accoutrements, uniforms, shoes, and the myriad of goods required by a warring nation. The technology that emerged during the previous decades combined with skilled laborers and created the agricultural and industrial foundation of the Union war effort.[15]

In 1861, however, that foundation remained unbuilt. The North possessed neither the strategy nor the capacity to wage the struggle that awaited, the daunting prospect of conquering the Confederacy. The mobilization of manpower and of resources into an organization or structure that achieved victory after four years of bloodshed was arguably the North's singular achievement. Appomattox resulted from military power and a capitalistic economy.[16]

Yet, Appomattox was not predetermined in 1861. Battles had to be won, popular support had to be sustained in the face of casualties and sacrifices. The Confederate government and military fought a valiant struggle despite the long odds against them. In the summer of 1864, during the war's darkest days, when the landscape seemed awash in blood, Abraham Lincoln's reelection hopes appeared doomed. But the capture of Atlanta, Georgia, and three victorious engagements in the Shenandoah Valley of Virginia within a month changed Northern sentiment toward the administration and brought Lincoln a second term, ensuring that there would be no outcome other than Union victory.[17]

Because of the agricultural and industrial wealth sustaining them, federal troops were able to move the conflict into the interior of the Confederacy, carrying destruction with them. "The American way of war that emerged from the conflict," historians Williamson Murray and Wayne Hsieh argue, "emphasized the logistical and operational projection of military power over continental distances along with a ruthless desire to bring the consequences of secession home to every hamlet in the Confederacy."[18]

These campaigns across hundreds of thousands of square miles of terrain scarred by rivers and tributaries and walled by mountain ranges relied on sinews that linked them to the rich soils of the Midwest and the factories of New England and the Mid-Atlantic. Although the national government interposed its demands and authority on the economy at a historic scale, the Union war effort rested almost entirely upon private enterprises. These businesses managed not only to fill War and Navy department contracts but also to meet civilian demands.[19]

The four-year conflict's impact on the Northern economy generates disagreement, if not controversy, among economists and historians.

Unquestionably, the nation's financial policies and institutions underwent a transformation; wartime profits fed future capital investments,
and Americans' view of the government and of the economy became
more national. Certain industries witnessed accelerated expansion and
consolidation, but an argument remains that the "war years were a period of relative economic stagnation in the North." Inflation rose 75
percent from 1861 to 1864, eroding real wages among workers perhaps
by 25 percent. Nevertheless, by 1865, the merchant economy of the past
was giving way to industrial capitalism. Organization on an unprecedented scale had achieved victory and heralded the future.[20]

SOUTHERN DELEGATES AT SECESSIONIST CONVENTIONS PERHAPS SHOULD
have listened, heeded the warning sounds. They were there in the
North—the blasts of furnaces, the hum of machinery, the singing of
iron rails, the shouts of farmers behind teams of horses and mules, the
whistle of steamships in harbors, the pounding of hammers on lumber,
the daily din of a society at work. But Southerners acted, triggering a
terrible reckoning, and the sounds of the North soon became deafening.

Some of the clang and hiss and voices belonged to a group of tin-
kerers, inventors, organizers, entrepreneurs, patriots, investors, and
visionaries. They might not have been the leading government contractors but definitely contributed to the war effort. They operated railroads,
cast big guns, designed repeating firearms, condensed milk, sawed lumber, cured meat, built warships, purified medicines, forged iron, made
horseshoes, supplied shoes, constructed wagons, and financed a war.[21]

For most of them, however, the four-year conflict proved to be a beginning, not an end. They fit well into the unfolding times. In a letter
to his brother, Major General William T. Sherman, Ohio senator John
Sherman exclaimed: "The truth is, the close of the war with our resources unimpaired gives an elevation, a scope to the ideas of leading
capitalists, far higher than anything ever undertaken in this country
before. They talk of millions as confidently as formerly of thousands."[22]

The passage of Union veterans down Pennsylvania Avenue signaled an ending and a beginning. Behind them lay the terrible reckoning between the North and South; ahead lay a new American age. At war's end, the Gilded Age beckoned when businessmen could talk readily of millions and when the country underwent more profound changes.

The war's scars needed time to heal, but the promise of a new nation awaited. In its unprecedented magnitude, the Civil War transformed America, redefining its ideals, its meaning, and awakening an industrial power. The shambling, uncertain country of 1861 gave way to one of incalculable possibilities, led, in part, by men shaped by the struggle's myriad exigencies. It had truly been a passage whose legacies recast America.

POSTSCRIPT

PHILIP D. ARMOUR MOVED IN 1875 FROM MILWAUKEE TO CHICAGO, where he founded Armour & Company. The meatpacking firm eventually became a family enterprise, with his brothers and sons as partners. Armour established himself as a pioneer in the industry, packing meat in tin cans and manufacturing glue, fertilizer, soap, and pharmaceuticals from animal parts. Like others, he shipped meat in refrigerated railroad cars. Armour and Gustavus Swift came to dominate the industry while they evidently conspired with competitors to divide markets and to fix prices.

A consummate businessman, Armour amassed a fortune from his multifaceted company. He also invested in railroads and banks and speculated and traded in commodity markets. An admirer of his contended that he was "something more than the richest man in Chicago . . . perhaps the greatest trader in the world." During the Panic of 1893, he prevented a major run on the city's banks by offering them gold and cash from his reserve. He donated millions to charities and established the Armour Institute of Technology, today the Illinois Institute of Technology after a 1940 merger of the Armour and Lewis institutes.

Philip Armour died of myocarditis on January 6, 1901, at his home at 2115 Prairie Avenue in Chicago. He was buried beside his son, Philip D. Armour Jr., in Graceland Cemetery. The so-called pork baron had a personal wealth estimated at $60 million (today, $1.75 billion).[1]

Gail Borden was a man undaunted by setbacks. His New York Condensed Milk Company prospered during the Civil War, supplying the

Union soldiers and sailors with its nutritious product. To meet the military's demands, he opened two other factories and licensed a pair of firms. With the war's end, his company had a huge surplus of milk amid the disbanding armies and navy.

Despite the postwar market conditions, Borden established Elgin Milk Condensing Company in Elgin, Illinois, in 1866. That same year, he partnered with Dr. John H. Currie, a New York chemist, to form Borden and Currie, which manufactured a beef extract. Like his meat biscuit, the extract never proved profitable.

During the postwar years, Borden returned frequently to Texas, building a house in the tiny settlement of Harvey's Creek in Colorado County. When his brothers and sons joined him, he renamed the town Borden. (A county northwest of Austin is named for him.)

He died of pneumonia at his home in Borden on January 11, 1874. A private funeral car carried his remains to Woodlawn Cemetery in White Plains, New York. On his tombstone are these words, "I tried and failed, I tried again and again and succeeded." That final success gave America "Eagle Brand."[2]

Henry Burden was seventy-four years old when the last Confederate army surrendered. His sales of horseshoes had risen to $1.3 million during the war's final year. He had taken his sons, James A. and I. Townsend, as partners in 1864, renaming the company H. Burden & Sons.

The Scottish immigrant and engineering genius lived less than six years after the war and died of heart disease on January 19, 1871, at his residence, Woodside, in Troy, New York. Funeral services were held in the Woodside Presbyterian Church, which he had had built, and the burial was in the Albany Rural Cemetery. An obituary in a newspaper asserted, "His name will descend to succeeding generations along with the names of Fulton and Morse, and other benefactors of mankind." The Burden Iron Works remained in the family until 1940.[3]

During the Gilded Age, **Andrew Carnegie** achieved the wealth and power he had sought since his youth. "Carnegie survived and triumphed in an environment rife with cronyism and corruption," in the estimation of biographer David Nasaw, who added that Carnegie was "ruthless" as a businessman.

At the peak of its size and capital in the 1890s, the Carnegie Steel Company was valued at $25 million (today, $15 billion). When his company sold out to the United States Steel Corporation in March 1901, Carnegie's share amounted to $226 million (today, $187 billion), making him likely the richest man in the world at the time.

Vilified in public as a "robber baron," Carnegie became the most generous philanthropist in the country, giving money for music halls, libraries, church organs, and educational programs, notably the Carnegie Institute in Pittsburgh. He considered Carnegie Hall an investment, not philanthropy.

Author of his autobiography and "The Gospel of Wealth," Andrew Carnegie died at a residence, Shadowbrook, near Lenox, Massachusetts, on August 11, 1919, at the age of eighty-three. The family held a small, private funeral for him, with burial in Sleepy Hollow Cemetery in White Plains, New York. He had given away $350 million (today, $180 billion) of his wealth.[4]

Jay Cooke emerged from the Civil War as the most famous banker in America. Jay Cooke & Company had earned a reputation for trustworthiness with its marketing of government bonds. Seeking new investment opportunities, Cooke signed a contract with the Northern Pacific Railroad to sell $100 million worth of its company's stock. The Philadelphia banker guaranteed $5 million.

The Northern Pacific's only asset was an immense land grant from Minnesota to Washington Territory. Sale of its bonds proved difficult. When Lakota Indians resisted railroad surveyors and the army through its lands, and Congress refused to guarantee the railroad's bonds, investors deserted the Northern Pacific. Cooke could not prevent the collapse and, on September 18, 1873, branches of Jay Cooke & Company suddenly closed, precipitating a banking crisis and the Panic of 1873. "The crash came like a thunderbolt from a clear sky," reported a newspaper.

Cooke repaid his creditors, and an investment in a Utah silver mine made him wealthy again. During his final years, he disappeared from public view, living with a daughter. He died on February 18, 1905, and was buried in Saint Paul's Episcopal Churchyard, Elkins Park, Pennsylvania. A devout Christian, he gave generously to his church and charities. His legacy remains in the democratic sale of government bonds.[5]

John Deere ceded daily management of his farm machinery company to his son Charles in 1858. Ten years later, Charles incorporated the firm, Deere & Company, granting his father a quarter of the shares and the titular post of president.

For the two decades after the Civil War, John Deere raised cattle and hogs on his farm east of Moline, Illinois, served as mayor of the city for a year, contributed to various charities, and invested money in small local businesses.

Deere died at his residence, Red Cliff, on May 17, 1886, at the age of eighty-two. "Probably no other funeral in Moline was ever attended by so many people or drew forth the public evidence of mourning," recalled a resident. A crowd of some four thousand folks paid respects as he was buried at Riverside Cemetery.[6]

After the Civil War, **James B. Eads** devoted his engineering talents to two major projects, bridging the Mississippi River and building a passage from the Atlantic to the Pacific. Though his efforts to construct a ship-and-railway route across Mexico were never realized, the Saint Louis or Eads Bridge still stands.

It took seven years, 1867–1874, from Eads's initial design to finish construction of the 6,442-foot steel span across the Mississippi River. Eads pioneered pneumatic caissons and cantilevered support methods. Major investors in the project included Andrew Carnegie, J. Edgar Thomson, and Thomas A. Scott. When finished, the bridge cost $10 million (today, more than $200 million). The Eads Bridge is on the National Registry of Historic Places.

His project for a ship-railway across Mexico never received congressional funding. In 1876, the editors of *Scientific American* had urged Eads to seek the presidency of the United States, calling him "a man of genius, of industry, and of incorruptible honor." In frail health, the world-renowned engineer traveled to Nassau in the Bahamas, where he died on March 8, 1887. His remains were returned to Saint Louis, with interment in Bellefontaine Cemetery.[7]

Abram S. Hewitt combined a career in business and in politics during the postwar years. He and Edward Cooper continued to manage the Trenton Iron Company, but Hewitt founded the New Jersey Steel & Iron Company to produce steel rails for railroads. He built the first open hearth furnace in America, which came to dominate the steelmaking process in the country.

A Jacksonian Democrat like his father-in-law, Peter Cooper, Hewitt was elected to Congress from the Tenth District in New York in 1874. He served six terms, highlighted by his efforts on behalf of Samuel Tilden in the disputed presidential election of 1876. In 1886, he ran for and was elected mayor of New York City. His administration was marked by honesty and organization. In August 1888, a newspaper claimed, "He is now the most popular mayor New York ever had." That fall, in a three-man race, Hewitt suffered defeat to a Tammany Hall candidate.

Hewitt devoted his final years to business interests, a pair of cattle companies, direction of Cooper Union, his beloved city, and philanthropy. He died of "obstructive jaundice" in his home on Lexington Avenue on January 18, 1903. Once called "New York's Grand Old Man," he was buried in the Cooper family plot in Greenwood Cemetery in Brooklyn. Among his nineteen pallbearers were Andrew Carnegie, J. P. Morgan, and William Dodge.[8]

Collis P. Huntington epitomized the vilified robber barons of the Gilded Age. A magazine of the era said of him: "He had a genius for money-making and could have earned a large fortune honestly had he chosen to be honest. . . . He did make a great deal of money honestly, but he stole more. Collis P. Huntington was a thief. That is the truth about him."

Huntington and his Associates did reap fortunes from their investments in the Central Pacific and Southern Pacific railroads. They bribed legislators, planted favorable newspaper stories, selected political candidates, influenced judges, and manipulated stock prices. Other rail-road owners and businessmen of the times adopted similar tactics. In time, the Associates controlled the railroad network in the southwest-ern and western states.

Collis Huntington died at his summer camp, Pine Knot, in the Adirondack Mountains of New York on August 13, 1900. He lost con-sciousness during a choking spell and never awoke. He was buried in Woodlawn Cemetery in New York City. The value of his estate was estimated at $100 million, or nearly $30 billion today. In an obituary a newspaper declared: "A man's success should be measured by the returns it brings to the world at large. Gauged by that standard Collis P. Hun-tington's life was a miserable failure."[9]

Cyrus McCormick entangled himself in a web of business inter-ests, Democratic politics, religious controversies, and legal feuds during the postwar years. While the farm machinery business and real estate holdings provided the foundation of his wealth, the native Virginian invested in railroads and mines in the decades after the conflict.

McCormick was a major stockholder and member of the board of directors of the Credit Mobilier Company, the firm that constructed the Union Pacific Railroad. Like other investors, he earned large profits with the company but managed to be spared when its scandalous actions be-came public. He owned stock in several other rail companies and silver and gold mines in the western United States and Central America.

The Great Chicago Fire of 1871 destroyed his factory and two thou-sand reapers. Seeing it as an opportunity, he and his brother Leland built a larger, more modern plant and resumed production a year later. The McCormick brothers succeeded in marketing their machinery in Europe while suing American competitors for patent infringements.

A devout Presbyterian and firm Democrat, McCormick involved himself in church controversies and local and national politics. He died at his residence from infirmities of old age on May 13, 1884, and was buried in Graceland Cemetery in Chicago. The man who fostered a revolution in farming was seventy-five years old.[10]

Gordon McKay revolutionized the shoemaking industry even further after the Civil War. He, with other inventors, obtained some forty patents for machinery related to the manufacture of shoes. He founded the McKay Sewing Machine Association, which leased his machines, and received a royalty on each pair of shoes.

By the late 1870s, McKay's machines were producing one-half of the nation's shoes, or 120 million pairs, yielding a royalty of $500,000. By 1881, the royalties exceeded $1 million annually. McKay augmented his income with profits from a Montana gold mine.

This inventive genius's final years were tarnished by a personal scandal. A widower, he married his housekeeper's twenty-one-year-old daughter, who had two children during the marriage. But later, in divorce proceedings, McKay charged his wife with infidelity and disowned the paternity of the children. When she married a German baron, he inexplicably gave her a $1 million wedding present.

Gordon McKay died at his "palatial home" in Newport, Rhode Island, on October 19, 1903, and was buried in the Pittsfield Cemetery in his hometown in Massachusetts. He willed the majority of his estate to Harvard University, where it endows forty engineering scholarships and fellowships today.[11]

Robert P. Parrott resigned the superintendency of the West Point Foundry in 1867 after a tenure of thirty-one years. Three years later he bought the shares in the foundry of Gouverneur and William Kemble for $80,000, becoming the "sole proprietor."

Parrott continued experiments in artillery and engines in the foundry's workshop. The inventor of his namesake cannon died on December 24, 1877, at the age of seventy-three. In his will, he bequeathed the firm to his nephews, who formed Pauling, Kemble & Company. The West Point Foundry remained in business until 1911. Robert P. Parrott was interred in Cold Spring Cemetery, Cold Spring, New York.[12]

Thomas A. Scott engaged in a different type of warfare in the years after the Civil War. Under his and J. Edgar Thomson's management, the Pennsylvania Railroad was widely regarded as the country's best railroad, with its tracks extending as far west as the Mississippi River and south to the Gulf of Mexico. Its capitalization exceeded $116 million in 1874.

When Thomson died in 1874, the company's stockholders elected Scott as president. At that time, however, he had also taken over the Texas and Pacific Railroad Company, which had plans to build a line from Louisiana to California along the country's southern border. For most of the 1870s, Scott fought against Collis P. Huntington and the Associates' Southern Pacific Railroad for congressional subsidies. At one point, Scott had two hundred lobbyists at work on convincing members of Congress.

Scott abandoned the struggle against the Associates in 1879, admitting defeat. He lived only two more years and died at the age of fifty-eight in his residence outside of Darby, Pennsylvania, on May 21, 1881. His death was attributed to "paralysis" likely caused by a cerebral hemorrhage. Perhaps the finest railroad executive of the era was buried in Woodlands Cemetery in Philadelphia.[13]

Christopher M. Spencer once told his daughter that when he had an idea for a new invention he "wanted to get it down on paper." For nearly six full decades after Appomattox, the American inventor of a repeating rifle continued to get things down on paper.

Spencer received forty-two patents in his lifetime for improvements in firearms, drop forging, textile manufacturing, and screw making. His most important contribution to automation in American industry came in 1873 with an automatic screw machine, which revolutionized screw making. A professor at the time called it one of the "great epoch making improvements in machine construction."

Unfortunately, his inventions never brought him wealth, and the companies he started rarely made a profit. Before he died, Spencer told his family, "I'd always hoped to leave you money, but the best I can say is I don't think I am leaving any enemies." The Connecticut Yankee died at his son's home in Hartford on January 14, 1922, at the age of eighty-nine. He is buried in Palisalo Cemetery, Windsor, Connecticut.[14]

Edward Squibb continued his life's work on the purification of drugs and on the improvement in medical procedures. He was both a pharmacist and a physician, experimenting with pharmaceuticals in his laboratory and serving as anesthetist in operating rooms.

While his Brooklyn laboratory struggled financially until the 1880s, Squibb worked tirelessly on refining chloroform and ether and on testing other drugs, from curare to morphine. He presented lectures, assisted in the revision of the US Pharmacopoeia, and self-published a magazine on various aspects of the drug industry. For half a century, he fought against adulterated pharmaceuticals and medical charlatans.

In 1892, he entered into a partnership with his sons, Edward H. and Charles F., renaming his business E. R. Squibb and Sons. He remained active in the laboratory until his passing at the age of eighty-one on the evening of October 25, 1900, in his home at 152 Columbia Heights, Brooklyn. He died of "cardiac dyspacea, due to occlusion of the coronary artery." He was buried in Greenwood Cemetery in Brooklyn. He left an estate estimated at $1 million, and a legacy, according to a fellow scientist, of "standards of purity for pharmaceutical products [that] were the highest attainable."[15]

Clement, John Mohler, and Peter Studebaker formed the Studebaker Brothers Manufacturing Company in March 1868. Each brother invested $25,000, borrowing money on personal notes. The oldest, Clement, served as president; John Mohler, treasurer; and Peter, secretary.

From its formation, the corporation prospered. Within three years, sales exceeded $600,000 annually, with a dividend of $107,000. A devastating fire at the factory in June 1872 nearly closed the business, and the Panic of 1873 reduced profits. The brothers advertised themselves as the "largest vehicle builders in the world." In 1896, the board of directors, over the opposition of Clement and John Mohler, invested $4,000 for the testing and building of a "horseless vehicle." Of the several thousand wagonmakers during the Civil War, only the Studebakers manufactured automobiles.

A fourth brother, Jacob, joined the company in 1870 and was the first to pass, dying on December 17, 1889, at the age of forty-two. Peter followed, suffering a heart attack on October 9, 1897, at the age of sixty-one. Clement suffered from unspecified illnesses for some time. He traveled to Europe for health reasons but, upon his return, collapsed and died on November 27, 1901. He was seventy years old. John Mohler succumbed to leukemia on March 16, 1917, at the age of eight-three. Jacob and Peter are buried in City Cemetery; Clement and John Mohler, in Riverview, South Bend, Indiana.[16]

J. Edgar Thomson remained as president of the Pennsylvania Railroad, overseeing its expansion and domination of the industry from the Atlantic Coast to the Mississippi River. A prudent businessman, he adopted measures that improved the company's performance and profitability. He lacked, however, the avarice that characterized other railroad barons of the era.

He was ill much of the time during his final years with the company and suffered several heart attacks. Thomson died on the night of May 27, 1874, "after a protracted illness," at the age of sixty-six. He bequeathed much of his wealth to the establishment of Saint John's Orphanage in Philadelphia. He was buried in Woodlands Cemetery in the city.[17]

Cornelius Vanderbilt strode across the postwar years like the business giant he had become. During the Civil War, he had begun crafting a railroad empire, but in the conflict's aftermath he consolidated it into a railroad system worth $90 million (today, $2 billion).

The New York Central Railroad system controlled rail traffic from New York City, along the shores of the Great Lakes, to Chicago. Vanderbilt acquired lines in Ohio, Indiana, and Illinois, and integrated them into the New York Central. He fought a public stockholders war with Daniel Drew and Jay Gould of the Erie Railroad that cost both parties money.

No industrialist or businessman of the 1870s rivaled Vanderbilt in his wealth and influence. The "Commodore" died from peritonitis, caused by a perforated colon, in his Manhattan residence on January 14, 1877, at the age of eighty-three years. A ferry, which he had created, carried his casket across the harbor to the Vanderbilt Mausoleum in New Dorp on Staten Island. He left his fortune in railroad and other securities, valued at $94 million at the time, to his son William.[18]

Frederick Weyerhaeuser fashioned an interlocking conglomerate of timber and lumber companies into "the second largest individual manufacturing industry in the United States." And as the newspaper reported, "There were very few people outside of the lumber trade who had ever heard of the man."

Weyerhaeuser and his partner and brother-in-law, Frederick Denkmann, organized or joined nearly fifty associations and corporations in the four decades after the Civil War. Their ownership of vast forests of timber extended from Wisconsin and Minnesota to the Pacific Northwest. At one point, Weyerhaeuser controlled twenty of the largest sawmills in the country, which were capable of producing seven million feet of sawed lumber daily.

The Weyerhaeuser Timber Company eventually formed the major firm in his timber empire. A hometown newspaper in Rock Island, Illinois, claimed that the German immigrant's achievements made him "the leading representative of the lumber trade in the United States and of the world." Frederick Weyerhaeuser died of pneumonia at his vacation home in Pasadena, California, on April 4, 1914, at the age of seventy-nine. He was buried in the Chippiannock Cemetery in Rock Island. He left behind an estate reportedly worth more than $500 million, or $12 billion today.[19]

ABBREVIATIONS

—ꝳ—

Works cited by the author and short titles are found in full in the bibliography. The following abbreviations are used in the notes.

AHEC   Army Heritage Education Center

B&L   *Battles and Leaders of the Civil War*

DU   Duke University

HBS   Harvard Business School

HSP   Historical Society of Pennsylvania

HSWP   Historical Society of Western Pennsylvania

LC   Library of Congress

MHM   Missouri History Museum

MNHS   Minnesota Historical Society

MNMP   Manassas National Battlefield Park

NC   Navarro College

NJSA   New Jersey State Archives

NMCWM   National Museum of Civil War Medicine

NYHS   New-York Historical Society

OR   US War Department, *War of the Rebellion: A Compilation of the Official Records of the Union and Confederate Armies*

PHM   Putnam History Museum

RBHPC   Rutherford B. Hayes Presidential Center

UM   University of Michigan

UME   University of Maine
WHS   Windsor Historical Society
WIHS   Wisconsin Historical Society
WWQR   *Walt Whitman Quarterly Review*

NOTES

---ᛗ---

Prologue

1. Laugel, *United States*, xxv, 38.
2. Frank L. Lemont to My Dear Mother, July 8, 1861, Lemont Letters, UME; Julius A. Murray to John, July 25, 1861, Murray Family Papers, WHS.
3. Laugel, *United States*, xxxvii, xo, 38, 179.
4. Ibid., xxvii, xxxix, xl.
5. Ibid., 122, 123; Nevins, *War*, 1:243n.
6. Laugel, *United States*, 168.
7. McPherson, *Battle Cry*, 6, 11–13.
8. Paludan, *"People's Contest,"* xxii, 106; Nevins, *War*, 1:247; Army, *Engineering Victory*, 54.
9. White, *Railroaded*, xxii; Chandler, *Visible Hand*, 14; Paludan, *"People's Contest,"* xxii; McPherson, *Battle Cry*, 14–15, 18–20.
10. Paludan, *"People's Contest,"* 152, 153, 161; Gates, *Agriculture and the Civil War*, 129, 132; Nevins, *War*, 3:218; Cronon, *Nature's Metropolis*, 228; Burlingame, *Lincoln's Journalist*, 27.
11. Paludan, *"People's Contest,"* xxii; Pittsburgh *Gazette*, July 28, 1862.
12. Paludan, *"People's Contest,"* 105, 106.
13. Huston, *Sinews*, 176, 177; Wilson, *Business*, 91, 92, 123; Nevins, *War*, 1:256; 3:251–256; Chandler, *Visible Hand*, 14.
14. Winik, *April 1865*, 379; Koistinen, *Beating Plowshares*, 76–78; Murray and Hsieh, *Savage War*, 48; Hacker, *Astride*, 48.
15. Paludan, *"People's Contest,"* xxxiii; Summers, *Plundering Generation*, 7, 14, 90, 151; McPherson, *Battle Cry*, 190.
16. Paludan, *"People's Contest,"* 13, 62; Laugel, *United States*, 179.
17. Winik, *April 1865*, 372.
18. Davis, *Look Away!* 9; McPherson, *Battle Cry*, 39.
19. McPherson, *Battle Cry*, 39, 40, 100.
20. Ibid., 9, 10, 100; Davis, *Look Away!* 9.
21. Davis, *Look Away!* 9, 10; McPherson, *Battle Cry*, 129, 232.
22. Davis, *Look Away!* 9–11; McPherson, *Battle Cry*, chaps. 4–7.

23. McPherson, *Battle Cry*, 231, 232; Davis, *Look Away!* 26.

24. Nevins, *War*, 1:243.

25. Murray and Hsieh, *Savage War*, 36.

Chapter One

1. Nevins, *Diary*, 127, 135; Goodheart, *1861*, 180.

2. Wert, *Brotherhood*, 5.

3. Goodheart, *1861*, 181; *B&L*, 1:84; James B. Flynn to most affectionate Parents, May 5, June 4, 1861, Flynn Papers, NC.

4. Horace Emerson to Brother, April 24, 1861, Emerson Letters, UM; William G. Davis to Parents, July 10, 1861, Davis Letters, MNMP.

5. Joseph B. Laughton to Father & Mother, July 10, 1861, Laughton Papers, DU.

6. Sears, *Lincoln's Lieutenants*, 37.

7. Wert, *Sword*, 6; Henry L. Martin, pseudonym "D. L. Dalton," to Jefferson Davis, June 29, 1861, Martin Letter, AHEC; James B. Flynn to affectionate Parents, May 18, 22, 1861, Flynn Papers, NC.

8. Nevins, *War*, 1:240; Staudemaus, *Mr. Lincoln's Washington*, 251; Stoddard, *Inside*, 15; Wert, *Sword*, 14.

9. Wert, *Sword*, 14.

10. Ibid., 14, 15.

11. Furgurson, *Freedom Rising*, 12; Leech, *Reveille*, 5, 6; Huston, *Sinews*, 168.

12. Winik, *April 1865*, 384, 385; Seymour *Tribune*, May 28, 1909; Goodheart, *1861*, 274.

13. Riddle, *Recollections*, 7–9.

14. Goodheart, *1861*, 274; Winik, *April 1865*, 386; Furgurson, *Freedom Rising*, 45.

15. Furgurson, *Freedom Rising*, 14, 15.

16. Quoted in Wert, *Sword*, 6.

17. Ibid.; John H. Burrill to Parents, July 5, 1861, Burrill Letters and Diary, AHEC.

18. Clark, *Railroads in the Civil War*, 31; Goodheart, *1861*, 194, 195.

19. Burlingame, *At Lincoln's Side*, 117; Burlingame, *Lincoln's Journalist*, 58.

20. Huston, *Sinews*, 168; Koistinen, *Beating Plowshares*, 134; Leech, *Reveille*, 5, 124, 379.

21. Wert, *Sword*, 7.

22. Ibid.; Army, *Engineering Victory*, 12, 72.

23. Wert, *Sword*, 7.

24. Ibid., 20–28; Furgurson, *Freedom Rising*, 80.

25. Army, *Engineering Victory*, 5, 6, 12; Wert, *Sword*, 20.

26. Murray and Hsieh, *Savage War*, 38–48; Koistinen, *Beating Plowshares*, 102, 131, 132.

27. Goodheart, *1861*, 275; Murray and Hsieh, *Savage War*, 40.

28. Sears, *Lincoln's Lieutenants*, 35.

29. Riddle, *Recollections*, 18.

30. Wilson, "Business," 1:139, 143; Huston, *Sinews*, 163; Nevins, *War*, 1:241; Murray and Hsieh, *Savage War*, 8; Koistinen, *Beating Plowshares*, 104.

31. Risch, *Quartermaster Support*, 339–341; O'Harrow, *Quartermaster*, 125, 126.

32. Riddle, *Recollections*, 179; Goodwin, *Team of Rivals*, 217, 246.

33. Riddle, *Recollections*, 179, 180.

34. Burlingame, *With Lincoln*, 59.

35. Burlingame, *Lincoln's Journalist*, 189, 196; Welles, *Diary*, 1:134.

36. Risch, *Quartermaster Support*, 340, 341; Wilson, *Business*, 24; O'Harrow, *Quartermaster*, 125, 126.

37. O'Harrow, *Quartermaster*, 105–110; Abraham Lincoln to My dear Sir, June 5, 1861, Lincoln Papers, LC.

38. O'Harrow, *Quartermaster*, 5, 7, 12, 116; quote in Furgurson, *Freedom Rising*, 52, 53; Welles, Diary, 62.

39. O'Harrow, *Quartermaster*, chaps. 4, 5, 8.

40. Huston, *Sinews*, 163; quote in Nevins, *War*, 2:473–475.

41. Wilson, *Business*, 6, 26, 27; Risch, *Quartermaster Support*, 348, 350; Huston, *Sinews*, 184.

42. Nevins, *War*, 2:472; Wilson, *Business*, 2, 35; Hattaway and Jones, *How the North Won*, 139; McPherson, *Battle Cry*, 325; Gallman, *Northerners at War*, 123.

43. Wilson, *Business*, 2, 73; O'Harrow, *Quartermaster*, 132, 134, 135; Koistinen, *Beating Plowshares*, 102; Hattaway and Jones, *How the North Won*, 139.

44. Hess, *Civil War Logistics*, 19.

45. Ibid., 21; O'Harrow, *Quartermaster*, 132.

46. Wilson, *Business*, 2, 35; O'Harrow, *Quartermaster*, 135.

47. Nevins, *Diary*, 173.

48. Nevins, *War*, 2:471; McPherson, *Battle Cry*, 325; Hattaway and Jones, *How the North Won*, 138.

49. Burlingame, *Lincoln's Journalist*, xvi, 167.

50. Ibid., 168.

51. Koistinen, *Beating Plowshares*, 103; Gallman, *Northerners at War*, 89; Nevins, *War*, 3:331; Goldfield, *America Aflame*, 302.

52. Paludan, *"People's Contest,"* 376; Army, *Engineering Victory*, 5, 6; Nevins, *War*, 3:331.

53. Huston, *Sinews*, 163; Hathaway and Jones, *How the North Won*, 138; McPherson, *Battle Cry*, 325.

54. Wert, *Brotherhood*, 54.

55. Wilson, *Business*, 1.

56. Army, *Engineering Victory*, 5, 39; Paludan, *"People's Contest,"* 376; Klein, *Change Makers*, xiv; Clark, *Railroads in the Civil War*, 6.

57. Klein, *Change Makers*, xii, 63, 103, 124; Paludan, *"People's Contest,"* 376; Nevins, *War*, 1:245; Ward, *That Man Haupt*, xiv.

Chapter Two

1. Ward, *J. Edgar Thomson*, 99; Altoona *Tribune*, February 3, 1954; Woods, "Up and Down," 1.

2. Altoona *Tribune*, February 3, 1954; Ward, *That Man Haupt*, 22; McIlhenny, "Early History," 28; Ward, *J. Edgar Thomson*, 99.

3. Ashmead, *History*, 727, 728; Delaware County *Daily Times*, February 22, 1964; Schotter, *Growth*, 33.

4. Ashmead, *History*, 727, 728; Delaware County *Daily Times*, February 22, 1964; Schotter, *Growth*, 33.

5. Ward, *J. Edgar Thomson*, 15, 16, 19, 26; Atlanta *Constitution*, April 12, 1907.

6. Ward, *J. Edgar Thomson*, 67; Ashmead, *History*, 728; Roberts, *Triumph I*, 60, 392; Woods, "Up and Down," 2; McIlhenny, "Early History," 24, 25.

7. Ashmead, *History*, 197, 728; McIlhenny, "Early History," 28; Ward, *That Man Haupt*, 22.

8. McIlhenny, "Early History," 25, 26; Roberts, *Triumph I*, 34; Schotter, *Growth*, 3, 4.

9. Altoona *Tribune*, February 3, 1954; Woods, "Up and Down," 2, 3; Ward, *J. Edgar Thomson*, 99; Philadelphia *Times*, April 14, 1896.

10. Ward, *J. Edgar Thomson*, 72, 78, 79, 90.

11. Ibid., 96; Ward, *That Man Haupt*, 25.

12. Ward, *J. Edgar Thomson*, 3.

13. Ibid., 6; Ward, *That Man Haupt*, 25; Ashmead, *History*, 729.

14. Ward, *J. Edgar Thomson*, 4–6, 10; Ashmead, *History*, 729.

15. Schotter, *Growth*, 7, 38, 39; Burgess and Kennedy, *Centennial History*, 66; Ward, *J. Edgar Thomson*, 104, 105, 134, 135; Baltimore *Sun*, January 8, 1858; *Dawson's Fort Wayne Daily Times*, March 2, 1860.

16. Ward, *J. Edgar Thomson*, 97; Nevins, *War*, 2:502; Ward, *That Man Haupt*, 25.

17. J. Edgar Thomson to Sir, January 4, 1854, Covode Papers, HSWP; Ward, *J. Edgar Thomson*, 113.

18. Ward, *J. Edgar Thomson*, 113–116.

19. Ashmead, *History*, 729; Ward, *That Man Haupt*, 25, 53.

20. Ward, *J. Edgar Thomson*, 120, 121; Louisville *Daily Courier*, January 29, 1859.

21. Riddle, *Recollections*, 180.

22. Nasaw, *Andrew Carnegie*, 69; *OR*, 2:603, 606, all series 1 unless otherwise designated; Kamm, "Civil War Career," 3; White, *Railroaded*, 3.

23. Kamm, "Civil War Career," 3, 4; Pittsburgh *Daily Commercial*, June 6, 1874; Clearfield *Republican*, June 1, 1881; White, *Railroaded*, 4.

24. Kamm, "Civil War Career," 2, 5; Pittsburgh *Daily Commercial*, June 6, 1874; Nasaw, *Andrew Carnegie*, 55, 56.

25. Ward, J. *Edgar Thomson*, 115, 116; White, *Railroaded*, 4; Kamm, "Civil War Career," 11, 13, 14.

26. Kamm, "Civil War Career," 13, 15, 18; White, *Railroaded*, 4, 5.

27. Nevins, *War*, 1:247, 2:501; Kamm, "Civil War Career," 23.

28. Ward, J. *Edgar Thomson*, 125; OR, 2:606.

29. Ward, J. *Edgar Thomson*, 126; Clark, *Railroads*, 18; Adams *Sentinel*, April 24, 1861.

30. McPherson, *Battle Cry*, 324; Ward, J. *Edgar Thomson*, 127; Nasaw, *Andrew Carnegie*, 71, 72; OR, 2:598.

31. Weigley, *Great Civil War*, 38, 39; OR, 2:597, 598, 601; Adams *Sentinel*, April 24, 1861; Nasaw, *Andrew Carnegie*, 69–72.

32. Pittsburgh *Daily Commercial*, June 6, 1874; Pittsburgh *Gazette*, April 14, 1896; Sipes, *Pennsylvania Railroad*, 14, 15; Schotter, *Growth*, 54, 55.

33. Herman Haupt to [John Covode], fragment of an April 1861 letter, Covode Papers, HSWP.

34. OR, series 3, 1:338.

35. Ibid., 325, 326; Clark, *Railroads*, 35; Whitten, *Emergence*, 16.

36. OR, series 3, 1:964; Schotter, *Growth*, 55; Basler, *Collected Works*, 4:471n.

37. Basler, *Collected Works*, 6:493n; OR, 10, pt. 2:243; Goodwin, *Team of Rivals*, 403.

38. Goodwin, *Team of Rivals*, 404, 405, 410–412.

39. Staudemaus, *Mr. Lincoln's Washington*, 62; Haupt, *Reminiscences*, 301.

40. Welles, *Diary*, 1:57, 67, 68; Riddle, *Recollections*, 317, 318.

41. Clark, *Railroads*, 62, 63; Huston, *Sinews*, 169; Hattaway and Jones, *How the North Won*, 120; Haupt, *Reminiscences*, xxix.

42. OR, 11, pt. 3:21, 28, 43; Huston, *Sinews*, 169; Wert, *Sword*, 65, 66.

43. OR, 10, pt. 2:10, 20, 171; series 3, 3, pt. 1:875–877; Basler, *Collected Works*, 6:493n; Kamm, "Civil War Career," 189; Clark, *Railroads*, 154; Indiana *Weekly Messenger*, April 12, 1862.

44. Thomas A. Scott to My dear fr, June 2, 1862, Lincoln Papers, LC.

45. OR, 19, pt. 2:209, 230, 250; Kamm, "Civil War Career," 141; Wert, *Sword*, 146.

46. OR, 27, pt. 3:66, 111, 134, 264, 391, 435, 553.

47. Ibid., 30, pt. 3:175, 871; Wert, *Sword*, 314, 315.

48. OR, 30, pt. 3:142–143, 175, 334, 360, 434; Basler, *Collected Works*, 6:493; Clearfield *Republican*, June 1, 1881.

49. Burgess and Kennedy, *Centennial History*, vi; Ward, J. *Edgar Thomson*, 132.

50. Ward, J. *Edgar Thomson*, 128, 129, 132; Clearfield *Republican*, June 1, 1881.

51. Ward, J. *Edgar Thomson*, 132; Clearfield *Republican*, June 1, 1881; Wilson, *History*, 1:416.

52. Schotter, *Growth*, 50, 52, 59, 60, 62; Sipes, *Pennsylvania Railroad*, 17; Ward, J. *Edgar Thomson*, 117; Lewisburg *Chronicle*, March 3, 1863; Philadelphia *Times*, April 14, 1896.

53. Wilson, *History*, 1:411, 412; Ward, J. *Edgar Thomson*, 130, 131, 133, 134.

54. Reading *Times*, August 15, 1871; Philadelphia *Times*, March 22, 1896; Hubbard, *Little Journeys*, 274; White, *Railroaded*, 4.

55. Reprinted in Reading *Times*, August 15, 1871; Ward, J. *Edgar Thomson*, 6.

56. Chandler, *Visible Hand*, 179; Ward, J. *Edgar Thomson*, xiv.

57. Ward, J. *Edgar Thomson*, 87; White, *Railroaded*, 3; Burgess and Kennedy, *Centennial History*, vi; Army, *Engineering Victory*, 300.

Chapter Three

1. Sandusky *Star-Journal*, November 28, 1901; Oberholtzer, *Jay Cooke*, 1:69, 71.

2. Sandusky *Star-Journal*, November 28, 1901.

3. Oberholtzer, *Jay Cooke*, 1:8, 28; Popowski, "Granddaddy," 29.

4. Cooke Memoir, 2, 6, Cooke Records, HBS; Oberholtzer, *Jay Cooke*, 1:1, 2, 4; Kirtland, *Family History*, 21; Louisville *Courier-Journal*, August 24, 1896; Sandusky *Register*, November 24, 1947.

5. Oberholtzer, *Jay Cooke*, 1:13, 29, 32, 33, 39; Sandusky *Register*, November 24, 1947.

6. Cooke Memoir, 18, 19, Cooke Records, HBS; Oberholtzer, *Jay Cooke*, 1:40–43; Sandusky *Register*, November 24, 1947.

7. Cooke Memoir, 20, Cooke Records, HBS; Popowski, "Granddaddy," 29; Oberholtzer, *Jay Cooke*, 1:52, 57.

8. Cooke Memoir, 29, Cooke Records, HBS; Sandusky *Register*, November 24, 1947; Popowski, "Granddaddy," 29; Oberholtzer, *Jay Cooke*, 1:81, 82.

9. Cooke Memoir, 21, Cooke Records, HBS; Oberholtzer, *Jay Cooke*, 1:83, 86, 87; Sandusky *Register*, November 24, 1947; Popowski "Granddaddy," 30.

10. Oberholtzer, *Jay Cooke*, 1:78; Josephson, *Robber Barons*, 36.

11. Cooke Memoir, 22, Cooke Records, HBS; Oberholtzer, *Jay Cooke*, 1:103.

12. White, *Railroaded*, 9; Cooke Memoir, 23, Cooke Records, HBS; Gallipolis *Journal*, January 8, 1863.

13. Cooke Memoir, 23, Cooke Records, HBS; Oberholtzer, *Jay Cooke*, 1:99, 100, 102.

14. Oberholtzer, *Jay Cooke*, 1:103, 104; Perrysburg *Journal*, August 22, 1865; Cooke Memoir, 36, 37, Cooke Records, HBS.

15. Oberholtzer, *Jay Cooke*, 1:106; Sandusky *Register*, November 24, 1947; Belmont *Chronicle*, May 25, 1865; Cooke Memoir, 10, 11, 37, Cooke Records, HBS.

16. Cooke Memoir, 37, Cooke Records, HBS; Belmont *Chronicle,* May 25, 1865; Josephson, *Robber Barons,* 55.

17. Koistinen, *Beating Plowshares,* 178; Oberholtzer, *Jay Cooke,* 1:128; Welles, *Diary,* 1:139.

18. Donald, *Lincoln,* 264; Staudemaus, *Mr. Lincoln's Washington,* 61, 176.

19. Sherman, *John Sherman's Recollections,* 1:251, 253, 254; Oberholtzer, *Jay Cooke,* 1:133; Paludan, *"People's Contest,"* 108.

20. Welles, *Diary,* 1:168; Lawson, *Patriot Fires,* 42; Oberholtzer, *Jay Cooke,* 1:133.

21. Oberholtzer, *Jay Cooke,* 1:92; Popowski, "Granddaddy," 30; Weigley, *Great Civil War,* 208; Kirtland, *Family History,* 21.

22. Cooke Memoir, 39, Cooke Records, HBS; Niven, *Salmon P. Chase,* 263.

23. Cooke Memoir, 40, Cooke Records, HBS.

24. Ibid., 28, 40; Niven, *Salmon P. Chase,* 263; Paludan, *"People's Contest,"* 115; Popowski, "Granddaddy," 29.

25. Oberholtzer, *Jay Cooke,* 1:145; Sandusky *Register,* November 24, 1947.

26. Oberholtzer, *Jay Cooke,* 1:143, 144; Josephson, *Robber Barons,* 55.

27. Oberholtzer, *Jay Cooke,* 1:147, 148; Popowski, "Granddaddy," 30, 31; Paludan, *"People's Contest,"* 115.

28. Sandusky *Register,* November 24, 1947; White, *Railroaded,* 10; Niven, *Salmon P. Chase,* 263.

29. Niven, *Salmon P. Chase,* 263; Oberholtzer, *Jay Cooke,* 1:158; Popowski, "Granddaddy," 31.

30. Oberholtzer, *Jay Cooke,* 1:159.

31. Ibid., 160; Koistinen, *Beating Plowshares,* 184.

32. Paludan, *"People's Contest,"* 110, 111; Stiles, *First Tycoon,* 350; Sherman, *John Sherman's Recollections,* 1:273; Lawson, *Patriot Fires,* 43, 44.

33. McPherson, *Battle Cry,* 443; Popowski, "Granddaddy," 31; Wilson, *Business,* 111.

34. Lawson, *Patriot Fires,* 44, 46; White, *Railroaded,* 10; Cleveland *Plain Dealer,* April 7, 1864; Jay Cooke-Garner, January 31, 1862; H. D. Cooke-Jay, March 5, 1862, Cooke Papers, HSP.

35. Lawson, *Patriot Fires,* 46; Weigley, *Great Civil War,* 208; Salmon P. Chase to My dear Cooke, February 7, 1862; Jay Cooke to Govr, February 8, 1862, Cooke Papers, HSP.

36. Salmon P. Chase to My dear Mr. Cooke, March 7, 1862; Jay Cooke to Govr, November 11, 1862, Cooke Papers, HSP; Weigley, *Great Civil War,* 208; White, *Railroaded,* 12.

37. Detroit *Free Press,* December 23, 1863; White, *Railroaded,* 13; Weigley, *Great Civil War,* 208; Koistinen, *Beating Plowshares,* 184.

38. Jay Cooke to S. P. Chase, November 11, 1862, Cooke Papers, HSP.

39. Oberholtzer, *Jay Cooke,* 1:253–255; Detroit *Free Press,* May 4, 1863; Junction City *Weekly Union,* August 19, 1865; Lawson, *Patriot Fires,* 59.

40. Koistinen, *Beating Plowshares,* 183; Oberholtzer, *Jay Cooke,* 1:187; H. D. Cooke to Jay, February 1, 11, 1862, Cooke Papers, HSP; Henry D. Cooke to Sir, January 6, 1864, Lincoln Papers, LC; Martin, *Pennsylvania History,* 556.

41. White, *Railroaded,* 11; Gettysburg *Compiler,* November 17, 1862; Koistinen, *Beating Plowshares,* 185; Paludan, *"People's Contest,"* 117.

42. Huston, *Sinews,* 183; Koistinen, *Beating Plowshares,* 185; Lawson, *Patriot Fires,* 49, 50, 53.

43. Oberholtzer, *Jay Cooke,* 1:230, 231, 234; Koistinen, *Beating Plowshares,* 184; Popowski, "Granddaddy," 32; Lawson, *Patriot Fires,* 48, 49.

44. Oberholtzer, *Jay Cooke,* 1:259, 260; Detroit *Free Press,* June 13, 1863.

45. Lawson, *Patriot Fires,* 46, 60, 61; New York *Times,* November 9, 1907; Oberholtzer, *Jay Cooke,* 1:244; Henry Cooke to Jay, March 6, 26, 1863, Cooke Papers, HSP.

46. Donald, *Inside,* 40; Cleveland *Daily Leader,* April 7, 1864; Oberholtzer, *Jay Cooke,* 1:319, 323, 325.

47. Popowski, "Granddaddy," 32; Koistinen, *Beating Plowshares,* 184, 187.

48. Sandusky *Register,* November 24, 1947.

49. Popowski, "Granddaddy," 33; Jay Cooke to Father, June 14, 1864, Cooke, Jay Family Papers, RBHPC.

50. Goodwin, *Team of Rivals,* 562–567, 631–633, 680.

51. Ibid., 634, 635.

52. Ibid., 636; Popowski, "Granddaddy," 32, 33; Oberholtzer, *Jay Cooke,* 1:131.

53. Popowski, "Granddaddy," 33.

54. Ibid., 34, 35; E. Cooke to My Dear Jay, November 21, 1864, Cooke, Eleutheros Papers, RBHPC.

55. E. Cooke to My Dear Jay, March 21, 1864, Cooke, Eleutheros Papers, RBHPC; Popowski, "Granddaddy," 34; Perrysburg *Journal,* August 22, 1865.

56. Washington *Evening Star,* August 3, 1864; Washington *National Republican,* September 8, 1864; Cooke Memoir, 65, Cooke Records, HBS; New York *Daily Tribune,* March 7, 1865; Popowski, "Granddaddy," 34, 35; Koistinen, *Beating Plowshares,* 185.

57. Goldin and Lewis, "Economic Cost," 304, 310; Paludan, *"People's Contest,"* 113.

58. Popowski, "Granddaddy," 32; Nelson and Sheriff, *People at War,* 134; Perrysburg *Journal,* August 22, 1865; Stiles, *First Tycoon,* 350.

59. Junction City *Weekly Union,* August 19, 1865; Milwaukee *Daily News,* July 16, 1865.

60. Popowski, "Granddaddy," 35; Louisville *Courier-Journal,* August 24, 1896.

61. Riverside *Press and Horticulturist,* September 30, 1902; Popowski, "Granddaddy," 35.

62. Lawson, *Patriot Fires,* 41; New York *Times,* November 9, 1907; Weigley,

Great Civil War, 209; Niven, *Salmon P. Chase,* 330; Donald, *Inside,* 40; Cozzens, *Earth,* 196.

63. Cooke Memoir, 2, Cooke Records, HBS; "Abraham Lincoln," 2, Cooke Papers, HSP.

64. Cooke Memoir, 83, Cooke Records, HBS; Indianapolis *Star,* May 13, 1864; E. Cooke to My Dear Jay, March 21, 1864, Cooke, Eleutheros Papers, RBHPC; Popowski, "Granddaddy," 29.

Chapter Four

1. Dorsey, *Road,* 4, 5; Nevada *Daily Mail,* March 11, 1887.

2. How, *James B. Eads,* 1; McHenry, *Addresses,* vii.

3. How, *James B. Eads,* 1; Davenport *Democratic Banner,* October 21, 1853; Davenport *Democrat,* March 11, 1887.

4. How, *James B. Eads,* 1, 2, 5; McHenry, *Addresses,* vii; Sellers, "Memoir," 51.

5. "Mud Clerk"; McHenry, *Addresses,* vii.

6. "Mud Clerk"; McHenry, *Addresses,* vii.

7. Dorsey, *Road,* 15–17; Jackson, *James B. Eads,* 4; How, *James B. Eads,* 10; Toledo *Blade,* December 8, 1910; "James Buchanan Eads."

8. Dorsey, *Road,* 23, 24; McHenry, *Addresses,* vii; Davenport *Democrat,* March 11, 1887.

9. McHenry, *Addresses,* vii; How, *James B. Eads,* 12; Sellers, "Memoir," 51, 52; Dorsey, *Road,* 26, 28.

10. Jones, *Civil War at Sea,* 1:106, 107; New Orleans *Times-Picayune,* September 17, 1858; How, *James B. Eads,* 12; Sellers, "Memoir," 52.

11. Dorsey, *Road,* 17–18.

12. Ibid., 18.

13. Ibid., 42, 43.

14. Ibid., 45, 46; How, *James B. Eads,* 19; Davenport *Daily Gazette,* June 18, 1858.

15. Alton *Weekly Telegraph,* July 1, 1858; Davenport *Daily Gazette,* June 18, 1858.

16. How, *James B. Eads,* 51, 52; McHenry, *Addresses,* 1, 5.

17. "Water Wheel Album"; "Henry Burden"; Proudfit, *Henry Burden,* 17, 84; Rolando, "Industrial Archeology," 27.

18. Proudfit, *Henry Burden,* 3; Rolando, "Industrial Archeology," 26.

19. Proudfit, *Henry Burden,* 3, 5, 7; Rolando, "Industrial Archeology," 26.

20. Rolando, "Industrial Archeology," 26; Proudfit, *Henry Burden,* 3.

21. Proudfit, *Henry Burden,* 3, 15, 32, 58; Weise, *City of Troy,* 43; Rolando, "Industrial Archeology," 26.

22. Weise, *City of Troy,* 43; Proudfit, *Henry Burden,* 15, 16.

23. Proudfit, *Henry Burden,* 4, 5, 48; Washington *Daily Globe,* September 26, 1854; "Burden Iron Works," 5.

24. Proudfit, *Henry Burden*, 5.

25. Ibid., 5.

26. "Burden Iron Works," 5; Proudfit, *Henry Burden*, 20, 59.

27. Rolando, "Industrial Archeology," 27; Proudfit, *Henry Burden*, 17; "Burden Iron Works," 5.

28. New York *Tribune*, September 6, 1859; Proudfit, *Henry Burden*, 4, 10; "Burden Iron Works," 5.

29. Rolando, "Industrial Archeology," 27; Proudfit, *Henry Burden*, 64, 65; New York *Times*, August 19, 2016.

30. Proudfit, *Henry Burden*, 82.

31. "Burden Iron Works," 5, 6; Weise, *City of Troy*, 46; article in Troy *Whig* and republished in Alton *Weekly Telegraph*, November 5, 1852.

32. Edward Bates to Sir, April 17, 1861, Eads Collection, MHM; New York *Times*, May 15, 1860.

33. Jones, *Civil War at Sea*, 1:106.

34. Ibid., 107.

35. Ibid., 107; Gideon Welles to Sir, May 14, 1861, Eads Collection, MHM.

36. Edward Bates to Sir, June 17, 1861, copy, Eads Collection, MHM.

37. Ibid.

38. John C. Fremont to Sir, [n.d.]; Barton Able to Sir, September 30, 1861; James B. Eads to M. C. Meigs, October 9, 29, 1861, Eads Collection, MHM.

39. OR, series 3, 2:816–832; O'Harrow, *Quartermaster*, 148.

40. O'Harrow, *Quartermaster*, 148; How, *James B. Eads*, 27, 28; OR, series 3, 2:816.

41. Jackson, *James B. Eads*, 11, 13; Saint Louis *Dispatch*, October 12, 2016; O'Harrow, *Quartermaster*, 148; Mattoon *Gazette*, August 15, 1861; OR, series 3, 2:817–832; McPherson, *Battle Cry*, 393.

42. Saint Louis *Dispatch*, October 12, 2016; Sellers, "Memoir," 52, 53.

43. Saint Louis *Dispatch*, October 12, 2016; Hattaway and Jones, *How the North Won*, 66; How, *James B. Eads*, 29; Sellers, "Memoir," 53.

44. How, *James B. Eads*, 30, 33; OR, series 3, 2:818; Saint Louis *Dispatch*, October 12, 2016; Sellers, "Memoir," 53; Jackson, *James B. Eads*, 13.

45. Sellers, "Memoir," 53; Saint Louis *Dispatch*, October 12, 2016.

46. O'Harrow, *Quartermaster*, 149; How, *James B. Eads*, 34; New York *Times*, December 7, 2013.

47. OR, 8:368, 505.

48. Ibid., 505, 535; Certification of Acceptance, January 15, 1862, Eads Collection, MHM; Findlay *Jeffersonian*, December 27, 1861; Hattaway and Jones, *How the North Won*, 66; New York *Times*, December 7, 2013.

49. Murray and Hsieh, *Savage War*, 132.

50. Cooling, *Forts*, 108–109, 152–160; New York *Times*, December 7, 2013.

51. New York *Times*, December 7, 2013.

52. Detroit *Free Press*, February 20, 1862.

53. Saint Louis *Dispatch*, October 12, 2016; James B. Eads to Sir, January 27, 1862, Eads Collection, MHM.

54. James B. Eads to Sir, January 27, 1862, Eads Collection, MHM.

55. Ibid.; James B. Eads to dear Col. [Blair], October 29, 1861; James B. Eads to My dear friend [Bates], November 10, 1861; Edward Bates to My Dr Sir [Eads], December 20, 1861; James B. Eads to Sir [Meigs], January 27, 1862; Edward Bates to Sir [Stanton], March 5, 1862, Eads Collection, MHM.

56. New York *Times*, December 7, 2013; Jones, *Civil War at Sea*, 2:179, 295, 422.

57. Syracuse *Daily Courier and Union*, April 16, 1862; Wyandotte *Commercial Gazette*, May 17, 1862; Pittsburgh *Daily Post*, June 3, 1863; Lawrence *Daily Kansas Tribune*, February 28, 1864; How, *James B. Eads*, 39, 40; *OR*, 22, pt. 2:278; McHenry, *Addresses*, vii.

58. Dorsey, *Road*, 81.

59. Davenport *Daily Gazette*, November 30, 1865; Carnegie, *Autobiography*, 114–115.

60. Rolando, "Industrial Archeology," 26; Pittsburgh *Gazette*, August 4, 1849; Washington *Evening Star*, July 14, 1857; Proudfit, *Henry Burden*, 46.

61. "Burden Iron Works," 4; New York *Tribune*, May 9, 1843, March 24, 1846; Nashville *Union and American*, October 12, 1858, December 30, 1858, March 29, 1859, May 1, 1859.

62. "Burden Iron Works," 5; New Orleans *Times-Picayune*, March 13, 1859; Weise, *City of Troy*, 46; Wilson, *Business*, 116.

63. Pittsburgh *Gazette News*, July 14, 1912; Proudfit, *Henry Burden*, 77; Geier, Scott, and Babits, *From These Honored Dead*, 178.

64. "Burden Iron Works," 7; Rolando, "Industrial Archeology," 27; Proudfit, *Henry Burden*, 71.

65. "Henry Burden"; Proudfit, *Henry Burden*, 5, 11; Nevins, *War*, 3:251; Geier, Scott, and Babits, *From These Honored Dead*, 181; Weise, *City of Troy*, 46.

66. "Burden Iron Works," 4, 5; Pittsburgh *Gazette News*, July 4, 1912.

67. Geier, Scott, and Babits, *From These Honored Dead*, 181; Troy *Times* quote in Proudfit, *Henry Burden*, 32.

Chapter Five

1. Bruce, *Lincoln and the Tools*, 187; Donald, *Lincoln*, 357; Wert, *Sword*, 71, 94.

2. Bruce, *Lincoln and the Tools*, 187; Wert, *Sword*, 49; Donald, *Lincoln*, 357.

3. Bruce, *Lincoln and the Tools*, 187, 188; Grace and Forlow, *West Point Foundry*, 8.

4. Walton, "West Point Foundry," 10; Soodalter, "Well Armed"; Walton, "Founding," 26, 27.

5. Walton, "Founding," 29–31; Grace and Forlow, *West Point Foundry*, 7.

6. Walton, "Founding," 35; Hornellsville *Weekly Tribune*, January 19, 1865; Grace and Forlow, *West Point Foundry*, 7, 19.

7. Grace and Forlow, *West Point Foundry*, 7, 16, 81; Soodalter, "Well Armed."

8. Grace and Forlow, *West Point Foundry*, 7, 8, 26, 27, 82; New York *Times*, July 26, 1855, December 24, 1858; Soodalter, "Well Armed."

9. Grace and Forlow, *West Point Foundry*, 30–32; Wilson, "Business," 1:324; Valentino, "Using Maps," 39.

10. Grace and Forlow, *West Point Foundry*, 8; Soodalter, "Well Armed"; Trepal, "Gun Foundry," 76.

11. Hacker, *Astride*, 77–78.

12. Ibid., 78.

13. Contract, December 19, 1850, Semmes Contract, NYHS.

14. Francis H. Smith to My dear General, January 28, 1878, Parrott Papers, PHM.

15. Ibid.

16. Bruce, *Lincoln and the Tools*, 23, 25, 26.

17. Ibid., 101; Huston, *Sinews*, 188, 189.

18. Hacker, *Astride*, 28–30, 32, 35.

19. Bruce, *Lincoln and the Tools*, 112, 116; Buckeridge, *Lincoln's Choice*, 14.

20. Taylor, "Christopher Spencer," 1, 2, WHS; New York *Tribune*, January 15, 1922; Buckeridge, *Lincoln's Choice*, 2, 4, 5.

21. Taylor, "Christopher Spencer," 2, 3; Roe, *English*, 175; Buckeridge, *Lincoln's Choice*, 5, 6.

22. Bartlett, "Appreciation," 1, 3.

23. Adler, *Guns*, 168; Taylor, "Christopher Spencer," 4, WHS; Hubbard, "Life," 2, WHS.

24. Taylor, "Christopher Spencer," 4, WHS; Adler, *Guns*, 168; Buckeridge, *Lincoln's Choice*, 6, 7; Cape Girardeau *Southeast Missourian*, March 4, 1977.

25. Taylor, "Christopher Spencer," 4, WHS.

26. Ibid., 5; Hubbard, "Abraham Lincoln," 3; Buckeridge, *Lincoln's Choice*, 10, 11; Bruce, *Lincoln and the Tools*, 114.

27. Buckeridge, *Lincoln's Choice*, 11.

28. Ibid., 12; Nelson, "Connecticut Arms," 32.

29. Soodalter, "Well Armed."

30. Robert P. Parrott to Sir, June 1, 1867, Parrott Papers, PHM; Grace and Forlow, *West Point Foundry*, 8; Walton, "West Point Foundry," 12; Wilson, "Business," 1:321; New York *Times*, July 14, 1861.

31. "Remarks from R. P. Parrott in relation to Rifled Cannon made by him," June 4, 1861, Parrott Papers, PHM.

32. Wilson, "Business," 1:321; Grace and Forlow, *West Point Foundry*, 8; Trepol, "Gun Foundry," 76; Soodalter, "Well Armed"; Bruce, *Lincoln and the Tools*, 186, 187; OR, 11:357.

33. Soodalter, "Well Armed"; Bruce, *Lincoln and the Tools*, 187.

34. Grace and Forlow, *West Point Foundry*, 8; Soodalter, "Well Armed"; Robert P. Parrott to A. B. Dyer, June 1, 1867; Robert P. Parrott to My dear General, November 4, 1862, Parrott Papers, PHM.

35. Wilson, "Business," 1:321; Grace and Forlow, *West Point Foundry*, 8; Soodalter, "Well Armed"; New York *Times*, September 17, 1863.

36. New York *Times*, September 17, 1863.

37. Nevins, *War*, 1:253, 356, 357; Koistinen, *Beating Plowshares*, 160, 163; Wilson, "Business," 1:355; Niven, *Connecticut*, 353; Nelson, "Connecticut Arms," 31.

38. Buckeridge, *Lincoln and the Tools*, 12, 203; Hubbard, "Life," 2, WHS; Nelson, "Connecticut Arms," 32; Niven, *Connecticut*, 383, 384; Beck, "Spencer's Repeaters"; Adler, *Guns*, 169, 170.

39. Taylor, "Christopher Spencer," 5, WHS; Nelson, "Connecticut Arms," 31, 32.

40. Huston, *Sinews*, 192; Taylor, "Christopher Spencer," 5, WHS; Bruce, *Lincoln and the Tools*, 203; Beck, "Spencer's Repeaters."

41. Bilby, *Small Arms*, 152, 153; Beck, "Spencer's Repeaters."

42. Bilby, *Small Arms*, 152, 153, 227, 228; Beck, "Spencer's Repeaters."

43. Bruce, *Lincoln and the Tools*, 253, 255; Bilby, *Small Arms*, 154, 155.

44. Bilby, *Small Arms*, 154, 155; Beck, "Spencer's Repeaters."

45. Bruce, *Lincoln and the Tools*, 255; Bilby, *Small Arms*, 155, 156.

46. Buckeridge, *Lincoln's Choice*, 14–15; Abraham Lincoln to My dear Sir, August 4, 1863, Lincoln Letter, NYHS.

47. Buckeridge, *Lincoln's Choice*, 15; Haupt, *Reminiscences*, 301; Laugel, *United States*, 234; Goldfield, *America Aflame*, 303.

48. Stoddard, *Inside*, 39; Bruce, *Lincoln and the Tools*, 76; Buckeridge, *Lincoln's Choice*, 15; Furgurson, *Freedom Rising*, 106.

49. Abraham Lincoln to My dear Sir, August 4, 1863, Lincoln Letter, NYHS.

50. Ibid.

51. Taylor, "Christopher Spencer," 6, WHS; Warren Fisher Jr. to Sir, August 13, 1863, Lincoln Papers, LC.

52. Taylor, "Christopher Spencer," 6, WHS; Bruce, *Lincoln and the Tools*, 102, 103; Furgurson, *Freedom Rising*, 13; Hubbard, "Abraham Lincoln," 3; Tambling, "Day Spencer Shot."

53. Taylor, "Christopher Spencer," 7, WHS; Bruce, *Lincoln and the Tools*, 263.

54. Taylor, "Christopher Spencer," 7, WHS.

55. Burlingame and Ettlinger, *Inside*, 75.

56. Ibid., 75; Tambling; "Day Spencer Shot."

57. Taylor, "Christopher Spencer," 7, WHS; Buckeridge, *Lincoln's Choice*, 18; Cleveland *Daily Leader*, July 3, 1863; Beck, "Spencer's Repeaters."

58. Grace and Forlow, *West Point Foundry*, 33; Wilson, "Business," 1:321, 325; Robert P. Parrott to Sir, October 5, 1864, Parrott Papers, PHM.

59. New York *Times*, September 17, 1865; *OR*, pt. 2, 35:143.

60. Soodalter, "Well Armed"; Robert P. Parrott to Capt. L. V. Benet, October 12, 1864, Parrott Papers, PHM; Naisawald, *Grape and Canister*, 28.

61. *OR*, 35, pt. 2:143; Robert P. Parrott to Capt. L. V. Benet, October 12, 1864, Parrott Papers, PHM.

62. Gillmore, *Engineer*, 350–354.

63. Hacker, *Astride*, 60.

64. Grace and Forlow, *West Point Foundry*, 9.

65. Robert P. Parrott to Sir, November 3, 1864, Parrott Papers, PHM; Wilson, "Business," 1:321.

66. New York *Times*, March 11, 1865; Soodalter, "Well Armed."

67. Wilson, "Business," 1:321; Grace and Forlow, *West Point Foundry*, 8.

68. Huston, *Sinews*, 186; Wilson, "Business," 1:321; Hacker, *Astride*, 36.

69. Bruce, *Lincoln and the Tools*, 286.

70. Ibid., 287.

71. Beck, "Spencer's Repeaters"; Buckeridge, *Lincoln's Choice*, 25, chaps. 9–14.

72. Wilmington *Daily Journal*, December 16, 1864; Buckeridge, *Lincoln's Choice*, 19.

73. Nelson, "Connecticut Arms," 32, 35; Beck, "Spencer's Repeaters"; Buckeridge, *Lincoln's Choice*, 25; Huston, *Sinews*, 192; Wilson, "Business," 1:357; *Soldier's Journal*, June 21, 1865; Adler, *Guns*, 170; New York *Tribune*, January 15, 1922.

74. Buckeridge, *Lincoln's Choice*, 6, 7; Bruce, *Lincoln and the Tools*, 288.

75. Hubbard, "Life," 3; Bartlett, "Appreciation," 3, WHS; Lewis, "C. M. Spencer."

Chapter Six

1. Blochman, *Doctor Squibb*, 121, 122; Florey, *Collected Papers*, 1:173.

2. Blochman, *Doctor Squibb*, 118–120, 151; Florey, *Collected Papers*, 1:173; Brooklyn *Daily Eagle*, October 27, 1900.

3. Blochman, *Doctor Squibb*, 2, 3.

4. Ibid., 3, 5; Florey, *Collected Papers*, 2:1418.

5. Philadelphia *Public Ledger*, March 21, 1845; Wilmington *Sunday Morning Star*, November 12, 1944; "Early Anesthesia."

6. "Early Anesthesia"; Florey, *Collected Papers*, 2:1419; Wilmington *Sunday Morning Star*, November 12, 1944; Blochman, *Doctor Squibb*, 2, 8, 10.

7. Blochman, *Doctor Squibb*, 8–11, 23, 36, 39; Florey, *Collected Papers*, 2:1419; "Early Anesthesia"; "Chapter 6," 169, 170.

8. Blochman, *Doctor Squibb*, 62, 63, 64; "Early Anesthesia"; "Chapter 6," 170; Florey, *Collected Papers*, 2:1419.

9. "Early Anesthesia"; Blochman, *Doctor Squibb*, 63, 64, 87.

10. "Chapter 6," 170; Blochman, *Doctor Squibb*, 87–89; "Early Anesthesia."

11. Blochman, *Doctor Squibb*, 96–99; "Chapter 6," 171; Florey, *Collected Papers*, 2:1419.

12. Blochman, *Doctor Squibb,* 80, 84, 105, 106; "Chapter 6," 171; Louisville *Daily Courier,* April 7, 1858.

13. Louisville *Daily Courier,* April 7, 1858; Blochman, *Doctor Squibb,* 108–110; "Chapter 6," 171.

14. Florey, *Collected Papers,* 2:1420, 1421; "Chapter 6," 171; Blochman, *Doctor Squibb,* 114–116, 118.

15. Nevins, *Abram S. Hewitt,* 41–43; Reading *Eagle,* August 3, 1902.

16. Nevins, *Abram S. Hewitt,* 82; Reading *Eagle,* August 3, 1902.

17. Nevins, *Abram S. Hewitt,* 3, 4, 6, 7, 13, 14; Pittsburgh *Press,* January 19, 1903; Smith, *Unveiling,* 3, 4.

18. Nevins, *Abram S. Hewitt,* 15, 16.

19. Ibid., 21, 22, 28, 31, 32; Smith, *Unveiling,* 4, 5.

20. Nevins, *Abram S. Hewitt,* 33, 34, 74.

21. Ibid., 48, 56, 58; Beckert, *Monied Metropolis,* 53.

22. Nevins, *Abram S. Hewitt,* 58, 59, 61; Beckert, *Monied Metropolis,* 54.

23. Mack, *Peter Cooper,* 200; Beckert, *Monied Metropolis,* 54; Nevins, *Abram S. Hewitt,* 65, 69, 71, 72.

24. Mack, *Peter Cooper,* 204, 205; Nevins, *Abram S. Hewitt,* 82, 83; Smith, *Unveiling,* 6.

25. Mack, *Peter Cooper,* 205.

26. Ibid., 205, 206; Cottrell, *Story,* 12; Nevins, *Abram S. Hewitt,* 86.

27. Mack, *Peter Cooper,* 208; Zink, "Iron & Steel"; Washington *National Intelligencer,* February 7, 1846; Baltimore *Sun,* December 3, 1846.

28. Cottrell, *Story,* 13; Mack, *Peter Cooper,* 205; Nevins, *Abram S. Hewitt,* 90; Zink, "Iron & Steel."

29. Florey, *Collected Papers,* 1:174; "Chapter 6," 171; Brooklyn *Daily Eagle,* October 27, 1900.

30. Brooklyn *Daily Eagle,* October 27, 1900; Florey, *Collected Papers,* 2:1413; "Chapter 6," 171.

31. "Chapter 6," 171; Wilmington *Sunday Morning Star,* November 12, 1944; Florey, *Collected Papers,* 1:174; Blochman, *Doctor Squibb,* 117, 151.

32. Smith, *Medicines,* 25; Brooklyn *Daily Eagle,* October 27, 30, 1900; "Early Anesthesia"; Blochman, *Doctor Squibb,* 152.

33. Brooklyn *Daily Eagle,* October 30, 1900.

34. Ibid.; Smith, *Medicines,* 19, 49.

35. Smith, *Medicines,* 25.

36. Ibid., 25, 27, 86n73.

37. Ibid., 25; "Chapter 6," 173; Blochman, *Doctor Squibb,* 133, 134; Florey, *Collected Papers,* 2:1421.

38. "Chapter 6," 173; Florey, *Collected Papers,* 2:1421; Blochman, *Doctor Squibb,* 133, 134.

39. Smith, *Medicines,* 3, 14, 15, 29, 30, 74.

40. Ibid., 8, 25, 79n67; Nevins, *War,* 3:314; "Bristol-Myers Squibb."

41. Smith, *Medicines,* 8; Squibb Pannier, NMCWM.

42. Smith, *Medicines,* 8, 9, 25.

43. Ibid., 25.

44. Cottrell, *Story*, 13.

45. Ibid., 3, 11; "Abram S. Hewitt"; Bishop, *History*, 544, 545; "Ringwood Manor" Papers, NJSA; Mack, *Peter Cooper*, 209, 210.

46. Nevins, *Abram S. Hewitt*, 100, 102; Zink, "Iron & Steel"; Milwaukee *Weekly Wisconsin*, June 14, 1854.

47. Beckert, *Monied Metropolis*, 63; Cottrell, *Story*, 13; New York *Tribune*, August 10, 1854; New Orleans *Times-Picayune*, December 26, 1858; Alexandria *Gazette*, August 12, 1859; Zink, "Iron & Steel."

48. Beckert, *Monied Metropolis*, 74; Zink, "Iron & Steel"; Nevins, *Abram S. Hewitt*, 175, 179, 186; Donald, *Lincoln*, 238.

49. Mack, *Peter Cooper*, 207; Nevins, *Abram S. Hewitt*, 147; Cottrell, *Story*, 13; Nevins, *Selected Writings*, ix; Miller, "Walt Whitman," *WWQR*, 96, 97; Baltimore *Daily Exchange*, October 15, 1859.

50. Nevins, *Selected Writings*, ix, 19; Baltimore *Daily Exchange*, October 15, 1859; Miller, "Walt Whitman," *WWQR*, 96, 97.

51. Nevins, *Abram S. Hewitt*, 94, 170, 171.

52. "Ringwood Manor" Papers, NJSA; New York *Times*, November 25, 1860; Baltimore *Daily Exchange*, January 28, 1861; Nevins, *Diary*, 115, 115n, 120.

53. Nevins, *Diary*, 120.

54. Nevins, *Abram S. Hewitt*, 193.

55. Ibid., 193.

56. Ibid., 194, 195, 197–199; Bruce, *Lincoln and the Tools*, 42; Nevins, *Selected Writings*, ix.

57. "Abram S. Hewitt"; Nevins, *Abram S. Hewitt*, 199, 201.

58. Nevins, *Abram S. Hewitt*, 201, 202; *OR*, series 3, 1:809, 810, 874.

59. *OR*, series 3, 1:884, 887, 892; "Abram S. Hewitt"; Nevins, *Abram S. Hewitt*, 203–205.

60. *OR*, series 3, 1:887.

61. Nevins, *Selected Writings*, ix; Nevins, *Abram S. Hewitt*, 206–210.

62. Nevins, *Abram S. Hewitt*, 210–212; New York *Times*, July 25, 1862; Pittsburgh *Gazette*, July 28, 1862; "Ringwood Manor" Papers, NJSA; Zink, "Iron & Steel."

63. Nevins, *Abram S. Hewitt*, 221, 222.

64. Ibid., 227–228n.

65. New York *Herald*, November 10, 1864; Paludan, *"People's Contest,"* 146; Ringwood Account Books and Journals, Ringwood Manor Papers, NJSA; Boston *Evening Transcript*, January 19, 1903.

66. Nevins, *Abram S. Hewitt*, 228.

Chapter Seven

1. Hutchinson, *Cyrus Hall McCormick*, 37, 38.

2. Ibid., 37, 38, 44, 46.

3. McCormick, *Century*, 6, 7.

4. Ibid., 8; *In Memoriam*, 5; Ott, "Producing a Past," 3.

5. Ott, "Producing a Past," 1–2; McCormick, *Century*, 1.

6. Ott, "Producing a Past," 3; McCormick, *Century*, 2, 3, 10; Cronon, *Nature's Metropolis*, 313; *In Memoriam*, 8.

7. Ott, "Producing a Past," 4, 5; McCormick, *Century*, 20.

8. McCormick, *Century*, 21, 23, 25, 43; McCormick American Reaper Memorandum, C. H. McCormick, September 19, 1863, McCormick Family Papers, WIHS.

9. McCormick, *Century*, 26, 44, 47; McCormick American Reaper Memorandum, C. H. McCormick, September 19, 1863, McCormick Family Papers, WIHS; *In Memoriam*, 10.

10. McCormick American Reaper Memorandum, C. H. McCormick, September 19, 1863, McCormick Family Papers, WIHS; McCormick, *Century*, 23, 24.

11. McCormick, *Century*, 26, 28, 29, 44; *In Memoriam*, 9.

12. Hutchinson, *Cyrus Hall McCormick*, 64; McCormick, *Century*, 29, 36, 37.

13. McCormick American Reaper Memorandum, C. H. McCormick, September 19, 1863, McCormick Family Papers, WIHS; Cronon, *Nature's Metropolis*, 313; McCormick, *Century*, 27.

14. McCormick, *Century*, 35; McCormick American Reaper Memorandum, C. H. McCormick, September 19, 1863, McCormick Family Papers, WIHS.

15. Goodwin, *Team of Rivals*, 173–175, 179.

16. McCormick, *Century*, 50; Hutchinson, *Cyrus Hall McCormick*, 71, 73.

17. McCormick American Reaper Memorandum, C. H. McCormick, September 19, 1863, McCormick Family Papers, WIHS; McCormick, *Century*, 37, 38; Cronon, *Nature's Metropolis*, 318; Nevins, *War*, 1:253.

18. Hutchinson, *Cyrus Hall McCormick*, 109, 110; McCormick, *Century*, 38.

19. Hutchinson, *Cyrus Hall McCormick*, 105, 105n, 106n.

20. Ibid., 85.

21. Nasaw, *Andrew Carnegie*, xi, 40; Louisville *Courier-Journal*, January 1, 1899.

22. Carnegie, *Autobiography*, 2, 4, 12; Nasaw, *Andrew Carnegie*, 1, 3, 7, 22, 24.

23. Hendrick, *Life*, 42; Nasaw, *Andrew Carnegie*, 34; Louisville *Courier-Journal*, January 1, 1899.

24. Nasaw, *Andrew Carnegie*, 36; Louisville *Courier-Journal*, January 1, 1899.

25. Louisville *Courier-Journal*, January 1, 1899.

26. Ibid.; Nasaw, *Andrew Carnegie*, 42, 45; Carnegie, *Autobiography*, 45, 47; Hendrick, *Life*, 56.

27. Josephson, *Robber Barons*, 42.

28. Louisville *Courier-Journal*, January 1, 1899; Carnegie, *Autobiography*, 62, 67.

29. Carnegie, *Autobiography*, 67.

30. Ibid., 73; Nasaw, *Andrew Carnegie*, 63, 64.

31. Nasaw, *Andrew Carnegie*, 59, 60; Louisville *Courier-Journal*, January 1, 1899.

32. Nasaw, *Andrew Carnegie*, 60; Louisville *Courier-Journal*, January 1, 1899.

33. Nasaw, *Andrew Carnegie*, 66, 68; Louisville *Courier-Journal*, January 1, 1899.

34. Nasaw, *Andrew Carnegie*, xi, 41, 67; Hendrick, *Life*, 83.

35. Hendrick, *Life*, 40; Bates, *Lincoln*, 20; Hubbard, *Little Journeys*, 276; Louisville *Courier-Journal*, January 1, 1899.

36. Bates, *Lincoln*, 15, 16, 21, 22; Leech, *Reveille*, 67.

37. Carnegie, *Autobiography*, 98; Bates, *Lincoln*, 35.

38. McPherson, *Battle Cry*, 280; Furgurson, *Freedom Rising*, 117; Bates, *Lincoln*, 22.

39. Bates, *Lincoln*, 25; Hendrick, *Life*, 93; Leech, *Reveille*, 67.

40. Wert, *Sword*, 7; Carnegie, *Autobiography*, 98, 99.

41. Carnegie, *Autobiography*, 97, 98.

42. Ibid., 105.

43. William S. McCormick to Brother, February 15, 1863, McCormick Family Papers, WIHS; Hutchinson, *Cyrus Hall McCormick*, 55.

44. William S. McCormick to Brother, February 15, 1863, McCormick Family Papers, WIHS.

45. Hutchinson, *Cyrus Hall McCormick*, 83.

46. McCormick, *Century*, 62–63; William S. McCormick to Brother, July 20, 1862, McCormick Family Papers, WIHS; Cronon, *Nature's Metropolis*, 124; Gates, *Agriculture and the Civil War*, 232, 233, 236, 237.

47. McCormick, *Century*, 63.

48. Ibid., 63.

49. Ibid.; Gates, *Agriculture and the Civil War*, 233.

50. Hutchinson, *Cyrus Hall McCormick*, 97n; William S. McCormick to Brother, July 9, 11, 20, October 8, 1862, McCormick Family Papers, WIHS.

51. Hutchinson, *Cyrus Hall McCormick*, 57; William S. McCormick to Brother, October 12, 1862; Leander J. McCormick to Brother, February 15, August 8, 1863; McCormick American Reaper Memorandum, C. H. McCormick, September 19, 1863, McCormick Family Papers, WIHS.

52. William S. McCormick to Brother, October 12, 1862, McCormick Family Papers, WIHS.

53. William S. McCormick to Brother, October 14, November 12, 19, 1862, January 4, 1863, ibid.

54. William S. McCormick to Brother, March 15, April 8, 1863, ibid.

55. William S. McCormick to Brother, December 11, 1862, February 15, March 1, April 8, 1863; William S. McCormick to Brother, March 15, 1863; Leander J. McCormick to [Brother], March 8, 1863, ibid.

56. Hutchinson, *Cyrus Hall McCormick*, 57, 59, 60, 123.

57. Ibid., 129; Smith, *Colonel*, 23–25.

58. Carnegie, *Autobiography*, 105, 135; Nasaw, *Andrew Carnegie*, 75.

59. Nasaw, *Andrew Carnegie*, 75, 80.

60. Nevins, *War*, 2:497, 507, 3:242.

61. Nasaw, *Andrew Carnegie*, 78; Louisville *Courier-Journal*, January 1, 1899.

62. Nasaw, *Andrew Carnegie*, 80; Carnegie, *Autobiography*, 116; Nevins, *War*, 3:252.

63. Nasaw, *Andrew Carnegie*, 80, 81; Carnegie, *Autobiography*, 105.

64. Carnegie, *Autobiography*, 106–109; Nasaw, *Andrew Carnegie*, 81, 87.

65. Nasaw, *Andrew Carnegie*, 82.

66. Ibid., 87, 88; Pittsburgh *Press*, July 7, 1933; Carnegie, *Autobiography*, 118.

67. Nasaw, *Andrew Carnegie*, 87, 88; Pittsburgh *Press*, July 7, 1933.

68. Carnegie, *Autobiography*, 135, 136; Carnegie, *"Gospel of Wealth" Essays*, x, 94.

Chapter Eight

1. "John Deere," *http://www.illinoisancestors.org/rockisland/pioneersfolder/johndeere.html*; Dahlstrom and Dahlstrom, *John Deere Story*, 9.

2. Dahlstrom and Dahlstrom, *John Deere Story*, 6, 9, 10; Broehl, *John Deere's Company*, 4.

3. Dahlstrom and Dahlstrom, *John Deere Story*, 5–6; Broehl, *John Deere's Company*, 4; Wagle, "John Deere."

4. Dahlstrom and Dahlstrom, *John Deere Story*, 5–6; Wagle, "John Deere."

5. Wagle, "John Deere"; Broehl, *John Deere's Company*, 11, 12; Dahlstrom and Dahlstrom, *John Deere Story*, 6, 7.

6. Wagle, "John Deere"; Broehl, *John Deere's Company*, 12, 13, 24; Abrams, "John Deere."

7. Broehl, *John Deere's Company*, 19; Wagle, "John Deere"; "John Deere," *http://www.illinoisancestors.org/rockisland/pioneersfolder/johndeere.html*; Sioux City *Journal*, November 30, 2016.

8. Wagle, "John Deere"; Dahlstrom and Dahlstrom, *John Deere Story*, 10, 11; Sioux City *Journal*, November 30, 2016; Broehl, *John Deere's Company*, 32.

9. Wagle, "John Deere"; Frazier, "John Deere"; Cronon, *Nature's Metropolis*, 99.

10. Broehl, *John Deere's Company*, 44, 45; Dahlstrom and Dahlstrom, *John Deere Story*, 13; Frazier, "John Deere"; "Original Steel Plow."

11. Frazier, "John Deere"; Broehl, *John Deere's Company*, 45; Dahlstrom and Dahlstrom, *John Deere Story*, 13, 14; Wagle, "John Deere."

12. Dahlstrom and Dahlstrom, *John Deere Story*, 14; Wagle, "John Deere."

13. Dahlstrom and Dahlstrom, *John Deere Story*, 19; Wagle, "John Deere"; Sioux City *Journal*, November 30, 2016.

14. Broehl, *John Deere's Company*, 71, 75, 76; Dahlstrom and Dahlstrom, *John Deere Story*, 21, 22, 26, 30; Wagle, "John Deere."

15. Broehl, *John Deere's Company*, 49; Drache, "Impact"; Chicago *Tribune*, May 27, 1994.

16. Broehl, *John Deere's Company*, 77; Davenport *Democratic Banner*, March 12, 1852; Emporia *Weekly News*, July 4, 1857.

17. Wakarusa *Kansas Herald of Freedom*, February 2, April 19, November 15, 1856.

18. Alton *Weekly Telegraph*, February 4, September 23, 1858; Chicago *Tribune*, March 30, 1858; Davenport *Quad-City Times*, September 17, 1859; Davenport *Morning Democrat*, October 8, 1860.

19. Chicago *Tribune*, February 24, 1859.

20. Dahlstrom and Dahlstrom, *John Deere Story*, 26, 30; Davenport *Quad-City Times*, March 4, 1859; Davenport *Morning Democrat*, May 2, 1859; Chicago *Tribune*, February 24, 1859.

21. Broehl, *John Deere's Company*, 100.

22. "John Deere: Self-Polishing Cast Steel Plow"; Wagle, "John Deere"; Chicago *Tribune*, February 24, 1859; Abrams, "John Deere."

23. Dahlstrom and Dahlstrom, *John Deere Story*, 33; Davenport *Quad-City Times*, March 4, 1859; Wagle, "John Deere"; Abrams, "John Deere."

24. Buffalo *Daily Republic*, March 26, 1858.

25. Wagle, "John Deere"; Chicago *Tribune*, February 24, 1859.

26. Broehl, *John Deere's Company*, 125, 126; Wagle, "John Deere"; Dahlstrom and Dahlstrom, *John Deere Story*, 37.

27. Broehl, *John Deere's Company*, 127, 128; Wagle, "John Deere"; Dahlstrom and Dahlstrom, *John Deere Story*, 38, 39.

28. Broehl, *John Deere's Company*, 132–135; Dahlstrom and Dahlstrom, *John Deere Story*, 41, 42.

29. Chicago *Tribune*, February 24, 1859; Dahlstrom and Dahlstrom, *John Deere Story*, 24.

30. Wilmington *Sunday Star-News*, February 17, 1952; Corle, *John Studebaker*, 35.

31. Corle, *John Studebaker*, 19, 21; Washington *Observer-Reporter*, January 21, 1978; Bryan *Times*, May 2, 2002.

32. Corle, *John Studebaker*, 19, 21; Washington *Observer-Reporter*, January 21, 1978; Bryan *Times*, May 2, 2002; Studebaker and Studebaker, *Studebaker Family*, 41, 43.

33. Washington *Observer-Reporter*, January 21, 1978; Corle, *John Studebaker*, 21, 22; Bonsall, *More Than They Promised*, 12, 13; Erskine, *History*, 3, 4; Milwaukee *Sentinel*, December 28, 1863.

34. Bonsall, *More Than They Promised*, 13, 14; Erskine, *History*, 3, 5; Milwaukee *Sentinel*, December 28, 1963; Corle, *John Studebaker*, 25.

35. Bonsall, *More Than They Promised*, 13; Corle, *John Studebaker*, 27, 30; Erskine, *History*, 5.

36. Bonsall, *More Than They Promised*, 12, 15.

37. Ibid., 15; Corle, *John Studebaker*, 30.

38. Bonsall, *More Than They Promised*, 13, 15; Erskine, *History*, 7; Studebaker and Studebaker, *Studebaker Family*, 55; Milwaukee *Sentinel*, December 28, 1963.

39. Erskine, *History*, 7; Bonsall, *More Than They Promised*, 16; Florence *Times*, September 23, 1910; Montreal *Gazette*, March 26, 1932.

40. Bonsall, *More Than They Promised*, 16; Erskine, *History*, 8.

41. Studebaker and Studebaker, *Studebaker Family*, 86; Erskine, *History*, 8; Bonsall, *More Than They Promised*, 17.

42. Bonsall, *More Than They Promised*, 17, 18; Studebaker and Studebaker, *Studebaker Family*, 86.

43. Bonsall, *More Than They Promised*, 18, 20; Washington *Observer-Reporter*, January 21, 1978; Erskine, *History*, 8; Wilmington *Sunday Star-News*, February 17, 1952.

44. Bonsall, *More Than They Promised*, 20; Guttman, "Studebaker Wagon"; Montreal *Gazette*, March 26, 1932.

45. Bonsall, *More Than They Promised*, 20, 21; "Clement Studebaker"; McPherson, *Battle Cry*, 45; Wilson, "Business," 1:102, 112.

46. Bonsall, *More Than They Promised*, 21; "Clement Studebaker"; Corle, *John Studebaker*, 75.

47. Corle, *John Studebaker*, 75, 76, 120; Erskine, *History*, 8; "Clement Studebaker"; Wilmington *Sunday Star-News*, February 17, 1952.

48. Bonsall, *More Than They Promised*, 22; Studebaker and Studebaker, *Studebaker Family*, 55; Pittsburgh *Press*, March 12, 1950.

49. Corle, *John Studebaker*, 133; Bonsall, *More Than They Promised*, 23; "Studebaker Brothers"; Wilmington *Sunday Star-News*, February 17, 1952.

50. Wilson, *Business*, 119.

51. Abrams, "John Deere"; Broehl, *John Deere's Company*, 143; Gates, *Agriculture and the Civil War*, 222, 223; Nevins, *War*, 3:236.

52. Gates, *Agriculture and the Civil War*, 222, 223; Nevins, *War*, 3:236.

53. Gates, *Agriculture and the Civil War*, 223, 225; Nevins, *War*, 3:236.

54. Dahlstrom and Dahlstrom, *John Deere Story*, 41, 42; Wagle, "John Deere"; Broehl, *John Deere's Company*, 148.

55. Dahlstrom and Dahlstrom, *John Deere Story*, 43; Wagle, "John Deere"; Nevins, *War*, 3:225.

56. Broehl, *John Deere's Company*, 148, 150.

57. Ibid., 148; Dahlstrom and Dahlstrom, *John Deere Story*, 45; Davenport *Quad-City Times*, December 2, 1863; Joliet *Signal*, April 19, 1864.

58. "Original Steel Plow."

59. McCormick, *Century*, 66.

60. Huston, *Sinews*, 216; Hagerman, "Field Transportation," 148.

61. Huston, *Sinews*, 216; Hagerman, "Field Transportation," 148.

62. O'Harrow, *Quartermaster*, 167; Guttman, "Studebaker Wagon."

63. Risch, *Quartermaster Support*, 373; Wilson, "Business," 1:368, 370; Parke, *Recollections*, v.

64. Corle, *John Studebaker*, 140, 141; Bonsall, *More Than They Promised*, 24; Wilmington *Sunday Star-News*, February 17, 1952.

65. South Bend *News-Times*, July 18, 1913; Corle, *John Studebaker*, 140.

66. Guttman, "Studebaker Wagon."

67. Hagerman, "Field Transportation," 171; Bonsall, *More Than They Promised*, 24.

68. Bonsall, *More Than They Promised*, 24; Corle, *John Studebaker*, 140; Wilson, "Business," 1:368.

69. Corle, *John Studebaker*, 141; Bonsall, *More Than They Promised*, 25.

70. Studebaker and Studebaker, *Studebaker Family*, 55.

71. Ibid., 83; Bonsall, *More Than They Promised*, 43.

Chapter Nine

1. Galveston *Daily News*, November 4, 1962; Frantz, *Gail Borden*, 67–69, 80.

2. Frantz, *Gail Borden*, 77–80.

3. Ibid., 5, 11, 33, 52; Paris *News*, June 27, 1985.

4. Frantz, *Gail Borden*, 4–11; Galveston *Daily News*, November 4, 1962.

5. Frantz, *Gail Borden*, 39, 40.

6. Ibid., 41, 42, 48.

7. Ibid., 40, 47–50.

8. Ibid., 52, 53, 55, 57; "Gail Borden Milks Success."

9. Frantz, *Gail Borden*, 59–61; Paris *News*, June 27, 1985.

10. Frantz, *Gail Borden*, 58, 59; "Gail Borden Milks Success"; Paris *News*, June 27, 1985.

11. "Gail Borden Milks Success"; Paris *News*, June 27, 1895; Frantz, *Gail Borden*, 59; Galveston *Daily News*, November 4, 1962.

12. Frantz, *Gail Borden*, 60, 61, 65; Paris *News*, June 27, 1985; Groesbeck *Journal*, June 28, 2001.

13. Frantz, *Gail Borden*, 69, 71; Groesbeck *Journal*, June 28, 2001; Schmidt, *Lincoln's Labels*, 42.

14. Frantz, *Gail Borden*, 63, 69, 79.

15. Ibid., 65–68, 79, 80.

16. Ibid., 84—86; Myers, *Print*, 127; Galveston *Daily News*, November 4, 1962; Groesbeck *Journal*, June 28, 2001.

17. Frantz, *Gail Borden*, 102–104.

18. Ibid., 104–107; Myers, *Print*, 128; Abilene *Reporter-News*, October 6, 1954; Galveston *Daily News*, November 4, 1962.

19. Frantz, *Gail Borden*, 106.

20. Ibid., 106, 107.

21. Ibid., 109.

22. Ibid., 110–112.

23. Ibid., 112, 113, 119; Groesbeck *Journal*, June 28, 2001; Paris *News*, June 27, 1985.

24. Galveston *Daily News*, November 4, 1962; Paris *News*, June 27, 1985; Frantz, *Gail Borden*, 129–131.

25. Frantz, *Gail Borden*, 176–180.

26. Ibid., 155, 158, 172, 190; Galveston *Daily News*, November 4, 1962.

27. Baker, *Year Worth Living*, 56.

28. Galveston *Daily News*, November 4, 1962; Frantz, *Gail Borden*, 173.

29. Frantz, *Gail Borden*, 203, 204; Groesbeck *Journal*, June 28, 2001.

30. Frantz, *Gail Borden*, 143, 204, 205; Stroudsburg *Jeffersonian*, April 4, 1850.

31. Frantz, *Gail Borden*, 206, 207.

32. Ibid., 209; Washington *Evening Star*, March 25, 1853; Burlington *Weekly Free Press*, July 29, 1853; Brownsville *Herald*, December 10, 1941; Schmidt, *Lincoln's Labels*, 42, 43.

33. Schmidt, *Lincoln's Labels*, 43; Frantz, *Gail Borden*, 219, 220; Brownsville *Herald*, December 10, 1941; Paris *News*, June 27, 1985.

34. Sumter *Watchmen and Southron*, November 18, 1903; Des Moines *Register*, April 29, 1960.

35. Berkshire *Eagle*, November 14, 1949; Lewis, "Gordon McKay"; Tenner, "Lasting Impressions," 37.

36. Lewis, "Gordon McKay"; Lebanon *Daily News*, August 2, 1962; Los Angeles *Times*, July 6, 1961; Hazard, *Organization*, 245.

37. Hazard, *Organization*, 245.

38. Ibid.; Des Moines *Register*, April 29, 1960; Lewis, "Gordon McKay"; Cronin, "McKay Stitcher."

39. Hazard, *Organization*, 245; Staunton *Spectator*, July 31, 1860; Reading *Times*, September 14, 1881; Wilmington *Morning News*, October 22, 1903; Sumter *Watchman and Southron*, November 18, 1903.

40. Sumter *Watchman and Southron*, November 18, 1903; Hazard, *Organization*, 73, 113; Nevins, *War*, 2:492.

41. Hazard, *Organization*, 73, 98, 99, 103, 105, 110.

42. Ibid., 113; Nevins, *War*, 2:492.

43. Sumter *Watchman and Southron*, November 18, 1903; Hazard, *Organization*, 113, 245.

44. Frantz, *Gail Borden*, 226; Schmidt, *Lincoln's Labels*, 45.

45. Baker, *Year Worth Living*, 104; Frantz, *Gail Borden*, 222, 223, 226; Schenkman, "Everyone Knows Elsie."

46. Schenkman, "Everyone Knows Elsie"; Frantz, *Gail Borden*, 224–226; Bridgeport *Post*, December 1, 1957.

47. Schenkman, "Everyone Knows Elsie."

48. Ibid., "Evaporated Milk's Connecticut Connection"; Brownsville *Herald*, December 10, 1941; Albuquerque *Journal*, June 29, 1953; Bridgeport *Post*,

December 1, 1957; Spartanburg *Herald-Journal*, April 29, 1982; Indianapolis *Star*, January 13, 2004; Norwalk, *The Hour*, August 18, 2006.

49. Frantz, *Gail Borden*, 226, 227; Schenkman, "Everyone Knows Elsie"; Orcutt, *History*, 84; Schenectady *Gazette*, May 12, 1982.

50. Frantz, *Gail Borden*, 238, 239, 241; "Evaporated Milk's Connecticut Connection"; Schenkman, "Everyone Knows Elsie."

51. Schenkman, "Everyone Knows Elsie"; Frantz, *Gail Borden*, 242, 245–247, 249–250; Brooklyn *Daily Eagle*, May 3, 1858; New York *Times*, May 12, 1858; Nevins, *War*, 2:480; Bridgeport *Post*, December 1, 1957.

52. Schmidt, *Lincoln's Labels*, 46; Frantz, *Gail Borden*, 254, 255; Bridgeport *Post*, December 1, 1952.

53. Frantz, *Gail Borden*, 255, 258, 260; Schmidt, *Lincoln's Labels*, 46; Bridgeport *Post*, December 1, 1957.

54. Schmidt, *Lincoln's Labels*, 46–47.

55. Ibid., 47.

56. Frantz, *Gail Borden*, 257, 258, 263.

57. Ibid., 261, 262; Bridgeport *Post*, December 1, 1957; Schmidt, *Lincoln's Labels*, 50.

58. Frantz, *Gail Borden*, 261, 263; Schmidt, *Lincoln's Labels*, 51, 52.

59. Paludan, *"People's Contest,"* 147.

60. Nevins, *War*, 2:492; Nelson and Sheriff, *People at War*, 242.

61. Hazard, *Organization*, 117, 118; "Gordon McKay"; "Short History"; Lewis, "Gordon McKay"; Nevins, *War*, 2:493.

62. Risch, *Quartermaster Support*, 361; "Short History."

63. Wilmington *Morning News*, October 22, 1903; Lewis, "Gordon McKay"; Wilson, "Business," 2:382; "Gordon McKay"; Des Moines *Register*, April 29, 1960.

64. Des Moines *Register*, April 29, 1960; Hazard, *Organization*, 117; Wilson, "Business," 1:382, 387n; Nelson and Sheriff, *People at War*, 242; Thomson, "Invention," 143; O'Harrow, *Quartermaster*, 135.

65. Paludan, *"People's Contest,"* 147; Sumter *Watchman and Southron*, November 18, 1903.

Chapter Ten

1. Leech and Conrad, *Armour*, 17, 24; Crawfordsville *Sunday Star*, January 14, 1901; Spokane *Daily Chronicle*, May 3, 1931.

2. Wildman, *Famous Leaders*, 3, 4; Hubbard, *Little Journeys*, 175; Spokane *Daily Chronicle*, May 3, 1931.

3. Leech and Carroll, *Armour*, 13, 14; Hubbard, *Little Journeys*, 168; Crawfordsville *Sunday Star*, January 14, 1901.

4. Leech and Carroll, *Armour*, 18.

5. Ibid., 14, 15.

6. Ibid., 15; McKinney, "House of Armour"; Hubbard, *Little Journeys*, 171; Chicago *Tribune*, August 8, 2014.

7. Leech and Carroll, *Armour,* 16–18; Hubbard, *Little Journeys,* 171; Crawfordsville *Sunday Star,* January 14, 1901; Chicago *Tribune,* August 8, 2014.

8. Spokane *Daily Chronicle,* May 3, 1931; Leech and Carroll, *Armour,* 19; Wildman, *Famous Leaders,* 3, 4.

9. Leech and Carroll, *Armour,* 19, 20; McKinney, "House of Armour."

10. McKinney, "House of Armour."

11. Ibid.; Wildman, *Famous Leaders,* 3; Leech and Carroll, *Armour,* 23.

12. McKinney, "House of Armour"; Leech and Carroll, *Armour,* 23, 24.

13. McKinney, "House of Armour"; Leech and Carroll, *Armour,* 24, 25, 34; Crawfordsville *Sunday Star,* January 14, 1901.

14. Leech and Carroll, *Armour,* 25, 34; Hubbard, *Little Journeys,* 175; Spokane, *Daily Chronicle,* May 3, 1931; McKinney, "House of Armour."

15. Leech and Carroll, *Armour,* 25, 28; "History Comes to Life."

16. Leech and Carroll, *Armour,* 25.

17. Ibid., 25, 28.

18. Ibid., 2, 3, 26–27; Crawfordsville *Sunday Star,* January 14, 1901; Spokane *Daily Chronicle,* May 3, 1931; Wildman, *Famous Leaders,* 6.

19. Leech and Carroll, *Armour,* 2, 3, 10; Skaggs, *Prime Cut,* 36, 48.

20. Leech and Carroll, *Armour,* 23–24.

21. Hidy, Hill, and Nevins, *Timber,* 3, 4.

22. Ibid., 4.

23. Ibid.

24. Ibid., 3, 4; Pittsburgh *Gazette Times,* April 5, 1914; Lewiston *Daily Sun,* April 2, 1914.

25. Pittsburgh *Gazette Times,* April 5, 1914; Rock Island *Argus and Daily Union,* October 11, 1907; Hidy, Hill, and Nevins, *Timber,* 4, 5.

26. Milwaukee *Sentinel,* January 8, 1912; Lewiston *Daily Sun,* April 2, 1914; Davenport *Democrat and Leader,* April 1, 1925; Hidy, Hill, and Nevins, *Timber,* 4, 5.

27. Hidy, Hill, and Nevins, *Timber,* 5.

28. Ibid., 5; Pittsburgh *Gazette Times,* April 5, 1914.

29. Hidy, Hill, and Nevins, *Timber,* 6.

30. Ibid., 6, 7.

31. Ibid., 6, 7; Milwaukee *Sentinel,* January 8, 1912; Rock Island *Argus and Daily Union,* October 11, 1907; Articles of Agreement, May 1, 1860, Weyerhaeuser Family Papers, MNHS.

32. Rock Island *Argus and Daily Union,* October 11, 1907; Lewiston *Daily Sun,* April 2, 1914; Hidy, Hill, and Nevins, *Timber,* 7, 8.

33. Articles of Agreement, May 1, 1860, Weyerhaeuser Family Papers, MNHS.

34. Ibid.; Hidy, Hill, and Nevins, *Timber,* 8.

35. Articles of Agreement, May 1, 1860, Weyerhaeuser Family Papers, MNHS; Hidy, Hill, and Nevins, *Timber,* 9; Davenport *Democrat and Leader,* April 1, 1925.

36. Hidy, Hill, and Nevins, *Timber*, 1–2, 18.

37. Wiley, *Life*, 237, 239.

38. Skaggs, *Prime Cut*, 36, 37, 48; Leech and Carroll, *Armour*, 10; Walsh, *Rise*, 57, 58.

39. Walsh, *Rise*, 67; Nevins, *War*, 3:233.

40. Walsh, *Rise*, 57, 58, 67; Leech and Carroll, *Armour*, 12; Hattaway and Jones, *How the North Won*, 141.

41. Walsh, *Rise*, 67; Janesville *Daily Gazette*, July 12, 16, 1863; Leech and Carroll, *Armour*, 28, 29; Crawfordsville *Sunday Star*, January 14, 1901.

42. Leech and Carroll, *Armour*, 29, 30, 54; Wildman, *Famous Leaders*, 6; Crawfordsville *Sunday Star*, January 14, 1901.

43. Wildman, *Famous Leaders*, 6, 7; Hubbard, *Little Journeys*, 166, 177; Sarasota *Herald-Tribune*, April 4, 1932; Leech and Carroll, *Armour*, 30, 35; Stoddard, *Men*, 203.

44. Stoddard, *Men*, 205; Lewis and Carroll, *Armour*, 54; Crawfordsville *Sunday Star*, January 14, 1901.

45. Leech and Carroll, *Armour*, 31; Spokane *Daily Chronicle*, February 4, 1931.

46. Leech and Carroll, *Armour*, 32, 33; Spokane *Daily Chronicle*, February 4, 1931; Crawfordsville *Sunday Star*, January 14, 1901.

47. Leech and Carroll, *Armour*, 12, 56; Walsh, *Rise*, 67; Hattaway and Jones, *How the North Won*, 141; Spokane *Daily Chronicle*, February 4, 1931; Crawfordsville *Sunday Star*, January 14, 1901.

48. Milwaukee *Journal*, June 13, 1899; Milwaukee *Sentinel*, January 8, 1912.

49. Hidy, Hill, and Nevins, *Timber*, 28; Toledo *Blade*, February 28, 1907.

50. Gates, *Agriculture in the Civil War*, 137; Nevins, *War*, 3:240.

51. Hidy, Hill, and Nevins, *Timber*, 30, 31.

52. Ibid., 29, 30.

53. Milwaukee *Sentinel*, January 8, 1912; Davenport *Democrat and Leader*, April 1, 1925; Milwaukee *Journal*, May 25, 1935.

54. Hidy, Hill, and Nevins, *Timber*, 31; Milwaukee *Journal*, June 13, 1899; Toledo *Blade*, February 28, 1907.

55. Toledo *Blade*, February 28, 1907; Spartanburg *Herald-Journal*, June 7, 1935; Davenport *Democrat and Leader*, April 1, 1925; Hidy, Hill, and Nevins, *Timber*, 31.

56. Spartanburg *Herald-Journal*, June 7, 1953; Rock Island *Argus and Daily Union*, June 16, 1904; Hidy, Hill, and Nevins, *Timber*, 30.

Chapter Eleven

1. Stiles, *First Tycoon*, 277.

2. Ibid., 277.

3. Ibid., chaps. 7–12; Stoddard, *Men*, 32; Saint Cloud *Democrat*, November 29, 1860.

4. Stiles, *First Tycoon*, 9, 11, 19, 20; Stoddard, *Men*, 32, 34; Doll, "Tales," 6, 7

5. Stiles, *First Tycoon*, 24, 26–28; Cleveland *Daily Leader*, April 14, 1864; Doll, "Tales," 7.

6. Nevins, *Diary*, xv; Lane, *Commodore Vanderbilt*, 10, 23, 31; Stiles, *First Tycoon*, 34, 36.

7. Stiles, *First Tycoon*, 37, 42, 61–63.

8. Ibid., 37, 71; Doll, "Tales," 7.

9. Stiles, *First Tycoon*, 5, 6, 159, 160; Summers, *Plundering Generation*, 260; Lane, *Commodore Vanderbilt*, 147, 148, 154, 240; Doll, "Tales," 7.

10. Stiles, *First Tycoon*, 217, 220, 225, 226, 320; Lane, *Commodore Vanderbilt*, 148.

11. Josephson, *Robber Barons*, 14; Detroit *Free Press*, March 13, 1860.

12. Stoddard, *Men*, 43; Renehan, *Commodore*, 243; Doll, "Tales," 8.

13. Lane, *Commodore Vanderbilt*, 185, 208, 211; Renehan, *Commodore*, 243, 244; Doll, "Tales," 8.

14. Doll, "Tales," 8.

15. Stiles, *First Tycoon*, 234, 320, 321.

16. Ibid., 114, 337; Kirkland, *Dream*, 10; Doll, "Tales," 8.

17. Pittsburgh *Post-Gazette*, August 15, 1900; Finlay, "Collis P. Huntington."

18. Lavender, *Great Persuader*, 2; Pittsburgh *Post-Gazette*, August 15, 1900; Finlay, "Collis P. Huntington."

19. Finlay, "Collis P. Huntington"; Wilkes-Barre *Times*, August 14, 1900.

20. Finlay, "Collis P. Huntington"; Josephson, *Robber Barons*, 34; Wilkes-Barre *Times*, August 14, 1900; Iola *Register*, August 15, 1900; San Francisco *Chronicle*, August 15, 1900.

21. Ambrose, *Nothing Like It*, 48; Finlay, "Collis P. Huntington"; Lavender, *Great Persuader*, 5.

22. Ambrose, *Nothing Like It*, 48.

23. Ibid., 49, 50; Iola *Register*, August 15, 1900; Lavender, *Great Persuader*, 7.

24. Ambrose, *Nothing Like It*, 50; Josephson, *Robber Barons*, 33, 34; Monroeville *Breeze*, August 30, 1900.

25. Ambrose, *Nothing Like It*, 49; Lavender, *Great Persuader*, 30, 31, 38.

26. Lavender, *Great Persuader*, 31, 32.

27. Ibid., 33, 34; Iola *Register*, August 15, 1900; Wilkes-Barre *Times*, August 14, 1900.

28. Lavender, *Great Persuader*, 33–34.

29. Ibid., 38–41.

30. Ibid., 42.

31. Ibid., 43, 44.

32. Ibid., 44, 45; Ambrose, *Nothing Like It*, 43, 53–55.

33. Ambrose, *Nothing Like It*, 54–59; Lavender, *Great Persuader*, 50, 51.

34. Ambrose, *Nothing Like It*, 57, 58; Lavender, *Great Persuader*, 51, 57.

35. Lavender, *Great Persuader*, 63, 64, 66, 67.

36. Ibid., 70, 72; Ambrose, *Nothing Like It*, 59.

37. Ambrose, *Nothing Like It,* 55, 59, 61, 62.

38. Lavender, *Great Persuader,* 92–94; "Collis P. Huntington."

39. "Collis P. Huntington"; White, *Railroaded,* 18.

40. Welles, *Diary,* 1:61, 62; Stiles, *First Tycoon,* 345.

41. Welles, *Diary,* 1:62, 63.

42. Ibid., 40; Stiles, *First Tycoon,* 345.

43. Lane, *Commodore Vanderbilt,* 176; Stiles, *First Tycoon,* 346.

44. Stiles, *First Tycoon,* 346; Lane, *Commodore Vanderbilt,* 175, 177; Stoddard, *Men,* 44; Lewisburg *Chronicle,* July 2, 1861; Clearfield *Raftsman's Journal,* May 1, 1861.

45. OR, series 3, 1:934, 935.

46. Ibid., 934; OR, series 1, 8:643; 11, pt. 2:299, 331; [Richard] Halsted to the President, March 15, 1862, Lincoln Papers, LC; Renehan, *Commodore,* 236; Lane, *Commodore Vanderbilt,* 177; Wert, *Sword,* 66.

47. OR, series 3, 2:525; Stiles, *First Tycoon,* 359–362; Lane, *Commodore Vanderbilt,* 178.

48. Stiles, *First Tycoon,* 363; Cleveland *Daily Leader,* April 14, 1864; Renehan, *Commodore,* 236, 237; Stoddard, *Men,* 45.

49. Stiles, *First Tycoon,* 358; OR, series 3, 2:713; Josephson, *Robber Barons,* 67.

50. Stiles, *First Tycoon,* 358; Josephson, *Robber Barons,* 67; Doll, "Tales," 7.

51. Stiles, *First Tycoon,* 369–371; Josephson, *Robber Barons,* 68; Renehan, *Commodore,* 245; Lane, *Commodore Vanderbilt,* 184.

52. Stiles, *First Tycoon,* 374–376; Josephson, *Robber Barons,* 68, 69, but misdates it to 1864; Renehan, *Commodore,* 247.

53. Stiles, *First Tycoon,* 376; Renehan, *Commodore,* 249; Cleveland *Daily Leader,* May 9, 1864.

54. Stiles, *First Tycoon,* 376, 377; Renehan, *Commodore,* 249; Cleveland *Daily Leader,* May 9, 1864.

55. Renehan, *Commodore,* 249; Cleveland *Daily Leader,* May 9, 1864.

56. Renehan, *Commodore,* 254–256; Josephson, *Robber Barons,* 69–71; Stiles, *First Tycoon,* 382–384.

57. Horace Greeley to My Dear Sir, November 23, 1864, Lincoln Papers, LC.

58. Washington *Evening Star,* July 14, 1865; Davenport *Daily Gazette,* August 1, 1865; Stiles, *First Tycoon,* 561.

59. Lavender, *Great Persuader,* 94–96; Ambrose, *Nothing Like It,* 73, 74; Monroeville *Breeze,* August 30, 1900.

60. Ambrose, *Nothing Like It,* 63.

61. Ibid., 73, 74; Lavender, *Great Persuader,* 98; Josephson, *Robber Barons,* 78; Stoddard, *Men,* 308.

62. Monroeville *Breeze,* August 30, 1900; Ambrose, *Nothing Like It,* 74.

63. Ambrose, *Nothing Like It,* 74; White, *Railroaded,* 18, 19.

64. Ambrose, *Nothing Like It,* 74, 75; Lavender, *Great Persuader,* 99, 100.

65. Lavender, *Great Persuader,* 103–105.

66. Josephson, *Robber Barons,* 78; Ramage, *Gray Ghost,* 301; "Collis P. Huntington."

67. Lavender, *Great Persuader,* 105, 106.

68. Ibid., 107, 108; Wilkes-Barre *Times,* August 14, 1900; Ambrose, *Nothing Like It,* 78.

69. Ambrose, *Nothing Like It,* 79, 80; White, *Railroaded,* 19; McPherson, *Battle Cry,* 451.

70. White, *Railroaded,* 19; McPherson, *Battle Cry,* 451; Ambrose, *Nothing Like It,* 80, 81.

71. White, *Railroaded,* 35, 37; Josephson, *Robber Barons,* 86, 87. These sources offered different amounts for the Associates' profits.

Epilogue

1. Wert, *Sword,* 410, 411; Winik, *April 1865,* 359; Furgurson, *Freedom Rising,* 385; Nevins, *Diary,* 589.

2. Wert, *Sword,* 411; Furgurson, *Freedom Rising,* 395, 396; Cleveland *Daily Leader,* May 24, 1865.

3. Columbus *Daily Ohio Statesman,* May 24, 1865; Harrisburg *Daily Independent,* May 23, 1906; Washington *Evening Star,* October 8, 1902; Furgurson, *Freedom Rising,* 395.

4. Cleveland *Daily Leader,* May 23, 1865; Columbus *Daily Ohio Statesman,* May 24, 1865; Akron *Beacon Journal,* March 5, 1915.

5. Sherman, *Memoirs,* 1:378; Seymour *Tribune,* May 28, 1909; Furgurson, *Freedom Rising,* 397; Harrisburg *Daily Independent,* May 23, 1906.

6. Winik, *April 1865,* 378.

7. Goldfield, *America Aflame,* 301; Laugel, *United States,* 109, 111.

8. Nevins, *War,* 3:215.

9. Ibid.

10. Ibid., 220; Goldfield, *America Aflame,* 10; Gates, *Agriculture and the Civil War,* 227.

11. Murray and Hsieh, *Savage War,* 87; Lawson, *Patriot Fires,* 7.

12. Whitten, *Emergence,* 13, 14; Bensel, *Yankee Leviathan,* 94.

13. Murray and Hsieh, *Savage War,* 87, 516; Wilson, *Business,* 38; Koistinen, *Beating Plowshares,* 185, 186; Lawson, *Patriot Fires,* 41.

14. Huston, *Sinews,* 176; Wilson, "Business," 1:315, 316; Paludan, *"People's Contest,"* 149; Murray and Hsieh, *Savage War,* 470, 516.

15. Murray and Hsieh, *Savage War,* 133, 515; Bensel, *Yankee Leviathan,* 94; Hacker, *Astride,* 26.

16. Cowley, *With My Face,* 71; Murray and Hsieh, *Savage War,* 515; Bensel, *Yankee Leviathan,* 94, 95, 97.

17. McPherson, *Battle Cry,* 760–781.

18. Murray and Hsieh, *Savage War,* 11–12.

19. Gallman, *Northerners at War,* 97, 102, 112.

20. Ibid., 94, 98, 99, 102; Koistinen, *Beating Plowshares*, 195, 196; Wilson, *Business*, 228; Goldfield, *America Aflame*, 308.

21. Wilson, *Business*, 214–215, 416.

22. Goldfield, *America Aflame*, 379.

Postscript

1. Leech and Carroll, *Armour*, chaps. V–XX; Skaggs, *Prime Cut*, 7; Cronon, *Nature's Metropolis*, 249; Clinton *Mirror*, February 2, 1901; Chicago *Tribune*, January 7, 1901; "Philip Armour's Grave."

2. Frantz, *Gail Borden*, 262–276; Bridgeport *Post*, December 1, 1957; Groesbeck *Journal*, June 28, 2001; "Gail Borden Milks Success."

3. "Henry Burden"; Weise, *City of Troy*, 46; Proudfit, *Henry Burden*, 6, 9, 12, 21, 22; "Burden Iron Works."

4. Nasaw, *Andrew Carnegie*, xxii, 357, 457, 506, 537, 538, 587, 742, 794, 799, 801.

5. White, *Railroaded*, 56, 57, 66, 82, 83; Cozzens, *Earth*, 207; Harrisburg *Telegraph*, September 19, 1873; Memphis *Daily Appeal*, September 19, 1873; Philadelphia *Times*, November 3, 1879; New York *Times*, November 19, 1907; Lawson, *Patriotic Fires*, 63.

6. Wagle, "John Deere"; Abrams, "John Deere"; Broehl, *John Deere's Company*, 161, 250–253; "John Deere."

7. How, *James B. Eads*, 60–66, 72, 119; Nasaw, *Andrew Carnegie*, 112, 134, 135; Dorsey, *Road*, chaps. IX–XIX; Davenport *Daily Gazette*, March 11, 1887; Davenport *Democrat*, March 12, 1887.

8. Zink, "Iron & Steel"; Nevins, *Abram S. Hewitt*, chaps. 13–30; Mack, *Peter Cooper*, 278; Boston *Evening Transcript*, August 20, 1888, August 1, 1902, January 20, 1903; Milwaukee *Journal*, January 10, 1903; Pittsburgh *Press*, January 19, 1903.

9. Scranton *Republican*, September 15, 1900; White, *Railroaded*, 115, 116, 201, 264, 265; San Francisco *Chronicle*, August 15, 1900; Ramage, *Gray Ghost*, 301; Iola *Register*, August 15, 1900; Wilkes-Barre *Times*, August 14, 1900; Richmond *Dispatcher*, September 2, 1900; Finlay, "Collis P. Huntington"; Atchison *Daily Champion*, August 18, 1900.

10. Hutchinson, *Cyrus Hall McCormick*, chaps. 5–17, 770, 771; White, *Railroaded*, 63, 64; *In Memoriam*, 23.

11. Lewis, "Gordon McKay"; Thomson, "Invention," 143, 146; Boston *Post*, November 17, 1880; Reading *Times*, September 14, 1881; Wichita *Daily Eagle*, April 27, 1899; Washington *Post*, February 5, 1910; Berkshire *Eagle*, November 4, 1949; "Gordon McKay."

12. "Robert P. Parrott"; Soodalter, "Well Armed"; Robert P. Parrott's Will, February 26, 1875, Parrott Papers, PHM; Grace and Forlow, *West Point Foundry*, 9, 88.

13. White, *Railroaded*, 35, 94, 121–130; Harrisburg *Telegraph*, June 4, 1874; Josephson, *Robber Barons*, 43, 79, 220; Clearfield *Republican*, June 1, 1881.

14. Taylor, "Christopher Spencer," 10–14; Taylor, "Character," 2; Hubbard, "Life," 3–5, WHS; Bridgeport *Evening Farmer*, July 22, 1915, April 7, 1916; Milwaukee *Sentinel*, January 15, 1922; New York *Tribune*, January 15, 1922; Saint Petersburg *Evening Independent*, January 20, 1922.

15. Blochman, *Doctor Squibb*, chaps. 10–20, quote on 350; Wilmington *Evening Journal*, October 27, 1900; Brooklyn *Daily Eagle*, December 21, 1900; Florey, *Collected Papers*, 2:1429.

16. Corle, *John Studebaker*, 146, 151, 213, 221, 300; Bonsall, *More Than They Promised*, 24–39; Studebaker and Studebaker, *Studebaker Family*, 55.

17. Ashmead, *History*, 728, 729; Ward, *J. Edgar Thomson*, 137, 140, 142, 216; New Orleans *Times Picayune*, February 1, 1860; Stroudsburg *Jeffersonian*, June 4, 1874; Washington *Post*, June 16, 1914.

18. Josephson, *Robber Barons*, 122, 134, 177, 182, 452; Stiles, *First Tycoon*, 7, 402, 561, 566.

19. Eau Claire *Leader*, April 4, 1909; Hidy, Hill, and Nevins, *Timber*, 50, 63, 74, 106, 212, 228; New Orleans *Times-Democrat*, April 5, 1909; Des Moines *Register*, May 26, 1935; Rock Island *Argus and Daily Union*, June 16, 1904; Lewiston *Daily Sun*, April 2, 1914; Ludington *Daily News*, April 4, 1914.

BIBLIOGRAPHY

Unpublished Sources

Army Heritage and Educational Center, Archives, Carlisle, Pennsylvania
    Civil War Documents Collection:
        Burrill, John H. Letters and Diary.
        Martin, Henry L. Letter.

Duke University, David M. Rubenstein Rare Book & Manuscript Library, Durham, North Carolina
    Special Collections:
        Laughton, Joseph B. Papers.

Harvard Business School, Baker Library, Cambridge, Massachusetts
    Historical Collections:
        Cooke, Jay & Company Records.

Rutherford B. Hayes Presidential Center, Library, Fremont, Ohio
    Charles E. Frohman Collection:
        Cooke, Eleutheros. Papers.
        Cooke, Jay. Family Papers.

Historical Society of Pennsylvania, Philadelphia, Pennsylvania
    Cooke, Jay. Papers. 0148.

Historical Society of Western Pennsylvania, Detre Library and Archives, Sen. John Heinz History Center, Pittsburgh, Pennsylvania
    Covode, John. Papers. MSS#18.

Library of Congress, Washington, DC
    Lincoln, Abraham. Papers.

Manassas National Battlefield Park, Library, Manassas, Virginia
    2nd Wisconsin Infantry File:
        Davis, William G. Letters.

Minnesota Historical Society, Saint Paul, Minnesota
    Weyerhaeuser Family Papers.

Missouri History Museum, Archives, Saint Louis, Missouri
    Eads, James Buchanan. Collection.

National Museum of Civil War Medicine, Frederick, Maryland
 Dammann Collection:
  Squibb Pannier.
Navarro College, Pearce Civil War Collection, Corsicana, Texas
 Flynn, James B. Papers.
New Jersey State Archives, Trenton, New Jersey
 Ringwood Manor. Papers.
New-York Historical Society, Gilder Lehrman Institute of American History, New York, New York
 Lincoln, Abraham, to Gen. Stephen A. Hurlbut, August 4, 1863, GLC00005.01.
 Semmes, Paul Jones. [Contract with Robert P. Parrott to buy 16 rifle cannons for Georgia], December 19, 1860, GLC00474.
Putnam History Museum, Cold Spring, New York
 Frederick Haida Collection:
  Parrott, Robert P. Papers
University of Maine, Raymond H. Fogler Library, Orono, Maine
 Special Collections, Paul W. Bean Civil War Papers, MS46:
  Lemont, Frank L. Letters, 1861–1864.
University of Michigan, William L. Clements Library, Ann Arbor, Michigan
 Emerson, Horace. Letters.
Windsor Historical Society, Windsor, Connecticut
 Christopher Miner Spencer Collection:
  Bartlett, W. A. "An Appreciation of Christopher Spencer."
  Hubbard, Guy. "The Life and Work of Christopher Miner Spencer," typescript.
  Taylor, Vesta Spencer. "Character Sketch of Christopher Miner Spencer."
  Taylor, Vesta Spencer. "Christopher Spencer: A Talk Given at a Meeting of the Windsor Historical Society," typescript.
Wisconsin Historical Society, Madison, Wisconsin
 McCormick Family Papers.
 Mead, Sydney B. "A Journal of the Marches, Reconnaissances, Skirmishes and Battles of the Second Regiment of Wisconsin Volunteer Infantry, June 11, 1861–March 29, 1864."
 Murray, Julius A. Family Papers.

Newspapers

Abilene (Texas) *Reporter-News*
Adams (Pennsylvania) *Sentinel*
Albuquerque (New Mexico) *Journal*
Alexandria (Virginia) *Gazette*
Alexandria (Virginia) *Soldier's Journal*
Alton (Illinois) *Weekly Telegraph*
Altoona (Pennsylvania) *Tribune*
Akron (Ohio) *Beacon Journal*
Atchison (Kansas) *Daily Champion*
Atlanta *Constitution*
Baltimore *Daily Exchange*

Baltimore *Sun*
Belmont (Ohio) *Chronicle*
Berkshire (Massachusetts) *Eagle*
Bismarck (North Dakota) *Tribune*
Boston *Evening Transcript*
Boston *Post*
Bridgeport (Connecticut) *Evening Farmer*
Bridgeport (Connecticut) *Post*
Brooklyn *Daily Eagle*
Brooklyn *Evening Star*
Brownsville (Texas) *Herald*
Bryan (Ohio) *Times*
Buffalo (New York) *Daily Republic*
Burlington (Vermont) *Weekly Free Press*
Burlington (Iowa) *Weekly Hawk-Eye*
Cape Girardeau *Southeast Missourian*
Charlotte (North Carolina) *Western Democrat*
Chicago *Tribune*
Clearfield (Pennsylvania) *Raftsman's Journal*
Clearfield (Pennsylvania) *Republican*
Cleveland *Daily Leader*
Clinton (Iowa) *Mirror*
Columbus *Daily Ohio Statesman*
Crawfordsville (Indiana) *Sunday Star*
Davenport (Iowa) *Daily Gazette*
Davenport (Iowa) *Daily Leader*
Davenport (Iowa) *Democrat*
Davenport (Iowa) *Democratic Banner*
Davenport (Iowa) *Morning Democrat*
Davenport (Iowa) *Quad-City Times*
Dawson's Fort Wayne (Indiana) *Daily Times*
Delaware County (Pennsylvania) *Daily Times*
Des Moines (Iowa) *Register*
Detroit *Free Press*
Eau Claire (Wisconsin) *Leader*
Emporia (Kansas) *Weekly News*
Findlay (Ohio) *Jeffersonian*
Florence (Alabama) *Times*
Gallipolis (Ohio) *Journal*

Galveston (Texas) *Daily News*
Gettysburg (Pennsylvania) *Compiler*
Groesbeck (Texas) *Journal*
Harrisburg (Pennsylvania) *Daily Independent*
Harrisburg (Pennsylvania) *Telegraph*
Hornellsville (New York) *Weekly Tribune*
Indiana (Pennsylvania) *Weekly Messenger*
Iola (Kansas) *Register*
Janesville (Wisconsin) *Daily Gazette*
Joliet (Illinois) *Signal*
Junction City (Kansas) *Weekly Union.*
Lane County (Kansas) *Journal*
Lawrence *Daily Kansas Tribune*
Lebanon (Pennsylvania) *Daily News*
Lewisburg (Pennsylvania) *Chronicle*
Lewiston (Maine) *Daily Sun*
London *Times*
Los Angeles *Times*
Louisville *Courier-Journal*
Ludington (Michigan) *Daily News*
Mattoon (Illinois) *Gazette*
Memphis (Tennessee) *Daily Appeal*
Milwaukee *Daily News*
Milwaukee *Journal*
Milwaukee *Sentinel*
Milwaukee *Weekly Wisconsin*
Monroeville (Indiana) *Breeze*
Montreal *Gazette*
Nashville *Union and American*
Nevada (Missouri) *Daily Mail*
New Orleans *Times-Picayune*
New York *Daily Tribune*
New York *Evening Post*
New York *Herald*
New York *Times*
New York *Tribune*
Norwalk (Connecticut) *The Hour*
Paris (Texas) *News*
Perrysburg (Ohio) *Journal*
Philadelphia *Times*

Pittsburgh (Pennsylvania) *Daily Commercial*
Pittsburgh (Pennsylvania) *Daily Post*
Pittsburgh (Pennsylvania) *Gazette News*
Pittsburgh (Pennsylvania) *Gazette Times*
Pittsburgh (Pennsylvania) *Post-Gazette*
Pittsburgh (Pennsylvania) *Press*
Pittston (Pennsylvania) *Gazette*
Reading (Pennsylvania) *Eagle*
Reading (Pennsylvania) *Times*
Richmond (Virginia) *Dispatch*
Riverside (California) *Press and Horticulturist*
Rock Island (Illinois) *Argus and Daily Union*
Saint Cloud (Minnesota) *Democrat*
Saint Louis *Dispatch*
Saint Petersburg (Florida) *Evening Independent*
Sandusky (Ohio) *Register*
Sandusky (Ohio) *Star-Journal*
San Francisco *Chronicler*
Sarasota (Florida) *Herald-Tribune*
Schenectady (New York) *Gazette*
Scranton (Pennsylvania) *Republican*
Seymour (Indiana) *Tribune*
Shiner (Texas) *Gazette*
Sioux City (South Dakota) *Journal*
South Bend (Indiana) *News-Times*
Spartanburg (South Carolina) *Herald-Journal*
Spokane (Washington) *Daily Chronicle*
Staunton (Virginia) *Spectator*
Stevens Point (Wisconsin) *Journal*
Stroudsburg (Pennsylvania) *Jeffersonian*
Sumter (South Carolina) *Watchman and Southron*
Syracuse (New York) *Daily Courier and Union*
Toledo (Ohio) *Blade*
Wakarusa *Kansas Herald of Freedom*
Washington (DC) *Daily Globe*
Washington (DC) *Evening Star*
Washington (DC) *Herald*
Washington (DC) *National Intelligencer*
Washington (DC) *National Republican*
Washington (Pennsylvania) *Observer-Reporter*
Washington (DC) *Post*
Wichita (Kansas) *Daily Eagle*
Wilkes-Barre (Pennsylvania) *Times*
Wilmington (North Carolina) *Daily Journal*
Wilmington (Delaware) *Morning News*
Wilmington (Delaware) *Sunday Morning Star*
Wilmington (North Carolina) *Sunday Star-News*
Wyandotte (Kansas) *Commercial Gazette*

Published Books and Articles

Adler, Dennis. *Guns of the Civil War*. Minneapolis, MN: Zenith Press, 2011.
Ambrose, Stephen E. *Nothing Like It in the World: The Men Who Built the Transcontinental Railroad, 1863–1869*. New York: Simon & Schuster, 2000.
Army, Thomas F., Jr. *Engineering Victory: How Technology Won the Civil War*. Baltimore: Johns Hopkins University Press, 2016.
Ashmead, Henry Graham. *History of Delaware County, Pennsylvania*. Philadelphia: L. H. Everts & Co., 1884.

Baker, William M. *A Year Worth Living: A Story of a Place and of a People One Cannot Afford Not to Know*. Reprint, London: Forgotten Books, 2015.

Basler, Roy P., ed. *The Collected Works of Abraham Lincoln*. 8 vols. New Brunswick, NJ: Rutgers University Press, 1953.

Bates, David Homer. *Lincoln in the Telegraph Office: Recollections of the United States Military Telegraph Corps During the Civil War*. Reprint, n.p.: Forgotten Books, 2012.

Beckert, Sven. *The Monied Metropolis: New York City and the Consolidation of the American Bourgeoisie, 1850–1896*. New York: Cambridge University Press, 2001.

Bensel, Richard Franklin. *Yankee Leviathan: The Origins of Central State Authority in America, 1859–1877*. New York: Cambridge University Press, 1995.

Bilby, Joseph G. *Small Arms at Gettysburg: Infantry and Cavalry Weapons in America's Greatest Battle*. Yardley, PA: Westholme Publishing, 2007.

Bishop, J. Leander. *A History of American Manufactures from 1608 to 1860*. Philadelphia: Edward Young & Co., 1866.

Blochman, Lawrence G. *Doctor Squibb: The Life and Times of a Rugged Idealist*. New York: Simon & Schuster, 1958.

Bonsall, Thomas E. *More Than They Promised: The Studebaker Story*. Stanford, CA: Stanford University Press, 2000.

Broehl, Wayne G. *John Deere's Company: A History of Deere and Company and Its Times*. Garden City, NY: Doubleday & Company, 1984.

Bruce, Robert V. *Lincoln and the Tools of War*. Indianapolis, IN: Bobbs-Merrill Company, 1956.

Buckeridge, J. O. *Lincoln Choice*. Harrisburg, PA: Stackpole Company, 1956.

Burgess, George H., and Miles C. Kennedy. *Centennial History of the Pennsylvania Railroad Company, 1846–1946*. Philadelphia: Pennsylvania Railroad Company, 1949.

Burlingame, Michael, ed. *At Lincoln's Side: John Hay's Civil War Correspondence and Selected Writings*. Carbondale: Southern Illinois University Press, 2000.

———. *Lincoln's Journalist: John Hay's Anonymous Writings for the Press, 1860–1864*. Carbondale: Southern Illinois University Press, 2006.

———. *With Lincoln in the White House: Letters, Memoranda, and Other Writings of John G. Nicolay, 1860–1865*. Carbondale: Southern Illinois University Press, 2000.

Burlingame, Michael, and John R. Turner Ettlinger, eds. *Inside Lincoln's White House: The Complete Civil War Diary of John Hay*. Carbondale: Southern Illinois University Press, 1999.

Carnegie, Andrew. *Autobiography of Andrew Carnegie*. Edited by John C. Van Dyke. Reprint, n.p.: n.p., n.d.

———. *The "Gospel of Wealth" Essays and Other Writings*. Edited by David Nasaw. New York: Penguin Books, 2006.

Chandler, Alfred D., Jr. *The Visible Hand: The Managerial Revolution in American Business.* Cambridge, MA: Harvard University Press, 1978.

Clark, John E., Jr. *Railroads in the Civil War: The Impact of Management on Victory and Defeat.* Baton Rouge: Louisiana State University Press, 2001.

Cooling, Benjamin Franklin. *Forts Henry and Donelson: The Key to the Confederate Heartland.* Knoxville: University of Tennessee Press, 1987.

Corle, Edwin. *John Studebaker: An American Dream.* New York: E. P. Dutton & Co., 1948.

Cottrell, Alden T. *The Story of Ringwood Manor.* Trenton, NJ: Trenton Printing Company, n.d.

Cowley, Robert, ed. *With My Face to the Enemy: Perspectives on the Civil War.* New York: G. P. Putnam's Sons, 2001.

Cozzens, Peter. *The Earth Is Weeping: The Epic Story of the Indian Wars for the American West.* New York: Alfred A. Knopf, 2016.

Cronon, William. *Nature's Metropolis: Chicago and the Great West.* New York: W. W. Norton & Company, 1991.

Dahlstrom, Neil, and Jeremy Dahlstrom. *The John Deere Story: A Biography of Plowmakers John & Charles Deere.* DeKalb: Northern Illinois University Press, 2005.

Davis, William C. *Look Away! A History of the Confederate States of America.* New York: Free Press, 2002.

Doll, Gaynelle. "Tales of the Commodore." *Vanderbilt Magazine* 77, no. 3 (Summer 1994).

Donald, David, ed. *Inside Lincoln's Cabinet: The Civil War Diaries of Salmon P. Chase.* New York: Longmans, Green and Co., 1954.

———. *Lincoln.* New York: Simon & Schuster, 1995.

Dorsey, Florence. *Road to the Sea and the Mississippi River: The Story of James B. Eads.* Reprint, Gretna, LA: Pelican Publishing Company, 1998.

Erskine, Albert Russel. *History of the Studebaker Corporation.* South Bend, IN: Studebaker Corporation, 1924.

Florey, Klaus, ed. *The Collected Papers of Edward Robinson Squibb, M.D.* 2 vols. New York: Squibb Corporation, 1988.

Frantz, Joe B. *Gail Borden: Dairyman to a Nation.* Norman: Oklahoma University Press, 1951.

Furgurson, Ernest B. *Freedom Rising: Washington in the Civil War.* New York: Alfred A. Knopf, 2004.

Gallman, J. Matthew. *Northerners at War: Reflections on the Civil War Home Front.* Kent, OH: Kent State University Press, 2010.

Gates, Paul W. *Agriculture and the Civil War.* New York: Alfred A. Knopf, 1965.

Geier, Clarence, Douglas D. Scott, and Lawrence E. Babits, eds. *From These Honored Dead: Historical Archaeology of the Civil War.* Gainesville: University Press of Florida, 2014.

Giesberg, Judith. *Army at Home: Women and the Civil War on the Northern Home Front.* Chapel Hill: University of North Carolina Press, 2009.

Gillmore, Quincy A. *Engineer and Artillery Operations Against the Defenses of Charleston Harbor in 1863.* New York: D. Van Nostrand, 1865.

Goldfield, David. *America Aflame: How the Civil War Created a Nation.* New York: Bloomsburg Press, 2011.

Goldin, Claudia D., and Frank D. Lewis. "The Economic Cost of the American Civil War: Estimates and Implications." *Journal of Economic History* 35, no. 2 (June 1975).

Goodheart, Adam. *1861: The Civil War Awakening.* New York: Alfred A. Knopf, 2011.

Goodwin, Doris Kearns. *Team of Rivals: The Political Genius of Abraham Lincoln.* New York: Simon & Schuster, 2005.

Grace, Trudie A., and Mark Forlow. *West Point Foundry.* Charleston, SC: Arcadia Publishing, 2014.

Hacker, Baron C., ed. *Astride Two Worlds: Technology and the American Civil War.* Washington, DC: Smithsonian Institution Scholarly Press, 2016.

Hagerman, Edward. *The American Civil War and the Origins of Modern Warfare: Ideas, Organization, and Field Command.* Bloomington: Indiana University Press, 1988.

————. "Field Transportation and Strategic Mobility in the Union Armies." *Civil War History* 34, no. 2 (June 1988).

Hattaway, Herman, and Archer Jones. *How the North Won: A Military History of the Civil War.* Urbana: University of Illinois Press, 1983.

Haupt, Herman. *Reminiscences of General Herman Haupt.* Milwaukee, WI: Wright & Joys, Co., Engravers, Printers, 1901.

Hazard, Blanche Evans. *The Organization of the Boot and Shoe Industry in Massachusetts Before 1875.* Reprint, New York: Augustus M. Kelley, 1969.

Hendrick, Burton J. *The Life of Andrew Carnegie.* London: William Heinemann, 1933.

Hess, Earl J. *Civil War Logistics: A Study of Military Transportation.* Baton Rouge: Louisiana State University Press, 2017.

Hidy, Ralph W., Frank Ernest Hill, and Allan Nevins. *Timber and Men: The Weyerhaeuser Story.* New York: Macmillan Company, 1963.

How, Louis. *James B. Eads.* Reprint, Freeport, NY: Books for Libraries Press, 1970.

Hubbard, Elbert. *Little Journeys to the Homes of the Great Businessmen.* New York: Wm. D. Wise, 1916.

Hubbard, Guy. "Abraham Lincoln and the Repeating Rifle: How an Inventor's Struggle for Recognition Was Assisted by the Action of the President." *Scientific American,* December 1921.

Huston, James A. *The Sinews of War: Army Logistics, 1775–1953.* Washington, DC: US Government Printing Office, 1966.

Hutchinson, William T. *Cyrus Hall McCormick Harvest, 1856–1884.* New York: D. Appleton-Century Company, 1935.

In Memoriam. Cyrus Hall McCormick. Reprint, n.p.: n.p., n.d.

Jackson, Rex T. *James B. Eads: The Civil War Ironclads and His Mississippi.* Westminster, MD: Heritage Books, 2007.

Johnson, Robert Underwood, and Clarence Clough Buel, eds. *Battles and Leaders of the Civil War.* 4 vols. Reprint, New York: Thomas Yoseloff, 1956.

Jones, Virgil Carrington. *The Civil War at Sea.* 3 vols. Reprint, Wilmington, NC: Broadfoot Publishing Company, 1990.

Josephson, Matthew. *The Robber Barons: The Great American Capitalists, 1861–1901.* New York: Harcourt, Brace & World, 1962.

Kamm, Samuel Richey. "The Civil War Career of Thomas A. Scott." PhD diss., University of Pennsylvania, 1940.

Kirkland, Edward Chase. *Dream and Thought in the Business Community, 1860–1900.* Chicago: Ivan R. Dee, 1990.

Kirtland, J. P. *A Family History: Genealogy of the Cooke Family.* n.p.: n.p., 1875.

Klein, Maury. *The Change Makers: From Carnegie to Gates, How the Great Entrepreneurs Transformed Ideas into Industries.* New York: Henry Holt and Company, 2003.

Koistinen, Paul A. C. *Beating Plowshares into Swords: The Political Economy of American Warfare, 1606–1865.* Lawrence: University Press of Kansas, 1996.

Lane, Wheaton. *Commodore Vanderbilt: An Epic of the Steam Age.* New York: Alfred A. Knopf, 1942.

Laugel, Auguste. *The United States During the Civil War.* Edited by Allan Nevins. Reprint, Bloomington: Indiana University Press, 1961.

Lavender, David. *The Great Persuader.* Niwot: University Press of Colorado, 1998.

Lawrence, Susan C., ed. *Civil War Washington: History, Place, and Digital Scholarship.* Lincoln: University of Nebraska Press, 2015.

Lawson, Melinda. *Patriot Fires: Forging a New American Nationalism in the Civil War North.* Lawrence: University Press of Kansas, 2002.

Le Duc, William G. *This Business of War: Recollections of a Civil War Quartermaster.* St. Paul: Minnesota Historical Society Press, 1963.

Leech, Harper, and John Charles Carroll. *Armour and His Times.* New York: D. Appleton-Century Company, 1938.

Leech, Margaret. *Reveille in Washington, 1860–1865.* New York: Harper & Brothers Publishers, 1941.

Lord, Francis A. *Lincoln's Railroad Man: Herman Haupt.* Rutherford, NJ: Fairleigh Dickinson University Press, 1969.

Mack, Edward C. *Peter Cooper: Citizen of New York.* New York: Duell, Sloan and Pearce, 1949.

Martin, Asa Earl. *Pennsylvania History Told by Contemporaries.* New York: Macmillan Company, 1925.

McCormick, Cyrus. *The Century of the Reaper: An Account of Cyrus Hall McCormick, the Inventor of the Reaper.* Boston: Houghton Mifflin Company, 1931.

McHenry, Estill, ed. *Addresses and Papers of James B. Eads, Together with a Biographical Sketch*. Reprint, n.p.: n.p., n.d.

McIlhenny, David Robert. "Early History of Pennsylvania Railroads." Master's thesis, Pennsylvania State University, 1932.

McPherson, James. *Battle Cry of Freedom: The Civil War Era*. New York: Oxford University Press, 1988.

Muler, Matt. "Walt Whitman and Abram S. Hewitt: A Previously Unknown Connection." *Walt Whitman Quarterly Review* 29, no. 3 (2012).

Murray, Williamson, and Wayne Wei-siang Hsieh. *A Savage War: A Military History of the Civil War*. Princeton, NJ: Princeton University Press, 2016.

Myers, John Myers. *Print in a Wild Land*. Garden City, NY: Doubleday & Company, 1967.

Naisawald, L. VanLoan. *Grape and Canister: The Story of the Field Artillery of the Army of the Potomac, 1861–1865*. Mechanicsburg, PA: Stackpole Books, 1999.

Nasaw, David. *Andrew Carnegie*. New York: Penguin Books, 2006.

Nelson, Dean E. "Connecticut Arms the Union." *Connecticut Explored* 9, no. 2 (Spring 2011).

Nelson, Scott Reynolds, and Carol Sheriff. *A People at War: Civilians and Soldiers in America's Civil War, 1854–1877*. New York: Oxford University Press, 2007.

Nevins, Allan. *Abram S. Hewitt: With Some Account of Peter Cooper*. New York: Octagon Books, 1967.

———, ed. *Diary of the Civil War: George Templeton Strong*. New York: Macmillan Company, 1962.

———, ed. *Selected Writings of Abram S. Hewitt*. Reprint, Port Washington, NY: Kennikat Press, 1965.

———. *The War for the Union*. 4 vols. New York: Charles Scribner's Sons, 1959–1971.

Niven, John. *Connecticut for the Union: The Role of the State in the Civil War*. New Haven, CT: Yale University Press, 1965.

———. *Salmon P. Chase: A Biography*. New York: Oxford University Press, 1995.

Oberholtzer, Ellis Paxson. *Jay Cooke: Financier of the Civil War*. Vol. 1. Reprint, n.p.: n.p., n.d.

O'Harrow, Robert, Jr. *The Quartermaster: Montgomery C. Meigs, Lincoln's General, Master Builder of the Union Army*. New York: Simon & Schuster, 2016.

Orcutt, Samuel. *History of Torrington, Connecticut, from Its First Settlement in 1737, with Biographies and Genealogies*. Albany, NY: J. Munsell, Printer, 1878.

Ott, Daniel Peter. "Producing a Past: Cyrus McCormick's Reaper from Heritage to History." PhD diss., Loyola University, 2015.

Paludan, Philip Shaw. *"A People's Contest": The Union and Civil War, 1861–1865*. Lawrence: University Press of Kansas, 1996.

Parke, John E. *Recollections of Seventy Years and Historical Gleanings of Allegheny, Pennsylvania*. Boston: Rand, Avery & Company, 1886.

Popowski, Howard. "Granddaddy of the Greenback: The Union's Jay Cooke." *Civil War Times Illustrated* 21, no. 8 (December 1982).

Proudfit, Margaret Burden. *Henry Burden: His Life and a History of His Inventions Compiled from the Public Press*. Reprint, London: Forgotten Books, n.d.

Ramage, James A. *Gray Ghost: The Life of Col. John Singleton Mosby*. Lexington: University Press of Kentucky, 1999.

Renehan, Edward J., Jr. *Commodore: The Life of Cornelius Vanderbilt*. New York: Basic Books, 2007.

Riddle, Albert Gallatin. *Recollections of War Times: Reminiscences of Men and Events in Washington, 1860–1865*. New York: G. P. Putnam's Sons, 1895.

Risch, Erna. *Quartermaster Support of the Army: A History of the Corps, 1775–1939*. Washington, DC: Center of Military History United States Army, 1989.

Roberts, Charles S. *Triumph I: Altoona to Pitcairn, 1846–1996*. Baltimore: Barnard, Roberts and Co., 1997.

Roe, Joseph Wickham. *English and American Tool Builders*. New Haven, CT: Yale University Press, 1916.

Rolando, Victor R. "The Industrial Archeology of Henry Burden & Sons Ironworks in Southwestern Vermont." *Journal of Vermont Archeology* 8 (2007).

Schmidt, James M. *Lincoln's Labels: America's Best Known Brands and the Civil War*. Roseville, MN: Edinborough Press, 2009.

Schotter, H. W. *The Growth and Development of the Pennsylvania Railroad Company*. Philadelphia: Press of Allen, Lane & Scott, 1927.

Schrader, Charles R. *United States Army Logistics, 1775–1992: An Anthology*. 3 vols. Washington, DC: Center of Military History United States Army, 1997.

Sears, Stephen W. *Lincoln's Lieutenants: The High Command of the Army of the Potomac*. Boston: Houghton Mifflin Harcourt, 2017.

Sherman, John. *John Sherman's Recollections of Forty Years in the House, Senate and Cabinet: An Autobiography*. 2 vols. Chicago: Werner Company, 1895–1896.

Sherman, William T. *Memoirs of Gen. W. T. Sherman, Written by Himself*. Vol. 1. 4th ed. New York: Charles L. Webster & Co., 1891.

Sipes, William B. *Pennsylvania Railroad: Its Origin, Construction, Condition, and Connections*. Reprint, Evansville, IN: Unigraphic, 1975.

Skaggs, Jimmy M. *Prime Cut: Livestock Raising and Meatpacking in the United States, 1607–1983*. College Station: Texas A&M University Press, 1986.

Smith, Charles Stewart. *Unveiling of the Statue of Abram S. Hewitt in the Chamber of Commerce of the State of New-York, May 11th, 1905*. New York: Press of the Chamber of Commerce, 1905.

Smith, George Winston. *Medicines for the Union Army: The United States Army Laboratories During the Civil War*. Madison, WI: American Institute of the History of Pharmacy, 1962.

~~Smith, Richard Norton. *The Colonel: The Life and Legend of Robert R. McCor-~~ *nel: The Life and Legend of Robert R. McCor-* ~~mick.~~ Northwestern University Press, 2003.

~~...~~ *ester Connecticut.* Manchester, CT: Centen-

's Washington: Selections from the Writings of ~~a~~ *spondent.* New York: Thomas Yoseloff, 1967.

Epic Life of Cornelius Vanderbilt. New York:

Vhite House in War Times. New York: Charles

en of Business. New York: Charles Scribner's

Railroads: Beanpoles and Cornstalks." *Civil* *cember* 1991).

nert Studebaker, eds. The Studebaker Family in City, OH: Studebaker Family National Associ-

ing Generation: Corruption and the Crisis of the k: Oxford University Press, 1987.

Tenner, Edward. "Lasting Impressions: An Ancient Craft's Surprising Legacy in Harvard's Museums—and Laboratories." *Harvard Magazine* 103, no. 1 (September–October 2000).

Thomson, Ross. "Invention, Markets, and the Scope of the Firm: The Nineteenth Century U.S. Shoe Machinery Industry." *Business and Economic History* 18 (1989).

Trepal, Dan. "The Gun Foundry Recast." *Journal of the Society for Industrial Archeology* 35, nos. 1 & 2 (2009).

US War Department. *The War of the Rebellion: A Compilation of the Official Records of the Union and Confederate Armies*. 128 vols. Washington, DC: US Government Printing Office, 1880–1902.

Valentino, Alicia B. "Using Maps to Aid Our Understanding of a Site's History." *Journal of the Society for Industrial Archeology* 35, nos. 1 & 2 (2009).

Walsh, Margaret. *The Rise of the Midwestern Meat Packing Industry*. Lexington: University Press of Kentucky, 1982.

Walton, Steven A. "Founding a Foundry: The Diary of the Setting-Out of the West Point Foundry, 1817." *Journal of the Society for Industrial Archeology* 35, nos. 1 & 2 (2009).

———. "The West Point Foundry in Larger Perspective." *Journal of the Society for Industrial Archeology* 35, nos. 1 & 2 (2009).

Ward, James A. *J. Edgar Thomson: Master of the Pennsylvania*. Westport, CT: Greenwood Press, 1980.

————. *That Man Haupt: A Biography of Herman Haupt*. Baton Rouge: Louisiana State University Press, 1973.

Weigley, Russell F. *A Great Civil War: A Military and Political History, 1861–1865*. Bloomington: Indiana University Press, 2000.

Weise, Arthur James. *The City of Troy and Its Vicinity*. Troy, NY: Edward Green, 1886.

Weld, Stephen Minot. *War Diary and Letters of Stephen Minot Weld*. 2nd ed. Boston: Massachusetts Historical Society, 1979.

Welles, Gideon. *Diary of Gideon Welles: Secretary of the Navy Under Lincoln and Johnson*. 3 vols. Boston: Houghton Mifflin Company, 1911.

Wert, Jeffry D. *A Brotherhood of Valor: The Common Soldiers of the Stonewall Brigade, C.S.A. and the Iron Brigade, U.S.A.* New York: Simon & Schuster, 1999.

————. *The Sword of Lincoln: The Army of the Potomac*. New York: Simon & Schuster, 2005.

White, Richard. *Railroaded: The Transcontinentals and the Making of Modern America*. New York: W. W. Norton & Company, 2011.

Whitten, David O. *The Emergence of Giant Enterprise, 1860–1914: American Commercial Enterprise and Extractive Industries*. Westport, CT: Greenwood Press, 1983.

Wildman, Edwin. *Famous Leaders of Industry: The Life Stories of Boys Who Have Succeeded*. Boston: Page Company, 1920.

Wiley, Bell Irvin. *The Life of Billy Yank: The Common Soldier of the Union*. Indianapolis: Bobbs-Merrill Company Publishers, 1952.

Wilson, Mark R. *The Business of Civil War: Military Mobilization and the State, 1861–1865*. Baltimore: Johns Hopkins University Press, 2006.

————. "The Business of Civil War: Military Enterprise, the State, and Political Economy in the United States, 1850–1880." PhD diss., University of Chicago, 2002. 2 vols. Ann Arbor, MI: ProQuest Information and Learning Company.

Wilson, William Bender. *History of the Pennsylvania Railroad Company, with Plan of Organization, Portraits of Officials and Biographical Sketches*. 2 vols. Philadelphia: Henry T. Coates & Company, 1899.

Winik, Jay. *April 1865: The Month That Saved America*. New York: Harper Collins Publishers, 2001.

Electronic Sources

"Abram S. Hewitt, 1822–1902." *http://www.ringwoodmanor.org/abram-s-hewitt.html*

Abrams, Michael. "John Deere." *https://www.asme.org/engineering-topics/articles/manufacturing-processing/john-deere*

Beck, A. M. "Spencer's Repeaters in the Civil War." *http://www.rarewinchesters.com/articles/art_spencercivilwar.shtml*

"Biography of Frederick Weyerhaeuser." *https://www.accessgenealogy.com/illinois/biography-of-frederick-weyerhaeuser.htm*

"Bristol-Myers Squibb: History." *http://www.b-ms.co.uk/ourcompany/Pages
/history.aspx*

"Burden Iron Works (Burden Iron Company)." *https://cdn.loc.gov/master/pnp
/habshaer/ny/ny0600/ny0671/data/ny0671data.pdf*

"Chapter 6—Unusual Jefferson Alumni, pp. 153–230" (2009). *Legend and Lore:
Jefferson Medical College.* Paper 7. *http://jdc.jefferson.edu/savacool/7*

"Clement Studebaker." *https://pabook.libraries.psu.edu/studebaker__clement*

Cronin, Andrea. "The McKay Stitcher: The Machine That Revolutionized
Footwear Production." *https://www.masshist.org/blog/1029*

Drache, Hiram M. "The Impact of John Deere's Plow." *http://www.lib.niu
.edu/2001/iht810102.html*

"'Drive On': The Genius of James Buchanan Eads." *http://civilwarnavy150
.blogspot.com/2011/07/drive-on-genius-of-james-buchanan-eads.html*

"Early Anesthesia at Jefferson, Or, 'Get a Whiff of This . . .'" *https://library
.jefferson.edu/archives/collections/highlights/Anesthesia*

"Evaporated Milk's Connecticut Connection—Who Knew?" *https://connecticut
history.org/evaporated-milks-connecticut-connection-who-knew/*

Finlay, Nancy. "Collis P. Huntington: The Boy from Poverty Hollow." *http://
connecticuthistory.org/collis-p-huntington-the-boy-from-poverty-hollow/*

Frazier, Ian. "John Deere Was a Real Person, His Invention Changed the Country." *http://www.smithsonianmag.com/history/john-deere-was-a-real-person
-his-invention-changed-the-country-4017033/*

"Gail Borden Milks Success." *http://www.texasingenuity.com/gail-borden.html*

"Gordon McKay (1821–1903)." *http://people.seas.harvard.edu/~jones/mckay
/mckay.html*

Guttman, Jon. "Studebaker Wagon: The Studie That Served on the Front
Lines." *Military History. http://www.historynet.com/studebaker-wagon-the
-studie-that-served-on-the-front-lines.htm*

"Henry Burden (1791–1871): Iron Titan, Horseshoe and Rail Spike Innovator."
http://www.timesunion.com/albanyrural/burden/

"History Comes to Life." *https://milwaukeehistory.net/education/milwaukee
-timeline/*

"James Buchanan Eads." *http://www.museum.state.il.us/RiverWeb/landings/Ambot
/TECH/TECH20.htm*

"John Deere." *http://www.illinoisancestors.org/rockisland/pioneersfolder/johndeere
.html*

"John Deere Biography: A Story Behind the Inventor." *http://blog.machinefinder
.com/9928/john-deere-biography*

"John Deere: Inventor of the Steel Plow." *http://www.robinsonlibrary.com/social
/industries/agricultural/deere.htm*

"John Deere: Self-Polishing Cast Steel Plow." *https://lemelson.mit.edu/resources
/john-deere*

Lewis, Harry R. "Gordon McKay: Brief Life of an Inventor with a Lasting
Harvard Legacy: 1821–1903." *http://harvardmagazine.com/2007/09/gordon
-mckay.html*

Long Spencer quote. *http://mrlincolnshightechwar.com/chapter_files/spencer_story.html*

McKinney, Megan. "House of Armour: Philip D." *http://www.classicchicago magazine.com/house-of-armour-philip-d/*

"The Original Steel Plow." *http://www.deere.com/en/our-company/history/john -deere-plow/*

"Ringwood Manor Iron Complex, 1740–1931." *https://www.asme.org/getmedia /3f9fc3b3-206d-426d-9559-9af57833957e/33-Ringwood-Manor-Iron-Complex .aspx*

"Robert Parker Parrott, 1804–1877." *http://www.civilwarartillery.com/inventors /parrott.htm*

Schenkman, A. J. "Everyone Knows Elsie: A Short History of the Borden Company." *http://newyorkhistoryblog.org/?s=Everyone+knows+elsie%3A ++a+short+history+of+the+borden+company*

Sellers, William. "Memoir of James Buchanan Eads, 1820–1887." *http://www .nasonline.org/publications/biographical-memoirs/memoir-pdfs/eads-james -b.pdf*

"A Short History of Abington, Massachusetts." *http://www.dyerlibrary.org /about/abington.html*

Soodalter, Ron. "Well Armed." *America's Civil War.* *http://www.historynet.com /well-armed.htm*

"The Studebaker Brothers Biographies." *http://genealogytrails.com/ind/stjoseph /studebakerbros.html*

Tambling, Richard. "The Day Spencer Shot Holes in Criticisms of His Rifle." *http://www.manchesterhistory.org/reprints/MHS3_Spencer_Lincoln.html*

Wagle, John S. "John Deere & Charles Deere." *http://anbhf.org/laureates /john-deere/*

"The Water Wheel Album: Page Three." *http://www.angelfire.com/journal /millbuilder/album3.html*

"Weyerhaeuser, Frederick (1834–1914)." *http://www.germanheritage.com /biographies/mtoz/weyerthaeuser.html*

Woods, Claire. "Up and Down and 'Round and 'Round and Back Again." *http://pabook2.libraries.psu.edu/palitmap/Horseshoe.html*

Zink, Clifford. "Iron & Steel: Entrepreneurs on the Delaware." *http://garden statelegacy.com/files/Iron___Steel_Zink_GSL223.pdf*

INDEX

—ɯɯ—

259